W9-CLC-253

David C. Fowler
Editor

Usage Statistics of E-Serials

Usage Statistics of E-Serials has been co-published simultaneously as *The Serials Librarian*, Volume 53, Supplement Number 9 2007.

Pre-publication
REVIEWS,
COMMENTARIES,
EVALUATIONS . . .

Usage Statistics
of E-Serials

Usage Statistics of E-Serials has been co-published simultaneously as *The Serials Librarian*, Volume 53, Supplement Number 9 2007.

Monographic Separates from *The Serials Librarian*®

For additional information on these and other Haworth Press titles, including descriptions, tables of contents, reviews, and prices, use the QuickSearch catalog at http://www.HaworthPress.com.

Usage Statistics of E-Serials, edited by David C. Fowler, MLS (Vol. 53 Suppl. 9, 2007). *"Provides the library community with valuable information from practitioners as to how institutions are addressing e-serials usage statistics. Especially thought-provoking offerings in this volume are the stewardship model in promoting database decision-making and maintenance; usage statistics as an economic factor in scholarly communications; the role of usage statistics in library promotional efforts; and the risks and rewards of assessment-driven decision making incorporating usage, inferential and experiential data." (Karen Rupp-Serrano, MLS, MPA, Head, Collection Development, University of Oklahoma Libraries)*

Electronic Journal Management Systems: Experiences from the Field, edited by Gary Ives, MLS (Vol. 47, No. 4, 2005). *"A valuable addition to the professional development collection of every academic library. Solutions to the challenges of 'back office' management of electronic subscriptions, as well as solutions for facilitating and streamlining access for library patrons are described." (Anne Prestamo, EdD, MLIS, BM, Associate Dean for Collection and Technology Services, Oklahoma State University Libraries)*

E-Serials Cataloging: Access to Continuing and Integrating Resources via the Catalog and the Web, edited by Jim Cole, MA, and Wayne Jones, MA, MLS (Vol. 41, No. 3/4, 2002). *"A very timely and useful reference tool for librarians. The best . . . on various aspects of e-serials: from standards to education and training, from policies and procedures to national and local projects and future trends. As a technical services librarian, I found the sections on policies and procedures and national projects and local applications very valuable and informative." (Vinh-The Lam, MLS, Head, Cataloging Department, University of Saskatchewan Library, Canada)*

Women's Studies Serials: A Quarter-Century of Development, edited by Kristin H. Gerhard, MLS (Vol. 35, No. 1/2, 1998). *"Candidly explores and analyzes issues which must be addressed to ensure the continued growth and vitality of women's studies. . . . It commands the attention of librarians, scholars, and publishers." (Joan Ariel, MLS, MA, Women's Studies Librarian and Lecturer, University of California at Irvine)*

E-Serials: Publishers, Libraries, Users, and Standards, edited by Wayne Jones, MA, MLS (Vol. 33, No. 1/2/3/4, 1998). *"Libraries and publishers will find this book helpful in developing strategies, policies, and procedures." (Nancy Brodie, National Library of Canada, Ottawa, Ontario)*

Serials Cataloging at the Turn of the Century, edited by Jeanne M. K. Boydston, MSLIS, James W. Williams, MSLS, and Jim Cole, MLS (Vol. 32, No. 1/2, 1997). *Focuses on the currently evolving trends in serials cataloging in order to predict and explore the possibilities for the field in the new millennium.*

Serials Management in the Electronic Era: Papers in Honor of Peter Gellatly, Founding Editor of The Serials Librarian, edited by Jim Cole, MA, and James W. Williams, MLS (Vol. 29, No. 3/4, 1996). *Assesses progress and technical changes in the field of serials management and anticipates future directions and challenges for librarians.*

Special Format Serials and Issues: Annual Review of . . . , Advances in . . . , Symposia on . . . , Methods in . . . , by Tony Stankus, MLS (Vol. 27, No. 2/3, 1996). *A thorough and lively introduction to the nature of these publications' types.*

Serials Canada: Aspects of Serials Work in Canadian Libraries, edited by Wayne Jones, MLS (Vol. 26, No. 3/4, 1996). *"An excellent addition to the library literature and is recommended for all library school libraries, scholars, and students of comparative/international librarianship." (Library Times International)*

Serials Cataloging: Modern Perspectives and International Developments, edited by Jim E. Cole, MA, and James W. Williams, MSLS (Vol. 22, No. 1/2/3/4, 1993). *"A significant contribution to understanding the 'big picture' of serials control. . . . A solid presentation of serious issues in a crucial area on librarianship." (Bimonthly Review of Law Books)*

The North American Serials Interest Group (NASIG) Series

Mile-High Views: Surveying the Serials Vista: NASIG 2006, edited by Carol Ann Borchert and Gary Ives (Vol. 52, No. 1/2/3/4, 2007). *Visionary perspectives, effective planning techniques, and practical strategies on technology and the state of serials from NASIG 2006.*

Roaring into Our 20's: NASIG 2005, edited by Margaret Mering and Elna Saxton (Vol. 50, No. 1/2/3/4, 2006). *A compilation of visionary papers from the North American Serials Interest Group's twentieth annual conference held May 2005 in Minneapolis, Minnesota.*

Growth, Creativity, and Collaboration: Great Visions on a Great Lake, edited by Patricia Sheldahl French and Margaret Mering (Vol. 48, No. 1/2/3/4, 2005). *"If any serials librarian wants one place to go to find the latest and greatest on serials issues, these proceedings are the first place to go. . . . A wide range of contributors from the who's who of the serials world." (Dan Tonkery, Vice President and Director of Business Development, EBSCO Information Services)*

Serials in the Park, edited by Patricia Sheldahl French and Richard Worthing (Vol. 46, No. 1/2/3/4, 2004). *Proceedings of the 18th Annual NASIG conference (2003, Portland, Oregon), focusing on the most significant trends and innovations for serials.*

Transforming Serials: The Revolution Continues, edited by Susan L. Scheiberg and Shelley Neville (Vol. 44, No. 1/2/3/4, 2003). *"A valuable and thought-provoking resource for all library workers involved with serials." (Mary Curran, MLS, MA, Head of Cataloguing Services, University of Ottawa, Ontario, Canada)*

NASIG 2001: A Serials Odyssey, edited by Susan L. Scheiberg and Shelley Neville (Vol. 42, No. 1/2/3/4, 2002). *From XML to ONIX and UCITA, here's cutting-edge information from leading serials librarians from the 16th NASIG conference.*

Making Waves: New Serials Landscapes in a Sea of Change, edited by Joseph C. Harmon and P. Michelle Fiander (Vol. 40, No. 1/2/3/4, 2001). *These proceedings include discussions of the Digital Millennium Copyright Act, and reports on specific test projects such as BioOne, the Open Archives Project, and PubMed Central.*

From Carnegie to Internet 2: Forging the Serials Future, edited by P. Michelle Fiander, Joseph C. Harmon, and Jonathan David Makepeace (Vol. 38, No. 1/2/3/4, 2000). *Current information and practical insight to help you improve your technical skills and prepare you and your library for the 21st century.*

Head in the Clouds, Feet on the Ground: Serials Vision and Common Sense, edited by Jeffrey S. Bullington, Beatrice L. Caraway, and Beverley Geer (Vol. 36, No. 1/2/3/4, 1999). *"Practical, common sense advice, and visionary solutions to serials issues afoot in every library department and in every type of library today. . . . An essential reference guide for libraries embracing electronic resource access." (Mary Curran, MA, MLS, Coordinator, Bibliographic Standards, Morisset Library, University of Ottawa, Ontario, Canada)*

Experimentation and Collaboration: Creating Serials for a New Millennium, Charlene N. Simser and Michael A. Somers (Vol. 34, No. 1/2/3/4, 1998). *Gives valuable ideas and practical advice that you can apply or incorporate into your own area of expertise.*

Pioneering New Serials Frontiers: From Petroglyphs to Cyberserials, edited by Christine Christiansen and Cecilia Leathem (Vol. 30, No. 3/4, and Vol. 31, No. 1/2, 1997). *Gives you insight, ideas, and practical skills for dealing with the changing world of serials management.*

Serials to the Tenth Power: Traditions, Technology, and Transformation, edited by Mary Ann Sheble, MLS, and Beth Holley, MLS (Vol. 28, No. 1/2/3/4, 1996). *Provides readers with practical ideas on managing the challenges of the electronic information environment.*

A Kaleidoscope of Choices: Reshaping Roles and Opportunities for Serialists, edited by Beth Holley, MLS, and Mary Ann Sheble, MLS (Vol. 25, No. 3/4, 1995). *"Highly recommended as an excellent source material for all librarians interested in learning more about the Internet, technology and its effect on library organization and operations, and the virtual library." (Library Acquisitions: Practice & Theory)*

New Scholarship: New Serials: Proceedings of the North American Serials Interest Group, Inc., edited by Gail McMillan and Marilyn Norstedt (Vol. 24, No. 3/4, 1994). *"An excellent representation of the ever-changing, complicated, and exciting world of serials." (Library Acquisitions Practice & Theory)*

Usage Statistics
of E-Serials

David C. Fowler
Editor

Usage Statistics of E-Serials has been co-published simultaneously as *The Serials Librarian*, Volume 53, Supplement Number 9 2007.

160101

The Haworth Information Press®
An Imprint of The Haworth Press, Inc.

www.HaworthPress.com

Usage Statistics of E-Serials has been co-published simultaneously as *The Serials Librarian*, Volume 53, Supplement Number 9 2007.

The development, preparation, and publication of this work has been undertaken with great care. However, the publisher, employees, editors, and agents of The Haworth Press and all imprints of The Haworth Press, Inc., including The Haworth Medical Press® and Pharmaceutical Products Press®, are not responsible for any errors contained herein or for consequences that may ensue from use of materials or information contained in this work. With regard to case studies, identities and circumstances of individuals discussed herein have been changed to protect confidentiality. Any resemblance to actual persons, living or dead, is entirely coincidental.

The Haworth Press is committed to the dissemination of ideas and information according to the highest standards of intellectual freedom and the free exchange of ideas. Statements made and opinions expressed in this publication do not necessarily reflect the views of the Publisher, Directors, management, or staff of The Haworth Press, Inc., or an endorsement by them.

The Haworth Press, Inc., 10 Alice Street, Binghamton, 13904-1580 USA

Library of Congress Cataloging-in-Publication Data

Usage statistics of e-serials / David C. Fowler, editor.
     p. cm.
    "Co-published simultaneously as The serials librarian, volume 53, Supplement number 9, 2007."
    ISBN: 978-0-7890-2987-4 (alk. paper)
    ISBN: 978-0-7890-2988-1 (pbk. : alk. paper)
    1. Electronic journals–Use studies. 2. Libraries–Special collections–Electronic journals. 3. Electronic journals–Statistics. I. Fowler, David C. II. Serials librarian.
    Z692.E43U83 2007
    070.5′797–dc22   2006036547

The HAWORTH PRESS *Inc.*

Abstracting, Indexing & Outward Linking

PRINT *and* ELECTRONIC BOOKS & JOURNALS

This section provides you with a list of major indexing & abstracting services and other tools for bibliographic access. That is to say, each service began covering this periodical during the year noted in the right column. Most Websites which are listed below have indicated that they will either post, disseminate, compile, archive, cite or alert their own Website users with research-based content from this work. (This list is as current as the copyright date of this publication.)

Abstracting, Website/Indexing Coverage . . . . Year When Coverage Began

- *International Bibliography of Book Reviews on the Humanities and Social Sciences (IBR) (Thomson) <http://www.saur.de>* 2006
- ***Academic Search Premier (EBSCO)** <http://search.ebscohost.com>* 2007
- ***Chemical Abstracts Service** <http://www.cas.org>* 1982
- ***CINAHL (Cumulative Index to Nursing & Allied Health Literature) (EBSCO)** <http://www.cinahl.com>* 1985
- ***CINAHL Plus (EBSCO)** <http://search.ebscohost.com>* 2006
- ***INSPEC (The Institution of Engineering and Technology)** <http://www.iee.org.uk/publish/>* 2002
- ***LISA: Library and Information Science Abstracts (ProQuest CSA)** <http://www.csa.com/factsheets/list-set-c.php>* 1990
- ***MasterFILE Premier (EBSCO)** <http://search.ebscohost.com>* 2006
- ***ProQuest Academic Research Library (ProQuest CSA)** <http://www.proquest.com>* 2006
- ***Research Library (ProQuest CSA)** <http://www.proquest.com>* 2006
- *Academic Search Alumni Edition (EBSCO) <http://search.ebscohost.com>* 2007
- *Academic Search Complete (EBSCO) <http://search.ebscohost.com>* . . . . *

(continued)

(continued)

(continued)

(continued)

*Exact start date to come.

Bibliographic Access

- **Cabell's Directory of Publishing Opportunities in Educational**
  Curriculum and Methods <http://www.cabells.com/>

- **Magazines for Libraries (Katz)**

- **MediaFinder <http://www.mediafinder.com/>**

- **Ulrich's Periodicals Directory: The Global Source for Periodicals**
  Information Since 1932 <http://www.bowkerlink.com>

As part of Haworth's continuing commitment to better serve our library patrons, we are proud to be working with the following electronic services:

AGGREGATOR SERVICES

EBSCOhost

Ingenta

J-Gate

Minerva

OCLC FirstSearch **FirstSearch**

Oxmill

SwetsWise SwetsWise

LINK RESOLVER SERVICES

1Cate (Openly Informatics)

ChemPort (American Chemical Society) **ChemPort**

CrossRef

Gold Rush (Coalliance) Gold Rush

LinkOut (PubMed)

LINKplus (Atypon)

LinkSolver (Ovid)

LinkSource with A-to-Z (EBSCO)

Resource Linker (Ulrich)

SerialsSolutions (ProQuest) **SerialsSolutions**

SFX (Ex Libris) $S\cdot F\cdot X$

Sirsi Resolver (SirsiDynix) SirsiDynix

Tour (TDnet)

Vlink (Extensity, formerly Geac) ((extensity))

WebBridge (Innovative Interfaces) WebBridge

ABOUT THE EDITOR

David C. Fowler, MLS, has been an assistant professor and the electronic resources librarian at the University of Oregon Libraries in Eugene since early 2006. From 1999 until early 2006, he was the electronic resources coordinator for acquisitions in the collections and technical services division of the Parks Library at Iowa State University in Ames. His professional experience began when he became the serials services librarian at Texas A&M University at Corpus Christi. His work has been published in *Collection Management,* the *Journal of Academic Librarianship,* and *Library Resources & Technical Services.* He has previously edited another Haworth Press book in this series, *E-Serials Collections Management: Transitions, Trends, and Technicalities.* He holds an MLS degree from the State University of New York–Albany, and BA in criminal justice from the University of Alaska–Anchorage. His work in the field has given him a wide array of experience in electronic serials acquisitions, cataloging, collection management, licensing, and statistics gathering.

To my wife, Elizabeth–for her love,
support, and insight

Usage Statistics
of E-Serials

CONTENTS

Contributors

Carol Abatelli is the Head of Collections and Electronic Resource Management at Eastern Connecticut State University's J. Eugene Smith Library. Over the course of her career, she has held professional library positions at The Cooper Union, SUNY Purchase College, and at several other academic institutions. She has also served as a public library director and has worked as a corporate researcher in the telecommunications industry. She holds an MLS from Long Island University and an MA in humanities from Manhattanville College.

Elise Anderson is the Collection Management Analyst at Wake Forest University. She earned an MS in zoology after conducting field research and statistical analyses on the resource consumption patterns of a marine invertebrate. Since 1997, she has been tracking and studying the information resource consumption patterns of large primates. Before joining Z. Smith Reynolds Library, Elise worked as an information specialist for several organizations, including The Nature Conservancy, Sterling C. Evans Library at Texas A&M University, and the Environmental Resource Center (Houston).

Gayle Baker is a professor and the Electronic Services Coordinator at the University of Tennessee Libraries. She has served as an adjunct faculty member at the University of Tennessee, School of Information Sciences and at the University of Alabama School of Library and Information Studies. In addition to an MLS, Baker has earned an MS in computer and information science from the Ohio State University. Prior to entering the library profession, she was a computer programmer/ analyst for several years.

Celia Bakke is currently Head of Planning and Organizing Electronic Resources at the Dr. Martin Luther King Jr. Library at San Jose State University. She has also served as the Head of Technical Services and taught cataloging classes for the SJSU School of Library and Information Science and UC Berkeley Extension.

Rickey Best holds a master's degree in library and information studies from the University of California, Berkeley, and a master's degree in history and archival management from the University of California, Riverside. He has served as Dean of the Library at Auburn University at Montgomery since 1997. Prior to this, he was the Archivist and Special Collections Librarian and also the Head of Technical Services for Auburn University at Montgomery.

Angela Boots was formerly a graduate trainee information assistant at Cancer Research, UK. She has recently completed her master's in information management at Metropolitan University, London. She was involved in the management of online and print journal subscriptions, including the routine collection and evaluation of online journals usage statistics. Angela now works at the University of London.

Martin P. Brändle is an information specialist and the Deputy Chief at the Chemistry Biology Pharmacy Information Center of ETH, Zürich. He is a native of Bern, Switzerland. He studied chemistry and finished his studies with a PhD in physical chemistry at the University of Bern. From 1995 until 1997, he was an Alexander-von-Humboldt fellow in the Quantum Chemistry group of Professor Joachim Sauer, at the Max-Planck-Society, Berlin. He then was a postdoctoral student at ETH Zürich in the group of Professor Reinhard Nesper at the Laboratory of Inorganic Chemistry from 1997 to 1999. In 2000, he moved to the Information Center as the IT coordinator. In 2002, he graduated as information specialist in after-diploma study in information and documentation at HTW Chur. His current activities include teaching chemical information, subject specialist, development of information systems, and projects involving XML in chemistry. He has delivered several lectures at international conferences and workshops, published fourteen articles and a book chapter, and co-authored a book.

Julia Chester is the Director of Knowledge Management, Cancer Research UK, London. She has been involved in information management in a variety of organizational settings for many years. Prior to joining Cancer Research UK, she was Head of Defence Medical Libraries for the Ministry of Defence and provided information services for the British Army, Royal Navy, and Royal Air Force, both at home and abroad.

Janet K. Chisman is the Head of Serials & Electronic Resources at Washington State University, Libraries, Serials & Electronic Resources Unit, Pullman, WA. She received her degree from the University of Illinois–Urbana Champaign.

Susanne K. Clement started in 2003 at the University of Kansas as a social science librarian and was appointed as the head of collection development in early 2004. She is also the liaison to the departments of political science and communication studies. Prior to joining KU, she worked for nearly eight years for an association as a professional librarian where she developed and operated its library, archives, historical preservation program, museum, and bookstore.

Donnice Cochenour is an associate professor at Colorado State University Libraries where she has been Serials Librarian since 1990. She received her MLIS in library and information science from the University of Hawaii and a certificate of advanced studies in library studies from the University of Oklahoma.

Joan E. Conger, MLIS, MA, OD, is a veteran of electronic resource management in libraries. She has written a book on *Collaborative Electronic Resources Management: From Acquisitions to Assessment,* published by Libraries Unlimited, Englewood, CO, in late 2004. She is a doctoral student in organization behavior and occasionally speaks, facilitates organization change efforts, and writes for professional publications.

Eleonora Dubicki, MLS, MBA, is an assistant librarian at the Monmouth University Library in West Long Branch, NJ. She holds an MLS from the School of Communication, Information, and Library Studies at Rutgers University, and an MBA from Rutgers Business School–Newark.

Randle Gedeon is the Acquisitions and Serials Librarian at Western Michigan University, a position he has held since 2000; prior to that, he was the Education Librarian at WMU. Previous professional positions he has held also include: Education Resources Coordinator at Northeastern State University (Oklahoma), and Reference Librarian at John Carroll University. He holds an MLS from Kent State University, MAEd from Baldwin-Wallace College, and a BA from Muskingum College.

Alea Henle is working on a doctorate in history at the University of Connecticut, researching information issues in early America. Previously employed at Colorado State University as an assistant professor and electronic resource librarian, she received her MS from Simmons Graduate School of Library and Information Science.

Susan L. Kendall is currently the Government Publications Coordinator and Reference Librarian at the Dr. Martin Luther King Jr. Library at San Jose State University. She has been at San Jose State University for six years. Before coming to San Jose State, she worked at the Nevada State Library & Archives, the University of Dallas Library, and the University of Nevada, Las Vegas Library.

Donald W. King (MS, Statistics) is a visiting scholar at the University of North Carolina (UNC) at Chapel Hill's School of Information and Library Science. He has devoted forty-five years to describing and evaluating information and communication processes. In addition to working on the MaxData project at the University of Tennessee, he is coprincipal investigator on two Institute of Museum and Library Services-funded projects to examine the future of librarians (UNC) and the impact of online systems (University of Pittsburgh), as well as another study to measure the return-on-investment in public libraries (Commonwealth of Pennsylvania). He has co-authored or edited sixteen books and hundreds of formal publications, many recently with Carol Tenopir.

Dr. Arun Kumar is a media specialist at the Chemistry Biology Pharmacy Information Center, Swiss Federal Institute of Technology, Zürich. He received his BSc and MSc in chemical engineering from Punjab University, Chandigarh (India), and his PhD in liquid-liquid extraction from Swiss Federal Institute of Technology, Zürich. Prior to joining the Information Center in 2000, he worked at the Technical Chemistry Laboratory of the same institute for twenty-two years. His major experiences were in the fields of liquid-liquid extraction, coalescence in droplet dispersions and foams, and calculations of shapes of fluid-liquid interfaces. Presently, he is responsible for management and cataloging of e-serials and e-books, installation and administration of databases, and providing assistance to clients of the Information Center in using the information resources. He has published about forty papers and two book chapters. He is a visiting professor of Sri Sai Institutes of Engineering and Pharmacy, Pathankot (India).

Maribeth Manoff is an associate professor and the Coordinator for Networked Service Integration at the University of Tennessee Libraries. She is responsible for many of the Web-based services provided by the libraries, including the Web site, the online public access catalog, electronic journal and article access via link resolver software, and federated searching capabilities. Her research interests are focused on emerging technologies, specifically, the use of technology to improve access to electronic resources.

Melissa K. McBurney works at Columbia Basin College as a medical librarian. At the time of the writing of this chapter, she worked at the Pacific Northwest National Laboratory as the manager of the Technical Library's Electronic & Technical Services group where she had oversight for the library's catalog and Web pages; the purchasing of books, journals and electronic resources for the library collection; and the licensing of electronic products. She has also worked in the reference department of North Carolina State University's library and published a book on electronic resources for engineers. She has a BA in political science from North Carolina State University and an MS in library science from the University of North Carolina at Chapel Hill.

Kitty McClanahan is a doctoral student in information science at the University of Tennessee. She has a master's degree in library and information science from the University of Kentucky, and a BA in economics from the California State University, Northridge. Prior to returning to graduate school, she was an operations executive for a market research consulting firm.

Norm Medeiros is Associate Librarian of the College & Coordinator for Bibliographic and Digital Services at Haverford College (PA), where he oversees technical services, coordinates the library's digital initiatives, and serves as economics bibliographer. Norm has published and presented papers in the areas of electronic resources management, metadata for resource discovery, and technical services administration. He recently served as project leader for a two-year CLIR-funded grant that sought to redesign the processes involved in managing electronic resources in the Tri-College Consortium of Bryn Mawr, Haverford, and Swarthmore Colleges. Norm is a Massachusetts native and an alumnus of the University of Rhode Island's Graduate School of Library and Information Studies. He and his family live in Wilmington, Delaware.

Heather Morrison is a project coordinator with BC Electronic Library Network, a consortium of postsecondary libraries in British Columbia, Canada. Heather's previous experience includes coordinating projects for The Alberta Library (TAL), a multitype library consortium in Alberta. While at TAL, Heather conducted research on various business models for a licensing program to include a wide variety of sizes and types of libraries. Heather served for many years as the Access Services Coordinator for Concordia University College of Alberta, and was an active volunteer with the NEOS Library Consortium during this time. Heather's numerous publications and presentations focus mainly on scholarly communications, particularly open access. Links to many of Heather's works can be found through her blog, "The Imaginary Journal of Poetic Economics," found at http://www.poeticeconomics. blogspot.com. Heather is very involved as a volunteer with library associations, particularly in the areas of academic librarianship and information policy, and serves as the Chief E-LIS Editor for Canada.

Professor David Nicholas is the Director of the School, Chair of Library and Information Studies and Director of CIBER (Centre for Information Behavior and the Evaluation of Research http://www. ucl.ac.uk/ciber/). He is also Director of the UCL Centre for Publishing. Previously, he was Head, Department of Information Science, City University, and prior to that, MA Course Tutor, School of Information and Communication Studies, University of North London. His research interests include the impact of ICTs on strategic user groups, policy implications of digital environments, digital libraries/Web sites uses and evaluations, digital information consumers, digital health services, deep log analysis, scholarly communication, information needs analysis, and information-seeking behavior.

Christine F. Noonan is an information specialist at Pacific Northwest National Laboratory in Richland, Washington. Christine works as the

Hanford Technical Library's Transformative Technologies lead where she is responsible for maintaining and developing the electronic collection infrastructure to meet customer need by leading the implementation of and training for new electronic services. Before working in library and information science, Christine worked as a cultural anthropologist. Her professional interests include user-centered design, Library 2.0, and e-metrics. She holds BS and MA degrees in anthropology and a master's in library and information science.

Eleanor J. Read is an associate professor and the Social Science Data Services Librarian at the University of Tennessee Libraries. She provides traditional and specialized reference services to faculty and students in sociology and psychology, and to researchers with numeric data needs. Prior to becoming a librarian in 2000, she worked as a statistician on environmental cleanup and health effects research projects for the Department of Energy and for the Environmental Protection Agency.

Emma Shaw was formerly a graduate trainee information assistant at Cancer Research UK. She recently completed her master's in information management at Metropolitan University, London. Much of her experience has been in assisting in the practical provision of general library services, alongside promoting and assisting in the use of electronic resources. Emma now works in the Search Services team at the Royal Society of Medicine Library.

Carol Tenopir is a professor at the School of Information Sciences at the University of Tennessee, Knoxville, and the Interim Director of Research for the College of Communication and Information. Her areas of teaching and research include information access and retrieval, electronic publishing, the information industry, online resources, and the impact of technology on reference librarians and scientists. She is the author of five books, including, *Communication Patterns of Engineers* (IEEE/Wiley InterScience, 2004) with Donald W. King. Since 1983, she has written the "Online Databases" column for *Library Journal*.

Chris Wilson is Resources Manager, Library & Information Services, Cancer Research UK, London. He has responsibility for managing information services, and converting the service from a print-based traditional model into a virtual library in a short time. He is currently developing and testing a range of tools and techniques for managing an online journals collection.

Introduction

Back in the early days of electronic resources, librarians were preoccupied grappling with the acquisitions issues associated with determining what access their institution was entitled to (paid, free, free with print), somehow acquiring that access, and then, maintaining it with a certain degree of predictability; in those days statistics were not even considered. In the adolescence of the electronic era, libraries became more concerned with moving their print resources to online versions, and seeking out the best financial deals possible through better negotiation and consortial participation. Statistics gathering then seemed to gain more relevance. Now that the electronic era is in its early middle age, librarians are building upon those experiences, and looking to either develop the necessary tools in-house, and/or acquire those tools from publishers and vendors, which will enable them to properly evaluate the level of usage of their electronic resources and make informed and reasoned collection development decisions concerning their electronic resources.

This volume will look at various experiences from the field of electronic resources usage, statistics collection, and management. Alea Henle and Donnice Cochenour discuss issues involved in the processing, standardizing, and dissemination of usage statistics; Randle Gedeon presents a case study that examines the cost associated with the selection, acquisition, maintenance, and renewal of subscription-based aggregated packages of e-journals, juxtaposed against the savings of canceling print journals; Susanne Clement from the University of Kansas discusses the stewardship model used at that university and how it has incorporated a consistent methodology of evaluating and interpreting data

[Haworth co-indexing entry note]: "Introduction." Fowler, David C. Co-published simultaneously in *The Serials Librarian* (The Haworth Information Press, an imprint of The Haworth Press, Inc.) Vol. 53, Supplement No. 9, 2007, pp. 1-3; and: *Usage Statistics of E-Serials* (ed: David C. Fowler) The Haworth Information Press, an imprint of The Haworth Press, Inc., 2007, pp. 1-3. Single or multiple copies of this article are available for a fee from The Haworth Document Delivery Service [1-800-HAWORTH, 9:00 a.m. - 5:00 p.m. (EST). E-mail address: docdelivery@haworthpress.com].

Available online at http://ser.haworthpress.com
doi:10.1300/J123v53S09_01

about the content and usage of databases as part of the renewal decision; Carol Tenopir et al. look forward to the MaxData Project, which runs from 2005 to 2007, and will assist librarians in their justifications and decision making by comparing different types of data collection and data analysis methods; Carol Abatelli reports on the results of the Council of Connecticut Academic Library Directors (CCALD) e-resource management survey, which requested information about how the libraries manage their e-resource collections; and Arun Kumar and Martin Brändle discuss an in-house current-awareness module, MyCLICAPS, developed by the Chemistry Biology Pharmacy Information Center at ETH, Zürich.

The editor examines statistics options currently provided by a major electronic resources management firm, Serials Solutions; Christine Noonan and Melissa McBurney examine how usage statistics influence collection development decisions at a major National Laboratory; Susan Kendall and Celia Bakke look at how San Jose State University tracks electronic resources from the Federal depository program; Heather Morrison examines how usage statistics could form the basis for a usage-based pricing system, and the librarians at Cancer Research, UK, provide a case study that looks at the practical experiences in using journal usage statistics to assess the usefulness of electronic journals as part of the annual renewal or cancellation cycle.

Rickey Best from Auburn University, Montgomery, examines how his library determines the value of the information on cost ratios for access to the electronic databases and for cost of access of the articles; Eleonora Dubicki reports on how libraries can monitor and analyze usage statistics with the goal of best directing promotional efforts for electronic resources; Norm Medeiros discusses how a new method of calculating cost-per-use metrics is needed; Elise Anderson looks at the further steps required in the development of electronic usage statistics; and Joan Conger looks at how usage statistics contribute to library decision making within the context of comprehensive assessment. Finally, Janet Chisman examines SUSHI (Standardized Usage Statistics Harvesting Initiative), an exciting new resource in this field that holds much promise for the future.

Most of the authors in this volume responded to a call for papers issued by the editor in late 2004, and I greatly appreciate their hard work and tenacity. I am also grateful to Jim Cole at The Haworth Press, who presented the idea for this volume to me, and gave encouragement throughout.

David C. Fowler, MLS
Assistant Professor and Electronic Resources Librarian
University of Oregon Libraries
Eugene
December 2005

Chapter 1

Practical Considerations in the Standardization and Dissemination of Usage Statistics

Alea Henle
Donnice Cochenour

INTRODUCTION

The importance of usage statistics has risen with the increasing prevalence of electronic resources. The Association of Research Libraries (ARL) E-Metrics Project,[1] the International Coalition of Library Consortia (ICOLC) guidelines,[2] and the Counting Online Usage of NeTworked Electronic Resources (COUNTER) initiatives,[3] among others, have made great strides toward achieving the goals of having uniform definitions of terms involved in usage statistics, and having more uniformity among publishers and aggregators providing those statistics. However, such initiatives operate on a macro level while individual libraries deal with usage statistics on a micro level. The statistical environment has changed and continues to change, but the fact remains that each library must formulate its own approach toward processing, standardizing, and disseminating usage statistics, whether this involves manual labor, in-house design and/or creation of a "data farm," in which

[Haworth co-indexing entry note]: "Practical Considerations in the Standardization and Dissemination of Usage Statistics." Henle, Alea, and Donnice Cochenour. Co-published simultaneously in *The Serials Librarian* (The Haworth Information Press, an imprint of The Haworth Press, Inc.) Vol. 53, Supplement No. 9, 2007, pp. 5-23; and: *Usage Statistics of E-Serials* (ed: David C. Fowler) The Haworth Information Press, an imprint of The Haworth Press, Inc., 2007, pp. 5-23. Single or multiple copies of this article are available for a fee from The Haworth Document Delivery Service [1-800-HAWORTH, 9:00 a.m. - 5:00 p.m. (EST). E-mail address: docdelivery@haworthpress.com].

external database software is adopted, or some combination of these solutions. This chapter will discuss issues to be considered in the processing, standardizing, and dissemination of usage statistics, regardless of the method utilized, with relevant comments interlaced within the text, arising from the recent micro level statistical review conducted by Colorado State University Libraries (CSUL).

LITERATURE REVIEW

Published materials on the discussion of usage statistics thus far have understandably focused on the macro level. Articles addressing standardization across publishers, ARL's E-Metrics, and the COUNTER initiative comprise most of the recent library statistical literature, along with comparisons of local and publisher collected statistics.[4] There is very little literature that focuses on standardization, processing, and dissemination at the micro level.

A notable exception to the literature's trend toward the macro level is outlined in an article describing Yale University's collection and dissemination of statistics. In *Against the Grain,* Jennifer Weintraub discusses specific local decisions regarding processing and disseminating statistics, including the dissemination of direct links to aggregator and publisher statistical sites when access is via Internet Protocol (IP) recognition, or separated from administrative functions, and notes that "most statistics that are sent directly to me eventually become an Excel file." Important data were transformed into graphs "as a visual aid for the selectors."[5]

Writing in *E-Serials Collection Management: Transitions, Trends, and Technicalities,* Joanna Duy also refers to the value of maintaining "a spreadsheet or database about each electronic resource and how to obtain its usage data."[6] On the subjects of standardization and dissemination, Duy notes that while usage data can be passed on in the aggregator or in the publisher-provided format, she suggests "[a]lternatively . . . [to] use the data to format reports that summarize key measures in a standardized and more easy-to-read report format." One value of such specific, micro level comments lies in their ability to confirm local practices and/or suggest new avenues. At the time of the writing of this chapter, CSUL reformats usage data into spreadsheets that are fairly uniform, allowing selectors to easily identify data of interest. Although most data are not transformed into graphs currently, the tables can easily be transformed into graphs on demand using the tools built into the spreadsheet software, in CSUL's case, Microsoft Excel. While CSUL does not currently maintain usage statistics access information in a database–an idea clearly worthy of further consideration–the library does track and document information about the statistics maintained, including the start and end dates of available usage data and the frequency with which the spreadsheets are updated.

Unsurprisingly, the American Publishers Association (APA) has recognized the intricacies involved in providing usage statistics and defining their worth. In 2004, the APA published a monograph on statistics that included guidance and comments for publishers.[7] Most of the chapters in this document focus on macro level aspects of usage statistics and/or micro level aspects targeted toward nonlibrary audiences. However, the chapter written by librarians and about librarians addresses the evolution of processing and standardization.[8] While discussing the evolution of statistics-handling at Arizona State University Library, Wonsik Shim, Kurt Murphy, and Dennis Brunning mention some of the processing, standardization, and dissemination decisions made behind the scenes–either before or during implementation of Arizona State University Library's electronic use management information database. The references are brief, as processing is not the focus of the chapter, but given the dearth of additional resources, they do provide some data on local decisions. For example, a tracking database is loaded with "usage data by quarter and year" that can be produced into standard and customized reports. The database "is kept in a BRS Onsite database (formerly produced by the Bibliographic Retrieval Service, and later by Dataware Technologies, Inc.)" and librarians are provided with spreadsheets embedded with formulae to generate usable data, whenever queries are made.

PRACTICE AT THE LOCAL LEVEL: STANDARDIZATION

Why should we consider standardization before processing? Is that an instance of putting the cart before the horse? Although an ever-increasing number of aggregators and publishers offer COUNTER-compliant reports on usage statistics, there are still many variant methods of delivering usage statistics. Statistics are meaningless if they cannot be used. Therefore, identifying a desirable end product to meet local needs is a primary consideration. This applies equally to the adoption of a commercial statistical product, the development of an in-house "data farm," or the design of internal spreadsheets and/or databases that can be processed manually. Flexibility in the design process is necessary to deal with the inevitable differences in aggregator and publisher end products, but the ideal situation would be to identify a solution that will provide meaningful and uniform data for all resources. The processing and standardization of usage statistics is an area that is ripe for technological innovation. Several library service vendors have already taken note of this need. Innovative Interfaces, Inc. (III),[9] plans to include a statistical component in the 2005 update to the Electronic Resources Management product and in the fall of 2005, MPS Technologies (MacMillan Publisher Services)[10] will launch a commercial service called "ScholarlyStats" to collect and consolidate e-journal and database usage statistics reports.[11]

Two topics discussed in the following text, (1) current use/desired use and (2) budget/time/personnel issues, provide the underlying framework that drives micro level statistical standardization. On the one hand, desired use identifies the goal: statistics that will support the collection development process. On the other, the resources and constraints faced by the institution define the practical possibilities between current reality and the desired vision. Other narrower formatting considerations include time, ease of use, and categories for inclusion/exclusion.

Current Use versus Desired Use

During the recent statistical review at CSUL, individual meetings were scheduled with the subject selectors. The selectors were asked two basic questions:

1. How did they use the statistics that was currently available (and what changes did they not want)?
2. In an ideal world, what statistics would they like to see, and how would they like to access them?

Although at least one presumption proved true–that the science selectors were generally more interested in statistics than were selectors in the arts and humanities–the results provided a more varied picture than might have been predicted. Even places where the meetings did no more than confirm perceptions, they helped shape a standardization design targeted toward end use and included the selectors in the design process. They offered some surprises as well. For example, one of the arts selectors initially indicated that she did not use statistics at all. A conscious decision was made to meet with her again after completing the meetings with other selectors to review the emerging design consensus. After seeing the potential layout of database statistics for a publisher of primary source materials, the selector expressed interest in a design that would allow one to view, separately, a subset of the statistics relating to a specific subject (Figure 1.1) and any further requested statistics for another unrelated and comparatively expensive database.

One science selector expressed an interest in seeing statistics for turnaways not only by month but also by day and by hour. Two other selectors barely touched the issue of turnaways and instead focused their discussion on accessing journal use by subject rather than by aggregator or publisher.

Two additional considerations play an important role in the question of current use versus desired use. First, addressing the preferences of the individual(s) responsible for the processing affects the success of the review, especially if the review is conducted by others. In CSUL's case, the statistical preferences of the electronic resources librarian included centralization of data in a flexible format, standard designs requiring minimal reformatting, and identification of desired data reports. Second, accrediting organizations and/or regulatory agencies may require usage statistics reporting on an institutionwide scale. The member libraries of the ARL provide usage data as part of the Supplementary Statistics report. State universities are often required to report to their respective state agencies; these reports may require inclusion of usage data. In addition, departmental and university accreditation reviews may

FIGURE 1.1. Sample publisher spreadsheet documenting database-specific information. Data for all databases are provided on the "All" worksheet. Data for the drama databases only are broken out and provided separately, as shown, on the "Drama" worksheet.

	A	B	C	D	E	F	
1	Database	Date	Visits	Queries	Menu Selections	Viewed Items	
2	Asian American Drama	2004-01					
3	Asian American Drama	2004-02					
4	Asian American Drama	2004-03					
5	Asian American Drama	2004-04					
6	Asian American Drama	2004-05					

ALL **Drama** Notes

require evidence of resource utilization, and local administration may require annual reports on utilization of the library's resources. Known reporting requirements can be integrated into any redesign, simplifying the collection and dissemination of such reports (Figure 1.2).

The meetings and subsequent interactions with selectors, along with the reporting and processing requirements, established common interests for all groups as well as areas of specialized concerns. Although some of the identified goals are not currently possible or practical to achieve at CSUL, they could potentially be realized in the near future. Overall, the result of these meetings, along with the considerations outlined next, was a micro level design that addressed current needs. The design was also flexible enough to integrate with unforeseen future developments, a likely occurrence given the evolving technological environment. Last, but not least, the design incorporated local reporting requirements.

Budget/Time/Personnel

Vital questions involved in this aspect of a micro level statistical review project included: Who would undertake the review? Who would design and/or maintain the resultant standards and process the aggregator and publisher-provided statistics accordingly? How much time would be involved in the review process and in the implementation of the end products? How much time would be required on an ongoing basis? Finally, what, if any, actual funds would be needed?

Practical issues, as in most parts of the academic world, play a strong role in the design and implementation phases of standardization. Even

FIGURE 1.2. Sample overall spreadsheet, organized around ARL E-Metrics. The Logins, Queries and Items Requested worksheets contain usage data by month. The Notes worksheet contains any definitions provided by the publisher/aggregator and documents how the ARL E-Metrics categories are applied. The ARL worksheet contains the Fiscal Year data for all categories.

	A	B	C	D	E	F	G	H	I	J	K	L	M	N	O	P
1						Statistics -- Logins / Sessions										
2	Year					Monthly								Calendar	Fiscal YTD	
3		Jan	Feb	Mar	Apr	May	Jun	Jul	Aug	Sep	Oct	Nov	Dec	YTD	Totals	Year
4	2002													0		
5	2003													0	0	2002-2003
6	2004													0	0	2003-2004
7																

Logins / Queries / Items Requested / Notes / ARL /

for those institutions endowed with money and personnel to design a statistical database, the time issue, however, remains. How long will it take to have the database up and running? It may be long enough to justify an interim solution. Moreover, while major aggregators and publishers increasingly convert to COUNTER-compliant reports, a myriad of smaller publishers continue to provide a diversity of statistical formats and interfaces, which increases the level of complexity to be addressed manually or electronically. In a climate of dwindling funds and staffing, allocation of the resources required to create and maintain an in-house database may be beyond the foreseeable horizon for a given institution. Although, as noted previously, at least two statistical products are in the pipeline, commercial products are likely to focus on existing report standards (such as COUNTER), leaving non-COUNTER data to be addressed separately. Cost/benefit analysis of the commercial products, when available, may promote their adoption, but price could prove a stumbling block for libraries justifying additional purchases. The micro level review process provides an opportunity to collect data on existing expenditures in time and personnel, which will be of use in evaluating implementation of commercial ventures and/or investing in an in-house electronic solution.

Time

The issue of time arises in terms of integrating statistical data across years–although periodicity can also be a consideration. CSUL's preference is to utilize monthly data that can be summed according to need, with data by day and/or time of day restricted to specific aggregators, publishers, and subjects such as ISI Web of Knowledge turnaways. Aggregators and publishers vary widely in their presentation of statistics. Some only provide monthly data–one month at a time or for multiple months–and others allow those accessing the statistics to choose the timeframe (one, two, three, or more months) and then provide cumulated totals. COUNTER reports are based on providing monthly statistics, one calendar year at a time. In all these scenarios, integrating statistics across years requires an additional investment of staff processing time. Is it worth it? The tradeoff lies in its flexibility. That is, initial integration allows one to compare and contrast statistics, including formatting graphs and other visual aids, across years with minimal notice, rather than combining separate reports at the eleventh hour. For CSUL, a compromise between processing and flexibility emerged. At this time, the number of logins, the number of searches, and the types of items requested (full-text article requests, abstracts, etc.) are combined across years for databases and journals *at the publisher or aggregator level*. Journal article requests at the title level, whether or not they are derived from COUNTER Journal Report 1 (JR1): Number of Successful Full-Text Article Requests by Month and Journal, are combined across years while all types of items requested, such as abstracts, tables of contents, and specific types of full-text downloads, are not combined, unless the total number of journals involved is minimal or has not changed (Table 1.1 for COUNTER report definitions). This is due to the fact that most reports are currently manually processed–a fact which has not escaped the notice of library service vendors. Future electronic resource management developments may resolve the issue. Alternatively, other vendors such as ISI may step into the breach and redress the situation. Although the mechanism for integration is not yet known, advance information indicates that the product will integrate JR1 at the database level, which will save considerable processing time. The product is initially focused on JR1, but further releases may extend functionality to address additional reports.

Initial information regarding the MPS Technologies' ScholarlyStats indicates that the project encompasses the goal of obtaining data for separate publishers and consolidating the results into comprehensive reports. The scope of this project clearly focuses on COUNTER reports, and will also incorporate non-COUNTER data, especially with regards to journals. The COUNTER reports designated for inclusion were not finalized at the time of writing this paper, but communication from MPS indicates that the extent of the project depends on library interest and will probably encompass all COUNTER reports eventually, as well as integrating non-COUNTER data into COUNTER report format.[12] After beta testing, MPS may offer a software toolkit both as a stand-alone product and also in conjunction with their processing service, if the interest expressed justifies it.[13]

Ease of Use

CSUL's practice is to provide most of the data in a tabular format that can easily be converted into other formats, with visual graphics provided for a few select resources and types of statistics. Due to budgetary constraints and existing university-wide software deals, the statistics

TABLE 1.1. COUNTER report definitions.

COUNTER report	Report title	Description	Definitions
Journal Report 1	Number of Successful Full-Text Article Requests by Month and Journal	Full-Text downloads in all formats	
Journal Report 1a	Number of Successful Full-Text Requests in html and PDF Formats	Full-Text downloads separated by format	
Journal Report 2	Turnaways by Month and Journal	Number of times a user was denied access where the user access model is based on a maximum number of concurrent users	A turnaway (rejected session) is defined as an unsuccessful log-in to an electronic service due to exceeding the simultaneous user limit allowed by the license
Journal Report 3	Number of Successful Item Requests and Turnaways by Month, Journal and Page-Type	Full-Text downloads totaled and separated by format plus additional request types from Abstracts to Table of Contents	Note: Not mandatory for compliance under the Code of Practice at this time. Vendors are encouraged to provide this report as able to do so.
Database Report 1	Total Searches and Sessions by Month and Database	Searches and user sessions accumulated by database	A session is one cycle of user activities that typically starts when a user connects to the service or database and ends by terminating activity that is either explicit (by leaving the service through exit or logout) or implicit (timeout due to user inactivity)
Database Report 2	Turnaways by Month and Database	Number of times a user was denied access where the user access model is based on a maximum number of concurrent users	
Database Report 3	Total Searches and Sessions by Month and Service	Searches and user sessions accumulated for the entire service	A service is a branded group of online information products from one or more vendors that can be subscribed to/licensed and searched as a complete collection, or at a lower level

are saved as spreadsheets. This enables selectors to have direct access to the raw data. While the data may be adjusted and reformatted into Web pages, graphs, and charts, such decisions are made on a case-by-case basis. Exceptions, once made, generally turn into regular features. As this indicates, the development of enhanced statistics is an organic, need-driven process. This provides an additional benefit of easier processing, since a good portion of available statistics are provided in spreadsheet-friendly formats. Maintaining data in uniform format allows for a few standardized designs, so that selectors can easily identify the specific data they are looking for, when comparing one provider to another.

CSUL generally provides usage statistics in one or more formats of three types of reports: Overall, Databases, and Journals. The Overall report is organized around the ARL E-Metrics categories (Figure 1.2). As an ARL library, CSUL reports these statistics annually, as Supplementary Statistics and the report format simplifies that task. When an aggregator or publisher does not provide sufficient data to warrant a Databases or Journals report, detailed information is included on the assorted tabs of the Overall report. Turnaways at the resource level are included in the Overall report. The Databases and Journals reports, as the names suggest, offers detailed information about respective databases and journals. The tables are organized horizontally or vertically, whichever format minimizes processing, and are easily sorted and filtered (Figures 1.3 and 1.4).

Aggregator and publisher data provided without dates–usually in month-by-month reports–are integrated by the simple expedient of adding a column/row, typing the date, and copying it as needed. Within the spreadsheets, full-text article request (JR1 or equivalent) statistics are maintained and updated on one worksheet, while additional statistics, such as COUNTER Journal Report 3: Full-Text Article Requests and Turnaways by Month, Journal, and Page-Type (JR3) are stored separately, when provided.

Subject- and/or department-specific listings for full-text article requests are still under development. Ideally, these should eventually be addressed by an in-house or a commercial statistical product. Until then, the journal spreadsheets include columns, which are hidden when not in use, that identify relevant titles for specific subjects and/or departments as shown in Figure 1.5. Re-sorting by a given column allows the relevant data to be batch-copied, and then pasted into a separate document-tracking usage by subject or department.

For example, the engineering sciences subject selector will review publisher packages, either title-by-title or by publisher catalog subject listings, and will identify journals of interest. After revealing the column(s) that designate subject coverage in each relevant aggregator or publisher spreadsheet, the data are re-sorted ("X" literally marks the journals), and the journals of interest can then easily be copied and pasted into another spreadsheet, this one geared toward the specific department(s). When statistics for new titles appear in the report, the titles

FIGURE 1.3. Sample processed COUNTER JR1–data aligned horizontally.

A	I	J	K	L	M	N	O	P	Q	R	S	T	U	V	W	X
Journal Name	1999								2000							
	Jun	Jul	Aug	Sep	Oct	Nov	Dec	CY	Jan	Feb	Mar	Apr	May	Jun	Jul	Aug
Total for all journals																
Agronomy Journal																
American Journal of Clinical Nutrition																
American Journal Of Pathology																
American Journal of Psychiatry																
American Journal of Public Health																
American Journal of Roentgenology																
American Journal of Sports Medicine																
Annals of the New York Academy of Sciences																
Biology of Reproduction																
Blood																
Cancer Epidemiology Biomarkers &																

FIGURE 1.4. Sample processed non-COUNTER report–data aligned vertically.

	A	B	C	D	E	F	G	H	I
	Date	Journal	Home Page	Current Issue Toc	All TOCs	Searches	Abstracts	Full Text HTML	PDF's
2	Jan-99	FASEB Journal							
3	Jan-99	Genes & Development							
4	Jan-99	Journal of Histochemistry and Cytochemistry							
5	Jan-99	Journal of Pharmacology and Experimental Therapeutics							
6	Jan-99	Molecular Pharmacology							
7	Jan-99	PNAS							
8	Jan-99	Totals							

are noted and e-mailed to the selector. These titles are then added to a subject column only if the selector indicates an interest. This feature is limited to JR1 data, since it features usage statistics for all available years and allows for comparison of use across e-journal providers. Similar to the other special features, this process also is need-driven. When selectors are sufficiently interested in viewing data by subject/department, the goal is to answer such interest. If a selector is willing to review a list of titles, whether a complete list or only those based on publisher-supplied subject categories, producing a corresponding, targeted spreadsheet requires relatively little effort and increases the selector's ease of use.

Statistical Categories for Inclusion/Exclusion

While many of the statistical categories offered by aggregators and publishers are similar across the spectrum, the issue of whether or not they are defined and collected similarly is another matter. Identifying which types of usage statistics to obtain, standardize, and disseminate is not a difficult matter and most likely varies little from library to library. For the most part, the E-Metrics, ICOLC, and COUNTER initiatives establish base-level usage statistics categories. A significant number of

FIGURE 1.5. Sample Vendor JR1 with subject/department columns unhidden.

	A	B	C	D	E	F	G	H	I
1	SASDW	SCEEW	SMEEW	SCBEW	SELDW				
2						Journal	Print ISSN	Online ISSN	Jan
3						Total			
4						Acta Oecologica		'1146609X	
5						Addictive Behaviors		'03064603	
6						Advanced Energy Conversion		'03651789	
7						Advances in Applied Mathematics		'01968858	
8						Advances in Free Radical Biology & Medicine		'87559668	
9						Advances in Mathematics		'00018708	
10		X				Advances in Water Resources		'03091708	
11						Ageing Research Reviews		'15681637	
12						Aggression and Violent Behavior		'13591789	
13	X					Agricultural and Forest Meteorology		'01681923	
14						Agricultural Economics		'01695150	
15	X					Agricultural Meteorology		'00021571	

FT / Non-FT-04 / Non-FT-03 / Non-Subscribed /

aggregators and publishers now offer an eclectic assortment of additional statistical data, and these comprise a grayer area. The discussions with subject selectors at CSUL provided the criteria by which additional use data were included or excluded. Standard data types form the majority of the included statistics–logins, turnaways, searches, content pages, abstracts, and full-text documents. A separate listing of the excluded reports is disseminated with the usage statistics, ensuring that selectors are aware that they exist.

PRACTICE AT THE LOCAL LEVEL: PROCESSING

The popular acronym KISS (Keep It Simple, Stupid) is a handy motto to bear in mind when considering the standardization and processing of usage statistics. Keeping report designs simple and flexible minimizes selector confusion by allowing them to readily identify desired statistics, no matter which aggregator or publisher's data they are consulting. Equally important is the ease of transfer of aggregator- and publisher-provided usage statistics into simple reports on a regular basis. In CSUL's case, the simplest reports for journal and database information are based on COUNTER reports as the evolving standard. Practically speaking, most usage statistics are processed and provided in tabular format, either horizontally (dates run across the report, usually COUNTER-compliant) (Figure 1.3) or vertically (types of statistics run across the report (Figure 1.4). In either case, it is relatively easy to add date fields, if these are not provided in the report; Figure 1.6 offers a non-COUNTER usage report as obtained from the publisher and saved in spreadsheet format, while Figure 1.4 shows the same report after processing.

The true difficulty lies in integrating reports across years. Indeed, the non-COUNTER-compliant reports are often easier to combine. They can extend through time, *ad infinitum,* and can also be easily sorted by various criteria. Although database usage statistics are not necessarily easy to integrate, their relative stability in aggregator or publisher affiliation and smaller numbers as compared to electronic journals, render them a lesser issue. Therefore, more attention is paid in this chapter to the difficulty of processing and integrating e-journal statistics.

While the calendar year design of COUNTER reports is understandable, this can prove cumbersome when applied in practice to e-journals,

FIGURE 1.6. Sample unprocessed non-COUNTER report–data aligned vertically.

Journal	Usage Month/Type	Home Page	Current Issue Toc	All TOCs	Unique TOCs	Searches	Abstra
Agronomy Journal	No usage was reported during January 1999.						
American Journal of Clinical Nutrition	No usage was reported during January 1999.						
American Journal Of Pathology	No usage was reported during January 1999.						
American Journal of Psychiatry	No usage was reported during January 1999.						
American Journal of Public Health	No usage was reported during January 1999.						
American Journal of Roentgenology	No usage was reported during January 1999.						
The American Journal of Sports Medi	No usage was reported during January 1999.						
Annals of the New York Academy of	No usage was reported during January 1999.						
Biology of Reproduction	No usage was reported during January 1999.						
Blood	No usage was reported during January 1999.						
Cancer Epidemiology Biomarkers & E	No usage was reported during January 1999.						
Cancer Research	No usage was reported during January 1999.						
Chest	No usage was reported during January 1999.						
Clinical Cancer Research	No usage was reported during January 1999.						

not because of the design itself, but because of certain unfortunate realities in the publishing market. In particular, this refers to the increasing consolidation of publishers and the continuous change in e-journal title lists offered by a particular aggregator or publisher. Tracking usage for a particular title or subject over time, using COUNTER reports, requires integrating the data line-by-line. In the absence of a sophisticated electronic mechanism to resolve this shortcoming, other options are not always ideal. Manually integrating reports is time consuming and not always practical. Even if an electronic mechanism for processing does exist, spot checks may be necessary to confirm that data are matched correctly. The easiest solution is to integrate reports only when specific data are required, and then only for requested titles. A potential compromise is to integrate only the JR1 report, either mechanically or manually.

A further complication of consolidation is caused by the very nature of serials: over time, journal titles change, split into multiple parts, merge, and change publishers. When a journal changes its title, related statistics are often collected under both titles. Subparts often receive separate statistical listings that appear as new, unrelated titles in the statistical reports, for instance, Parts A, B, etc., and/or additional or altered titles such as the *New Anatomist* issued in conjunction with the *Anatomical Record*. Meanwhile, statistics continue to be collected under the presplit title for earlier issues. Usage statistics of merged journals are collected under the new and former titles. When journals change publishers, access to issues and corresponding statistics are split between the old and new publishers. Also, more than one aggregator or publisher may provide access to issues of a given journal at the same time. Any of these issues produces fractures in a journal's usage statistics that may go unnoticed and, thus, produce a false picture of the actual importance of a title for the local collection. While such detailed statistics are valuable, compiling them to ascertain the use of a given subscription and/or subject becomes a more complicated affair. The task of integration across titles, as with integrating JR3 statistics, is too manually cumbersome to justify routine processing and is better saved for specific requests.

PRACTICE AT THE LOCAL LEVEL: DISSEMINATION

Posting usage statistics on a central Web site is a fairly simple measure of dissemination. Although some care may be required where access to usage statistics is restricted, staff Web sites offer a fairly stable environment to do so, and also allow for links to a variety of formats including internal databases and spreadsheets. With the upcoming statistical function of Innovative Interfaces' electronic resources management (ERM) module, libraries using this software will have the opportunity to store some usage statistics centrally, although it certainly seems advantageous to keep backup copies stored separately. Joanna Duy recommends keeping "information about how to access the statistics," as well as start and end dates, and "what kinds of measures are reported" in a simple database.[14] This can be developed internally, or stored within an electronic resources management system. CSUL is still in the process of implementing the Innovative Interfaces' ERM module, but already has allocated time to establish what information will be stored in the statistics field(s) provided: the URL for the statistical interface with logins and passwords (or other instructions; for example, the e-mail address for a specified individual to request data) and the server location where existing statistics and documented processing procedures are stored (Figure 1.7).

Offering a stable, reliable location for storing usage statistics is an important step, but an equally vital component is the human element. When one person consistently retrieves and processes statistics for given aggregator(s) or publisher(s), that person is usually best placed to notice any changes in usage. For example, a significant increase in turnaways for a particular resource at the very least deserves some attention, and may require action. In addition, a regular or semi-regular e-mail that alerts selectors about the availability of the latest monthly, quarterly, or semiannual statistics, provides a reminder, given that most subject selectors have many demands for their time and attention. Re-

FIGURE 1.7. Sample ERM usage statistics fields. The Usage Statistics field is repeatable. The first instance contains the URL to obtain statistics. The second contains the local address where processing instructions, processed reports, and archived original reports are stored. When the statistical login differs from the administrative, a third instance will contain the usage statistics username and password.

Administration	username: xxxxxxx; password: xxxxx
Usage Statistics	http://www.bioone.org/bioone/?request=report-login
Usage Statistics	http://server.colostate.edu/statistics/bioone.html

visiting selectors to ask the questions featured in the initial standardization phase is an additional tool in the never-ending quest to keep statistical information and interfaces evolving to suit present and projected needs.

AREAS FOR ACTION

As is true for any function in the midst of expansion, there are many areas for potential action at the macro and micro levels. Although the focus is at the individual library level, there are ways in which aggregators, publishers, and library service vendors could ease the local standardization and processing of statistics. Electing to adopt these or similar improvements would also benefit publishers by creating a clearer picture of evolving use over time, thereby justifying future library expenditures.

Journal Changes

Many of the frustrations of processing and integrating journal statistics arise from the issues mentioned in the aforementioned section, Practice at the Local Level: Processing, such as, title changes, journal mergers, subparts, and the addition or deletion of titles from a given publisher's product list. Clear information and documentation of these changes by publishers would reduce the need for individual libraries to independently research and compile them. In the print environment, this was of lesser importance and was usually handled by a library's serials agent. Now, many electronic packages are purchased directly from the publisher with no intervention by a serials agent, a situation that requires the publisher to assume responsibility for alerting libraries of any changes to their title list. The ability to combine statistics for previous titles/premerged journals into one listing offers at least one simple benefit for both publishers and libraries: the consolidated listing indicates the true level of interest in a given subject/ journal, an issue of no small importance for publishers. In an era of an increasing number of consortial deals, consolidated title-level statistics may provide libraries with incentives to actively support renewing such deals.

Reviewing the statistics might well reveal that, in the absence of such a deal, subscriptions to titles previously not thought to be of interest would cost significantly more, necessitating extensive budget discussions. For libraries, such documentation would ease the manual processing of composite statistics and provide a blueprint for electronic integration of statistics.

Subject-Specific Statistics

The increasing consolidation in the publishing world effectively combines statistics for multiple subjects into massive centralized lists. Given the smaller numbers, databases are more easily processed and sorted by subject, but even in this case, publishers and aggregators might offer libraries the option of presorting databases by area of interest during the process of obtaining statistics. With journals, especially with regard to publishers and aggregators providing access to hundreds or thousands of titles, the ability to easily sort by subject is even more desirable. Selectors are often reluctant to review long lists of titles, especially those irrelevant to their particular interests, and restrict such action to the most basic requirements. At least two entities already offer the ability to retrieve journal statistics by subject (JSTOR and Cambridge University Press). Most publishers offer lists of journal titles by subject in the marketing pages of their Web sites. Integrating these details with statistics is time-intensive and requires reconciling with different publishers' nonstandard subject classifications. As such, this would be a candidate for a centralized approach, either through service vendors or through an emergent standard.

Library Service Vendors

Many library service vendors will probably jump into the statistical market, following the initial forays of Innovative Interfaces and MPS. The current market is ripe for innovation, particularly in the arena of value-added reports. At the ground level, consolidation of statistical reports, across time and across publishers, provides a foundation for more sophisticated applications. Both these issues would fit well within the parameters of central vendors servicing multiple libraries. Service vendors could create, update, and apply subject taxonomies to journals and databases across publishers and platforms, allowing libraries and librarians to evaluate resources within discipline contexts. Equally, service vendors could create, update, and apply documentation, tracking journal histories through title changes, mergers, splits, and publisher shifts. One caution to note: since the usernames and passwords required to obtain usage statistics from publisher Web sites are often identical to the administrative usernames and passwords, any service vendor providing a service that includes extracting statistics from Web sites would need strong protection against the misuse of administrative functions. A better arrangement for publishers would perhaps be to separate access to the library's general administrative module from access to the statistical reports module.

CONCLUSIONS

As electronic resources expand to become the preferred format in libraries, aggregator- and publisher-supplied usage statistics will be one of the primary criteria in the collection management decision making process. Collecting and analyzing these statistics at the micro level will become essential to this decision process, if it has not already. Even with standardized definitions and report formats, as detailed in COUNTER and other guidelines, individual libraries will have to manipulate the data to meet local demands. Aggregators and publishers can simplify this process by listening to grassroots requests and continuing to evolve additional reporting features based on both popular need and a combination of interface and content. Commercial "integrated library systems" software vendors can increase the value of their products by developing data storage and integration tools to handle these standard reports. While some additional data processing, such as subject assignment, title history tracking, and the consolidation of standardized reports across vendors and time, can be handled at the universal level by those vendors who are inclined to move into this market, none of these will replace the requirement for the local library to determine how to format and present the data to meet local needs. An excellent method to accomplish this is through a local needs-assessment process that identifies all potential uses and users of the data, along with the preferred formats of the consolidated reports. From this process, the library will have a clear picture of the desired outcome and the actions necessary to reach that vision.

NOTES

1. Association of College & Research Libraries, "E-Metrics Activities," http://www.arl.org/stats/newmeas/emetrics/proj.html
2. International Coalition of Library Consortia, "Guidelines for Statistical Measures of Usage of Web-Based Information Resources (Update: December 2001)," http://www.library.yale.edu/consortia/2001webstats.htm, and "Guidelines for Statistical Measures of Usage of Web-based Indexed, Abstracted, and Full-Text Resources (November 1998)," http://www.library.yale.edu/consortia/webstats.html
3. Counting Online Usage of NeTworked Electronic Resources, "Code of Practice," http://www.projectcounter.org/code_practice.html
4. Articles on the macro level include Pesch, Oliver. "Usage Statistics: Taking E-Metrics to the Next Level" *The Serials Librarian*, 2004, 46 (1): 143-154, and Shim, Wonsik, and Charles R. McClure. "Improving Database Vendors Usage Statistics Reporting through Collaboration between Libraries and Vendors" *College and Research Libraries*, 2002, 63 (6): 499-514.
5. Jennifer, Weintraub. "Usage Statistics at Yale University Library." *Against the Grain*, December 2003-January 2004, 15 (6): 32, 34.
6. Joanna, Duy. *"Usage Data: Issues and Challenges."* In: *E-Serials Collection Management: Transitions, Trends, and Technicalities,* ed. David C. Fowler, 111-138 Binghamton, NY: Haworth Information Press, 2004.
7. Bernard, Rous, ed., *Online Usage: A Publisher's Guide.* New York: Association of American Publishers, Inc., 2004.
8. Wonsik, Shim, Kurt Murphy, and Dennis Brunning. "Usage Statistics for Electronic Services and Resources: A Library Perspective." In *Online Usage: A Publisher's Guide,* ed. Bernard Rous, 34-46. New York: Association of American Publishers, Inc., 2004.
9. Innovative Interfaces, Inc., http://www.iii.com/. Information concerning the statistical release was not available on the Web site when the article was written, and was gathered through CSUL's III sales representative.
10. MPS Technologies, http://www.mpstechnologies.com/
11. Martha Sedgewick, e-mail message to LIBLICENSE LISTSERV, May 9, 2005.
12. Martha Sedgewick, e-mail message to the authors, March 1, 2005, and personal communication, April 15, 2005.
13. David Sommer, personal communication, March 3, 2005.
14. Duy, 134.

doi:10.1300/J123v53S09_02

Chapter 2

Are We Really Balancing the Ledger with E-Journals?

Randle Gedeon

INTRODUCTION

Electronic journals have dramatically changed all the layers of the research landscape. This change affects how researchers conduct their research and how libraries support those research efforts. The acquisition and support of e-journals has required budgetary reallocations, personnel work shifts, and workflow altering in technical services departments. Additional resources for heightened access and support of e-journals have become a big market in the library industry. Link resolving software and open URLs, which allow the ability to link to the original content, are now ubiquitous. The landscape has now changed so dramatically in this regard that vendors offering noncompliant content can count on reduced rates of usage for their electronic products.[1] Negotiating and administering licenses represent significant legal and time commitments on behalf of universities. The confluence of these elements has created a market for electronic resource management (ERM) software. The process of managing e-journals thus continues to become an increasingly complicated and costly enterprise. These complications are further exaggerated by varied vendor/publisher guidelines, specifications, and expectations. That being said, e-journals provide considerable added benefits, including remote access for multiple users, desktop

[Haworth co-indexing entry note]: "Are We Really Balancing the Ledger with E-Journals?" Gedeon, Randle. Co-published simultaneously in *The Serials Librarian* (The Haworth Information Press, an imprint of The Haworth Press, Inc.) Vol. 53, Supplement No. 9, 2007, pp. 25-42; and: *Usage Statistics of E-Serials* (ed: David C. Fowler) The Haworth Information Press, an imprint of The Haworth Press, Inc., 2007, pp. 25-42. Single or multiple copies of this article are available for a fee from The Haworth Document Delivery Service [1-800-HAWORTH, 9:00 a.m. - 5:00 p.m. (EST). E-mail address: docdelivery@haworthpress.com].

convenience, the virtual elimination of theft and mutilation incidents, and the potential addition of multitudes of titles to library collections.

Library administrators once looked to electronic resources for possible measures of savings in library budgets. Minimal savings might still be found around the edges when converting print subscriptions to electronic equivalents, but conversely, additional costs associated with e-journals are now found lurking everywhere. It has been suggested that a series of myths still exist in the minds of many librarians regarding electronic resources: (1) these resources will resolve serials budget crises; (2) they require less work in technical services; (3) "Big Deal" style publisher packages save the library's money; and (4) moving to e-journals automatically removes the need for serials check-in.[2] The automatic presumption of savings is now readily disabused; converting print journal subscriptions to their electronic equivalents is now recognized as having come with additional costs and trade-offs.

PRICING MODELS

The "Big Deal" captured a lot of attention in the e-journal realm several years ago. Kenneth Frazier coined the term defining "Big Deals" as collections of online journals available for an established price (sometimes variable by institution, due to users populations and consortial arrangements), often at the cost of print subscriptions with an additional incremental percentage, with the rate of increase being determined contractually and smaller percentages of increase attached to lengthier contracts.[3] A groundswell against this model developed, citing the inability to remove unwanted titles, the developing sense of dependency directed toward a few large publishers, the fact that negotiating directly with publishers effectively kept trusted subscription agents out of the mix, and also the belief that this practice tends to homogenize journal collections.[4]

Many publishers also offered "free" access to the electronic version of a subscribed print title. We now see this practice ceasing with many publishers offering a "print plus online" option, where an additional percentage is tacked on to a print subscription for additional electronic access. An "E-Only" option has more recently surfaced in which the subscribing institution agrees to cancel all of their print subscriptions and move to an entirely electronic model in exchange for a contracted set rate of price increases. Over the last two years, the author's institution has pursued the E-Only model with a number of publishers, canceling in the process hundreds of print titles with major publishers like the American Chemical Society, Elsevier, IEEE, and Sage.

In tough economic times, the cost of journal content, regardless of format, will be of significant consideration. Shifting to the E-Only option only buys an institution some additional time. The savings that an institution might expect to realize by this change will, in all likelihood, work out to be well below the comparable annual rate of inflation for periodicals in any given year.

GAUGING USAGE

Publisher-provided statistics create a real briar patch to analyze. Little or no control is exercised over how and when data are provided to a subscriber. Not all publishers deliver comparable statistics in a uniform format, and some publishers offer no usage data at all.[5] Often, the data that the publisher provides are all there is to work with, and that can sometimes require librarians to "don green eyeshades" in order to assist with the interpretation. Certainly some institutions do generate statistics locally, but as Judy Luther points out, "once the patron enters a publisher site; that patron's movements are solely tracked by the publisher."[6] Another point to consider is that local institutional tracking statistics have found discrepancy in their data, when juxtaposed against publisher data; James Stemper and Janice Jaguszewski, who compared data from four different publishers, found a variance of up to 2 percent.[7]

Usage data provides a measure of activity that often is equated with the number of articles downloaded as PDF files, in HTML format, printed out by the user, or sent as e-mails; once again, the manner in which the information is portrayed varies by publisher. This activity can be interpreted in a many different ways, particularly when presented out of context. However, it does provide a measure on what the resources are or what resources are being utilized. Additional factors, such as cost or the amount of available content, are regularly offered as "context" in calculating the average cost per access or article, a practice associating cost with productivity either for the given article or service, and discounting all other noneconomic factors.[8] Using that cost context, the author's institution's 2004 use of Wiley InterScience (4658) or Emerald (2389) divided by the cost of the service provides an average cost per article.

A CASE STUDY

The context of this case study encompasses entire packages of e-journals, priced as whole units, with full-text activity in the form of PDF and HTML articles downloaded, e-mailed, or printed being considered. This arbitrary decision is based upon the following two points: (1) most e-journal packages offer some type of usage data and (2) fees are typically instituted for the entire package and not individual titles. Situational dynamics can place the cost of journal package within the budgetary context of the acquisitions budget, the serials budget, or the electronic serials budget.

Western Michigan University (WMU) enrolls approximately 28,000 students and is categorized by the Carnegie Foundation as Doctoral/Research Universities-Extensive. WMU offers 150 undergraduate programs, seventy master's programs, two specialist programs, and thirty doctoral degree areas. In support of these programs, the University Libraries subscribe to a variety of publisher e-journal packages including the ACM Digital Library; the American Chemical Society; BioOne; Emerald Library; IEEE Xplore; JSTOR: Arts & Sciences Collections I, II, III, IV, and Music Collection; Oxford University Press; Springerlink; Project Muse; PROLA (American Physical Society); and Science-Direct.

Waldo Library employs a library administrator, four support staff, a host of librarians, and a student worker, all of whom spend varied portions of their schedule in the support of its electronic journal service. Average personnel costs are represented as $35.00 per hour for a library administrator or senior librarian, $25.00 per hour for a librarian, $20.00 per hour for a senior staff member, and $6.50 per hour for a student worker.

What Does It Involve?

The process of selecting, licensing, accessing, maintaining, and ultimately renewing e-journals is a complicated and often expensive procedure. Vetting an electronic resource for potential purchase may require the time and research efforts of several librarians. Licensing a resource will require the time and expertise of an experienced librarian or library administrator, and in some cases, perhaps that of an attorney as well. Access to some resources may require the purchase of additional supporting software and hardware, with the attendant setting up and programming, along with all that is required for activation of a resource and bibliographic control. Maintenance involves updating the data through a variety of administrative modules, link checking, and post-setup troubleshooting. Renewing a resource may repeat some of the steps of the original vetting process, along with a review of the usage data relative to a given institution's curricular needs.

Whom Does It Involve?

Personnel costs represent a significant portion of the library budget, and what portion of that expense will be attributable to the provision of e-journals will vary by institution. Personnel costs represent a significant expense, but this financial outlay will always be a part of the cost of conducting library business. Some new positions may be authorized, although typically, existing personnel retool their existing skill sets to prepare for the additional challenge. The contents of job descriptions and the number of personnel supporting that part of the serials operation will depend on the institution's commitment to e-journals. Individuals, units, or departments may be charged with the responsibility.

At WMU, responsibilities for e-journal acquisition and maintenance are assigned diffusively. An administrator, the library faculty, several staff members, and a student assistant are all involved in the e-journal life cycle. The position of electronic resources librarian is a standard player in many library systems and currently represents an open position which this university has only recently been authorized to fill; the cataloger who had previously cataloged e-journals retired recently and has not yet been replaced, so other staff members have necessarily filled those gaps.

Current players in WMU's e-journals drama are the assistant dean for resources, who interfaces with vendors and consortia partners and disseminates information to concerned parties; the assistant dean also chairs the Libraries' Collection Development Committee, where major purchasing decisions are made. The acquisitions and serials librarian likewise deals with vendors, as well as facilitates orders, approves larger invoices, participates in the statewide collection development group, and serves as a voting member on both the Collection Development and Serials Committees. Most of the library faculty members serve as liaison to the various colleges and departments on campus. These librarians request trials and submit orders for e-journals and services on behalf of teaching faculty or in support of a curriculum. Many of these librarians serve on the previously mentioned vetting committees, considering these and other purchases, and later instructing patrons in their proper use. Several full-time staff members are central to the e-journal operation. The serial resources coordinator places orders with vendors or subscription agents, maintains order and vendor information in the integrated library system (ILS), performs copy cataloging of e-journals, liaisons with vendor support staff, cancels print subscriptions with vendors, closes print records as needed, and attends Serials Committee meetings as a nonvoting member. The serials resources coordinator also spends approximately two-thirds of his time working with e-resources. The electronic resources specialist spends all of his time in support of e-resources, serving as the designated troubleshooter. This position is the technical liaison with publishers, vendors, and the systems that WMU subscribes to, which supports them (such as EZ Proxy and SFX); the person in this position also runs reports and maintains the departmental Access '97 database. A senior staff member of the Cataloging Department spends approximately one-quarter of his or her time cataloging e-resources. The library systems manager spends approximately one-quarter of his or her time supporting the software and hardware required to run the ILS, EZ Proxy, and SFX installations. A student assistant, scheduled to work twelve hours a week, is responsible for checking Web links and for updating information in the departmental Microsoft Access '97 database.

Vetting Process

Practices vary by institution, but getting approval to purchase a journal or journal collection (print or electronic) at the author's institution requires that the requested item pass through multiple obstacles. Initially, a request is generated via an online or printed form. Requesters must provide a rationale for purchase and are asked to pass along any background information they may have. Also, they are asked to search the Online Public Access Catalog in order to avoid possible duplication with a preexisting subscribed resource before turning in the completed request to their departmental library liaison. The liaison is then asked to search *Ulrich's* or *The Serials Directory* for pricing information, to determine whether the title is refereed or not, to ascertain bibliographic information, and ascertain electronic availability. The request is then forwarded to the Serials Resources Department for further action and the liaison is then expected to present the request to the Serials Committee. Once the request is at the Serials Department, the provided information is verified, copyright and ILL files are checked for usage statistics, and publisher Web sites and Online Computer Library Center (OCLC) are also searched for further background information. Requests are then placed on the Serials Committee agenda. This committee meets every month and is comprised of five public services and technical services librarians and three Serials staff. This group meets for the purpose of considering e-resource requests that are under a predetermined price ceiling of $2,000.

Requests that are accepted by the Serials Committee are then passed along to the Collection Development Committee (CDC) for final approval. The CDC is comprised of the assistant dean for resources and six librarians, who represent a variety of disciplines as well as technical services. This group considers the requests approved by the Serials Committee and all other requests priced at over the $2,000 price ceiling and recommends trials before purchase. Once approved, the request is turned over to the Serial Resources Unit for purchase. The library liaison and requester are then informed of the decision.

Trials

Prior to purchase, collections of e-journals and databases are typically subject to a trial period at WMU. Trials determine a resource's usefulness, as well as the depth and breadth of its content, and may reveal how easy and intuitive its search interface is. Before the beginning of trial, a trial license may be signed, often determining such details as the scope of the participants involved (librarians, faculty, patrons, etc.) and duration of the trial (typically, one month). If the licensing terms are acceptable, the trial is setup and the institution is authenticated for access. Once available, input on the product is solicited from trial participants. These views and opinions, combined with those of the participating librarians, largely form the basis of the purchasing decision. If the trial is deemed successful, the Collection Development Committee then considers the purchase.

Licensing

A decision to purchase an e-resource leads to consideration of the licensing agreement, often a point of consternation for librarians. Lengthy, complicated agreements serving the publisher's best interests, and those which limit a library's ability to provide conventional service, have been a regular source of complaints. These agreements are typically found on the publisher's Web site, but this is certainly not always the case. Occasionally, these agreements are only available in abridged form or not readily available at all. These agreements are binding legal documents, and should be entered into and treated in a very serious fashion. The issues to be considered are the person designated to sign (typically, a senior collection development officer, or an administrator), how the agreements are monitored and tracked, and an appreciation for the consequences of a license violation. Reviewing a license may occupy many hours of a limited schedule for senior members of a library. It is important to keep in mind that the signatory for the library is not just representing the library; he or she is signing for the institution at large and for the Board of Trustees. The library is obligated to spell out to patrons any conditions of use in plain and clear language.

Many elements of these agreements are boilerplate in nature, with standard conditions of permitted use, method of authentication, length of term, format of materials, archival rights, technical support, and payment terms consistently found. If an institution has an expectation for training, or for the use of the material in e-reserves or ILL, it should be clearly spelled out in the agreement. A standard license agreement detailing twenty-five commonly found points in a basic contract between a publisher and an academic library can be found at http://www.library.yale.edu/~llicense/standlicagree.html.

Order Placement

With the order approved and the license agreement deemed agreeable, an order for the journal or collection is placed. At WMU, a purchase order is created in the ILS, requiring a bibliographic record for the item to reference. To accomplish this, a cataloging record must be downloaded, or a provisional record be created. With a purchase order (PO) and a PO number in hand, the vendor or publisher is contacted, the order is placed, and any authentication information is provided. The vendor then responds with activation information and the resource(s) are activated. A request to catalog the resource is then sent to the Cataloging Department, along with a screenshot of the initial publisher page for descriptive matter and another screenshot of the entry for inclusion in the Access database. The Web Office is also notified to link the item to any appropriate pages.

Access Database

The electronic resources specialist at WMU has developed an elaborate Access '97 database with multiple searchable fields for all purchased e-resources. A separate entry is made for each e-journal added to the database. An entry is made concurrent with the creation of the purchase order and placing the order with the vendor. The database contains fields indicating title, provider, publisher, e-ISSN, URL, proxy, accessibility, holdings, the scope of licensed coverage, availability elsewhere, and where it can be found. A field indicates whether an action in SFX needs to be taken and what is the SFX threshold. The first and the last year with volume and issue are listed. Additional fields include: print equivalent, print holdings, print call number, print purchase order number, print bibliographic record number, print ISSN number, the OCLC number, whether the item is intended to be cataloged, and on what date it has been sent for cataloging. The electronic resources specialist spends a significant amount of time inputting data into the database and keeping it current. This rich resource is consulted multiple times per hour during the course of a typical workday.

Administrative Modules

A newly established library with an e-journal service will require a designated person to work with the service provider's administrative module. The complexity of process depends upon the administrative features the publisher offers, or what they present up front for the e-resources person to work with. Most administrative modules require the input of institutional contact and directory information, proxy server data, IP information, interface display options, language, linking options, and subscription data. Again, the electronic resources specialist is the individual who spends a large amount of time activating, registering, and updating the e-journal services through these administrative modules.

Cataloging

Cataloging any product, not just an electronic resource or e-journal, is a complicated and involved process. The multistepped process begins with a formal request to catalog the resource. For example, consider the Wiley InterScience e-journal package, comprising 256 titles, purchased by WMU in 2004. At the beginning of the process, a working list of these Wiley titles is retrieved from the Access '97 database. The URL for a given title is copied from the Access database and then it is verified, as well as having the extent of availability and completeness of issues confirmed. The OCLC records (both print and electronic) are searched and printed. The Access database is then consulted for holdings information with specific attention to the exact month it starts and the frequency of its issues. Product information is checked for any background information on the originating society or publisher. The OCLC record is edited as required, including the removal of any items deemed unnecessary or that will be purchased from another vendor (e.g., the addition of a note in the 500 Field that could read, "Published on behalf of." Information for the specified title is added into the ILS constant data file, detailing a list of titles from the same source compiled onto one record, which sometimes requires the reordering of categories. Control headings are checked online, with special attention paid to the possibility of finding combined or special issues. The inputted data is validated in the ILS and then exported, with holdings being updated. The item is then saved and printed. The holdings display is examined and the record is linked to the print record with a note placed in the 530 field and the OCLC number is noted for the e-version. The URL is then added to the 856 field, and finally, a MARC (Machine-Readable Cataloging) error report is run to check for and adjust invalid indicators. If the record is error free, it is saved to the ILS database.

It takes approximately twenty to twenty-five minutes to copy catalog a single title. At that rate, it would take a notional cataloger more than eighty-five hours to catalog 256 titles in the Wiley InterScience Collection.

A-Z List

For several years, the author's institution subscribed to the TDNet service providing access to our collection of e-journals through an alphabetical listing. During the course of this relationship, the library was paying to have the service hosted remotely. Prior to subscribing, WMU received the sales pitch and conducted research on the product. Once the contract was signed, a committee of five public and technical services librarians worked to customize portions of the interface. Decisions had to be made on the color scheme, banner, virtual buttons, and any links to additional information. Help screens were created for searching the list and for searching within databases, as well as the method of connection, and an explanation of the results screen and search results display. The use and placement of informational icons would have been determined for use with specific titles or for all titles within a service. Several meetings of the committee were held to achieve consensus on these issues, with some time between meetings spent on investigating how other libraries were using and customizing the product.

Becoming established with TDNet required submitting three tab de-limited lists to the company. The first list contained all the aggregated collections with access to all titles. The second list contained individual titles within packages with access, which was only a fraction of the over-all total. The third list included aggregated databases with full-text con-tent. An additional file of print ISSN equivalents was also sent, allowing for linking between TDNet and the Western Michigan ILS. Also sent were image files defining banners, buttons, and the source HTML.

Maintaining the service involved refining the content to integrate with TDNet's requirements. All the aggregator content had to be check-ed and the linking status had to be confirmed. Individually subscribed e-journals had to be checked individually. Updates for new subscriptions and modified existing content were accomplished through the administra-tive module. These updates were performed weekly, and items re-quiring adjustments always could be found.

This service linked well to the content, but it did not provide sub-scription management. The nature of e-journal publishing adds another layer of complexity to the situation. Up to 100 publishers and services need to be tracked, with differing licensing terms, payment practices, and URL assignments. Status changes are not often readily apparent; the patron is denied access when one slips through the net that the li-brary has cast. Checking the links manually may often be the only way to ascertain that they are working correctly.[9]

A student assistant, working for the electronic resources specialist, methodically checks the links. It takes approximately four months (working twelve hours per week) to check through all the resources in the Access database. The link check involves looking at the publisher site for added issues or split-out journals. URLs are checked for correct-ness and for accessibility. Information from the Access database is often preferred to the original order information. Any changes in holdings and title data are affected in both the Access database and in the ILS catalog-ing module.

WMU cancelled its subscription to TDNet in December 2004, after previously setting up an SFX installation in the summer of 2004, with the addition of an A-Z list planned for the upcoming version (Version 3) of SFX.

SFX Setup

Setup for this service begins with supplying SFX tab-delimited lists of aggregator and journal packages, along with individually subscribed journal titles. Other data provided include the extent of full-text access, along with years and volume numbers, and information on closed subscriptions including cessation dates. These threshold data were loaded into WMU's profile, and downloaded with the basic software onto the library's server. On completion, the administrative module became available, and the data thresholds were given a brief examination. Most of the data were correct, but some additional editing was required.

Three public services librarians met many times, determining logic statements on the order of menu targets (what data appears first on the menu, and in which order), the appearance and placement of SFX logos and buttons, and writing explanatory material for linking to the library's Web site, and for a frequently asked questions (FAQ) page. In addition to time committed to meetings, these librarians checked other library SFX treatments and the SFX support site. Server files were subsequently edited in response to those decisions. HTML language behind the forms was created, the display logic tested, and the installation was then activated.

SFX Maintenance

Updates to the SFX database (knowledge base) are scheduled on a monthly basis for the addition of new targets and objects. Even with automatic activation, appended content must be verified; threshold data are checked for PERL format, and then data are compared once again in the Access database against the data in the SFX administrative module. Locally, upgrades can be applied systemically, or on a journal-by-journal basis. The addition of archival issues or the closing of titles requires changing the PERL code string in the threshold. A new purchase requires that the item be established in the knowledge base, and if it is not found in the administrative module, a request is sent to SFX Help. These titles are normally added automatically and only on rare occasions are they not found. Once that is accomplished, an entry is made in the Access database and the service is checked for activation. SFX is rechecked to make sure that the portfolio (the collection of objects) is activated. Next, the ISSNs are confirmed along with their SFX threshold values. The title fields are changed to active and are saved in a tab-delimited file, and then are updated in the SFX data loader.

The library's electronic resources specialist spends several hours a week maintaining the institution's SFX data. During the months of initial setup, twenty to thirty hours of the electronic resources specialist's time were consumed with tasks related to it.

EZ Proxy

Another effort, which supported the remote use of electronic resources and e-journals, was the purchase of EZ Proxy software and a server for running it. Previously, the library had used an unpopular freeware application that required patrons to reconfigure their browsers in order to utilize it. The decision to purchase EZ Proxy was arrived at in the summer of 2003. Setup of the product took most of September and October 2003. During this period, the electronic resources specialist was spending about half of his time, or approximately twenty hours a week, on this project.

Initially the EZ Proxy software was downloaded onto the library's server, which made its administrative module available. Configuration files were created for all packages, databases, and individual journal subscriptions. Some services and titles presented special difficulties that required a certain amount of experimentation, typically involved reading and responding to error messages and then restarting the server. Helpful clues and information about working with some of the more difficult titles and services can be found on the EZ Proxy LISTSERV. WMU's configuration file for EZ Proxy has 578 entries at the time of this writing, most of which are fairly stable resources. Updates are now performed several times a week in order to add new resources or to adjust existing configurations. Maintaining this data now takes the electronic resources specialist several hours a week.

Local Hosting

Western Michigan locally hosts both the SFX and EZ Proxy services, but had paid to have TDNet hosted remotely. The library systems manager maintains the servers and software, and his available skills, ability, and time allow the library to be able to do this. The library systems manager's participation in these projects entails initially installing the operating system (typically requiring a full day), then initially installing the software, then configuring and customizing it (one to two weeks). Once established, maintaining these systems involves the weekly updating of the operating systems (one hour per machine), updating the software (two hours per month), conducting major annual upgrades (one week), and low level technical support (two hours per month on each system). Purchasing a server requires finding the time to obtain specifications on the hardware, finding a location to house it, and obtaining a network jack. These factors must be considered when deciding to pay for the remote hosting. Five years ago, WMU's library system maintained five servers; this institution now maintains twenty servers with no additional staffing required to support them.

Serials Workflow

The decision to purchase and support access to the electronic versions of journals affects budget allocations, changes the nature of the work for some librarians and staff, and alters the workflow for serials staff. The decision to cancel print subscriptions while pursuing publisher's "E-Only" options adds the additional duty of closing out corresponding print records and volumes. As previously mentioned, over the course of the last two years, the author's institution has pursued the "E-Only" option with the American Chemical Society, Elsevier, IEEE, Sage, and Wiley, which has totaled innumerable e-journal titles and a similar number of cancelled print titles.

Closing Out Print

Once the decision is made to pursue the "E-only" option, the publisher is notified for activation, and the serials vendor also is notified to cancel the print titles. Receipt of print issues will continue until volumes are complete, and in some cases issues may continue past the established cutoff date. Timing for completing volumes can translate into a potentially large, one-time project for the serials department and bindery operation in late winter or early spring which may be repeated for a few years, depending on the number of E-Only options selected and a given institution's schedule for print cancellations.

Procedurally, pop-up notes are cut and pasted into the check-in records of the e-journal package titles, which refer the title to staff upon check-in. Receipt history is checked, and the display is changed if the information is correct. The check-in pattern is then closed. Noting the call number, the issues are then removed from the shelf, and the shelf label is removed. The corresponding purchase order is completed and the last volume received is indicated on the cataloging record. The record is saved and then printed, making note of the OCLC number, followed by its closure on the union list. The completed volume is bound together with a bindery slip and taken to the bindery unit. Title counts are kept for statistics. Completing a title takes a staff member about ten minutes. This procedure is repeated hundreds of times annually.

The print volume is then processed for the commercial bindery for the last time. The shelf list record is closed, and a record is kept in the dead file for possible later reference, should the library decide to later resubscribe to the print copy. This is potentially an area of significant savings. Between the fiscal years 2002-2003 and 2003-2004, the library's bound periodical count was reduced by 592 volumes. Additional decreases in the bound volumes were expected and realized.

The short-term view is that the bindery unit will remain quite busy as the flood of canceled print titles comes in for the final bound volume. The long-term view sees hundreds of titles no longer bound at the cost of more than $7.00 per volume. Consequently, the library has seen a slight reallocation of staff time in the bindery unit, with one of the two staff members now able to spend twenty-five percent of her schedule in another unit. A further adjustment is possible as the library cancels additional print subscriptions in the future.

Serials Check-In

Receiving hundreds fewer print titles means that many titles will no longer be physically checked-in. WMU now schedules one-third fewer student hours for check-in, due to this reduced volume. Those hours are balanced against the addition of student hours in Electronic Resources for tasks such as link checking, so there is no perceived savings of time. The print volumes that are still subscribed to require the student assistant to type the title into the serials acquisitions check-in module and to match the issue in hand against the expected pattern. With a match, the issue is accepted and the module is reset for the next issue. The call number is written on an adhesive patch and adhered to the upper right hand corner of the issue. Designated issues are tattle-taped or given a routing slip. Issues are then date-stamped and sorted into piles by location. The library has found that a reasonably efficient student can check-in approximately forty issues per hour, so canceling hundreds of print titles reduces some of the library's need for student hours dedicated to the check-in process.

Storage

Fewer bound serials ease some of the pressure on swelling shelves and shrinking storage facilities. It is difficult to generalize about the costs or savings associated with this reduced number of bound periodicals, but some of the cost factors to consider include shelving or compact shelving, the upkeep or rental of storage facilities, climate control, and the logistics involved in packing and transporting these volumes to such a facility. Jennifer Hain-Teper and Stephanie Atkins found the weighted cost of processing a bound serial to storage priced at $1.87 per unit, with this processing including selection, bar-coding, updating holdings, packing, shipping, and unloading.[10] Electronic access to a significant portion of a library's journals may reduce some of these costs, but will not eliminate them.

CONCLUSIONS

So we conclude with the question, are libraries really balancing their serials ledgers with e-journals? On the face of it, this certainly does not appear to be the case. The costs associated with selection, activation, access, maintenance, programming, and support are considerable. Western Michigan's institutional decision to locally host the supporting software, and the purchase and maintenance of servers for running it represent a considerable ongoing expense.

Subscriptions to publishers' monolithic e-journal packages do provide access to a wide array of titles, many of which might be found quite useful, while other included titles may not be so highly regarded. These packages are available for a subscription cost, which in all likelihood greatly exceeds the sum total of all the desired titles had they been selected individually. When a library factors in an inflationary increase of at least 5 percent annually, the financial commitment to e-journals takes on even greater significance. Pursuing the "E-Only" option with these publisher packages represents a large institutional commitment toward this format, changing how an institution builds its journal collection. This move leads to a reduction in student hours needed for checking in print journals, storage costs, space issues, and bindery costs, savings that are not entirely inconsequential, but are also not particularly large.

It is fairly clear that, on a purely financial basis, the costs associated with the procurement of e-journals outweigh any savings associated with the cancellation of related print titles. This begs the question if these titles are actually worth the additional costs, which then brings libraries back to e-journals usage. Any e-journal activity, whether portrayed as a PDF or HTML article, or an article printed or e-mailed, provides a potential gauge on what electronic resources students and faculty are actually using. In the earlier cited examples of Emerald and Wiley, WMU saw annual institutional use running into thousands of uses, with other services indicating similar levels of activity.

NOTES

1. Jill Emery, Claire Ginn, and Dan Tonkery, "Expose Yourself to Electronic Journals: Report of a program at the 2003 NASIG Conference." *The Serials Librarian* 46, no. 1/2 (2003): 101.

2. Ibid, 102.

3. Kenneth Frazier, "The Librarian's Dilemma: Contemplating the Costs of the "Big Deal," *D-Lib Magazine* 7, no. 3 (2003), http://www.dlib.org/dlib/march01/frazier/03frazier.html.

4. Ibid, 2.

5. Betty Galbraith, "Journal Retention Decisions Incorporating Use-Statistics as a Measure of Value," *Collection Management* 27, no. 1 (2002): 82.

6. Judy Luther, "White Paper on Electronic Journal Usage Statistics." *The Serials Librarian* 41, no. 2 (2001): 127.

7. James A. Stemper and Janice M. Jaguszewski, "Usage Statistics for Electronic Journals: An Analysis of Local and Vendor Counts." *Collection Management* 28, no. 4 (2003): 11.

8. Karla L. Hahn and Lila A. Faulkner, "Evaluative Usage-Based Metrics for the Selection of E-Journals." *College & Research Libraries* 63, no. 3 (2002): 218-219.

9. Randle Gedeon and George Boston, "Western Michigan Universities" "Electronic Journal Finder." *Acquisitions Librarian* 33/34, (2005): 97-106.

10. Jennifer Hain-Tepper and Stephanie S. Atkins, "Time and Cost Analysis of Preparing and Processing Materials for Off-Site Shelving at the University of Illinois at Urbana-Champaign Library." *Collection Development* 28 no. 4 (2003): 58.

REFERENCES

Atkins, Stephanie S., and Jennifer Hain Teper. Time and Cost Analysis of Preparing and Processing Materials for Off-Site Shelving at the University of Illinois at Urbana Champaign Library. *Collection Management* 28(4): 43-65.

Emery, Jill, Claire Ginn, and Dan Tonkery. 2004. Expose Yourself to Electronic Journals. Report of a Program at the 2003 NASIG Conference. *The Serials Librarian* 46(1/2): 99-105.

Frazier, Kenneth. The Librarians' Dilemma: Contemplating the Costs of the "Big Deal" *D-Lib Magazine* 7(3): 1-9. computer file, Access: File size: 29363 bytes http://www.dlib.org/dlib/march01/frazier/03frazier.html.

Galbraith, Betty. 2002. Journal Retention Decisions Incorporating Use-Statistics As a Measure of Value. *Collection Management* 27(1): 79-90; Related Resources: http://www.library.ucsb.edu/islt/00-winter/article1.html; http://www.wisc.edu/wendt/journals/costben/mcostben.html; http://www.library.ucsb.edu/islt/00-fall/refereed.html.

Gedeon, Randle and George Boston. 2005. Western Michigan University Libraries' "Electronic Journal Finder." *Acquisitions Librarian* 33/34: 97-106.

Hahn, Karla L., and Lila A. Faulkner. 2002. Evaluative Usage-Based Metrics for the Selection of E-journals. *College & Research Libraries* 63(3) (May): 215-227.

Luther, Judy. 2001. White Paper on Electronic Journal Usage Statistics. *The Serials Librarian* 41, (2): 119-148; Related Resource: http://www.albany.edu/imlsstat; http://www.press.umich.edu/jep/04-02/index.html.

Stemper, James A. and Janice M. Jaguszewski. 2003. Usage Statistics for Electronic Journals: An Analysis of Local and Vendor Counts. *Collection Management* 28(4): 3-22; Related Resources: http://www.projectCounter.org; http://www.alpsp. org/seminars/previous/koh-1120402.ppt; http://www.stat.umn.edu/macanova/.

doi:10.1300/J123v53S09_03

Chapter 3

Shared Purchase-Shared Responsibility: A Stewardship Tool for Consistent E-Usage Evaluation

Susanne K. Clement

INTRODUCTION

As electronic databases absorb an ever-increasing amount of a library's former print resources, it is important that librarians look for systematic methods to evaluate how well these resources meet our users' needs. Unlike print resources, where librarians have the ability to analyze (however imperfect these metrics may be) how often a book has been checked out of the library or how often a periodical has been reshelved, analyzing the usage and the usefulness of databases present fairly different problems. What kinds of usage statistics are available; what patterns emerge, both monthly and yearly? Is information available about turnaways? Are users finding the information they want? Finally, do the results from gathering usage statistics, whether from internal or external sources, justify the cost of collecting usage statistics? Even surveys of users may not produce the information that is needed about individual database use. Collection development librarians have always had to rely on their professional knowledge and subject

[Haworth co-indexing entry note]: "Shared Purchase-Shared Responsibility: A Stewardship Tool for Consistent E-Usage Evaluation." Clement, Susanne K. Co-published simultaneously in *The Serials Librarian* (The Haworth Information Press, an imprint of The Haworth Press, Inc.) Vol. 53, Supplement No. 9, 2007, pp. 43-53; and: *Usage Statistics of E-Serials* (ed: David C. Fowler) The Haworth Information Press, an imprint of The Haworth Press, Inc., 2007, pp. 43-53. Single or multiple copies of this article are available for a fee from The Haworth Document Delivery Service [1-800-HAWORTH, 9:00 a.m. - 5:00 p.m. (EST). E-mail address: docdelivery@haworthpress.com].

Available online at http://ser.haworthpress.com
© 2007 by The Haworth Press, Inc. All rights reserved.
doi:10.1300/J123v53S09_04

expertise or experience in order to understand how patrons are most likely to use library resources. However, in the current environment of proliferating and competing electronic resources, and where access rather than ownership of information has become the norm, it is even more important that librarians effectively use what data are available. The stewardship model is one tool that incorporates a consistent method of evaluating and interpreting data about the content and usage of the database itself.

BACKGROUND

As university libraries increase their collections of electronic resources, they often have to forego traditional monographic and serial funding models. Individual subject funds may no longer be sufficient to pay for the ongoing expenditure of electronic resources, particularly multidisciplinary databases.[1] Over the past few years, libraries have had to be creative in their materials funding structures in order to adequately meet the electronic information resource needs of their campuses. Several years ago, the University of Kansas (KU) Libraries adopted a mix of using subject collection funding and central collection funding for electronic information acquisition. This was actually no different from what many other libraries were doing at the time.[2] The criterion was established at KU that all databases (both subject and aggregate) costing more than $2,000 would be transferred to the central collection fund; databases costing less than $2,000 would be paid by subject collection funds, or by the reference collection fund. Any databases that subsequently increased in cost would be transferred to the central collection fund once the price breached the $2,000 threshold. The subject collection fund would have a corresponding permanent reduction of $2,000.

As more databases have been transferred to central collection funding, it became apparent that subject bibliographers, who had already been struggling to meet the myriad demands that modern librarianship had added to their responsibilities, had become less involved in the evaluation of these centrally funded databases when compared to the evaluation of material purchased with individual subject collection funds. With the passage of time and various staffing changes, many bibliographers who were charged with oversight for a particular database no longer appreciated or understood the original justification for the acquisition of that resource.

Unlike print journals, most of which are renewed annually through vendors and paid for through individual bibliographer's subject funds, the centrally paid electronic resources were not getting the scrutiny they required or deserved. For databases serving a single (or only a few) discipline(s), the subject bibliographers tended to take a better interest. For the many multidisciplinary and aggregate databases that provided access to hundreds of journals, it was hard to find even a small group of bibliographers who were willing to take ownership of the content of those databases. Bibliographers were especially reluctant to recommend canceling a database or advocating a potential alternative product. When discussing multidisciplinary databases, they tended to look only for the subject coverage with which they were familiar, and did not think it prudent to comment on someone else's subject area. As is well known, the large aggregate databases often have uneven subject coverage, and this fact only increased bibliographers' reluctance to recommend a review, especially in cases where they perceived a database's weaker areas to be in another bibliographer's subject specialty. KU therefore looked for an efficient method that would ensure that centrally funded databases were evaluated as rigorously and as regularly as the ones for which the bibliographers had direct subject responsibility. After considerable discussion, the KU Libraries developed a policy of database stewardship.

STEWARDSHIP MODEL

In the stewardship model, all electronic resources listed in the centrally administered collection budget (at KU, this is called the Electronic Information Fund, or EIF) have been assigned to a steward.[3,4] (Figure 3.1) The head of collection development is responsible for making such stewardship assignments in consultation with the Resource Development Council and is also in charge of overseeing all stewardship activities. Stewardship assignments are reviewed annually. When the content of an electronic resource is directly connected with a particular subject fund, the steward will be the bibliographer for that fund. Stewards assigned to broader discipline-based and multidisciplinary resources are expected to carry out their stewardship responsibilities in consultation with other interested bibliographers. In case of interdisciplinary products, the steward does not necessarily have to be a bibliographer, but it could be another staff member, who knows the resource well, uses it frequently, and thus, can fulfill stewardship responsibilities better than could a bibliographer who was unfamiliar with it.

The chief role of a steward is to assess, on an annual basis, the continued utility and the need for the assigned product. The depth, complexity, and duration of this assessment depend upon the resource. A large

FIGURE 3.1. KU Libraries database stewardship template.

Database:

Steward:

*Subscription Expires:	
*Platform or Provider:	
*Access through Consortium (name)?	

Scope: Coverage
         Full-text/ abstract/ citation?
         Audience or user group
         Ease of use
         URL to vendor site describing
         product	

Is the resource stand-alone or part of a larger product (e.g., OCLC FirstSearch)?	
Access information: Unlimited Web Limited Web (number of seats) Other	
Is KU LINK (open URL) enabled in this resource?	

**Use patterns (select what applies):
         Monthly
         Yearly
         Other
         Turn-aways	

***Price: Last FY year This FY year	

Cost/use (calculate by dividing number of searches and downloads into the cost of the database):
         Cost/searches
         Cost/downloads	

Number of titles indexed or abstracted [info from provider]:
         Last year
         This year	

****Number of titles covered in full-text:
         Last FY year
         This FY year	

Alternative Product Information

Is there an alternative product or products? (Repeat this as many times as necessary): 　　　Product name 　　　Provider/Platform: 　　　Does KU have access? 　　　If yes, how?	
Horizon product: Are you aware of a future product that might be considered a competitor? If so when are details about this product expected?	

KU Website information

If the information on KU's Website describing the database is not current, indicate date you made/requested update?	
Are subject headings for databases in Jupiter up-to-date? Indicate date of latest update.	

(Jupiter is a database application program for subject specialists to enter information about open access resources)

Recommendation:

Do you recommend continuation of this product?	
Comments:	
If recommending cancellation or platform change, what other bibliographers, if any, have been involved in this decision	

*'s provides links to the staff intranet where bibliographers can access the in-formation.

and expensive interdisciplinary product, especially one that is available on alternative platforms, will require a more extensive review than a small, inexpensive, discipline-specific product. This assessment should be based on established criteria for reviewing electronic resources and should include scope and coverage, usage statistics, and information about possible alternative resources. In addition, comments about the resource from users and library staff and its usefulness in information literacy instruction should also be a part of any evaluation. Though consortial arrangements usually may determine the timing of implementation of a change with regard to the resource, electronic resources purchased through consortial agreements are also assessed and stewarded similar to any other resources that are paid for solely by the library. To assist bibliographers with this evaluation, a template was developed for each database, so that each evaluation is organized uniformly and consistently, thereby making it easier to review and compare databases.

SCOPE AND COVERAGE

Databases are rarely static. In addition to adding titles or expanding the years of coverage, librarians are all familiar with vendors who have merged products, or those who have extracted journals from one product to create new products for the expressed purpose of providing more choice and making it easier for libraries to target specific disciplines.[3] Librarians are also well acquainted with journal titles shifting among databases, as vendors lose or gain licensing rights to titles. Being able to track whether a database maintains its consistency over time is important and it is therefore beneficial to systematically track the scope and coverage of the content. A variety of questions should be addressed and incorporated into the scope and coverage section of the template:

- What journals were added or deleted?
- If journals are dropped, will archival coverage continue for the years previously covered?
- Is the coverage full-text, citations, or abstracts? What is the proportion of full-text to citations or abstracts?
- Have there been significant changes to the length of a title embargo?
- Have there been any changes to the primary audience of this database?
- Is the database stand-alone, or is it part of a larger purchase/package?
- How easy is it to use? Has the vendor or owner made changes to the interface that makes searching easier, or is it less user-friendly?
- What kind of platform is used for the database?

- Is it compatible with other programs used to search across aggregate databases, such as Serial Solutions?
- If the library does not have unlimited access to a database, how many simultaneous users are there, and what is the turnaway rate?

This evaluation process can assist in making an informed retention decision. Systematically recording coverage, scope, and audience establishes useful benchmarks. For some databases, it may take several evaluations before noticeable patterns of change emerge, but the process should make it easier to see if a database continues to meet users' needs.

USAGE STATISTICS

Usage statistics should be one of the more important indicators of how well an electronic product is meeting users' needs. Yet, usage statistics are anything but easy to interpret, and comparing similar databases from different vendors can often be nearly impossible. Most librarians, who have been using usage statistics for some time, know that it is often like comparing apples and oranges. Vendors' use of terminology can often be baffling, and even the most rigorous research often leaves more questions unanswered, instead of providing a satisfactory explanation of how users access, navigate, and utilize the information available in the databases.[4] What does it mean, for instance, when a database has very few downloads–is it failing to meet users' needs, or are they using it only to browse what is available in a certain discipline? What does it mean if a database has a high number of downloads compared to total number of searches–is the user only accessing particular journal titles within that database and ignoring the rest?

The inconsistency in the way the numbers are being reported by publishers and vendors does not make it any easier to make sense of the usage statistics. An international initiative to address the problem of interpreting electronic usage data was launched in 2002, and publishers are slowly modifying their data extraction to become COUNTER compliant.[5] Usage statistics reports that adhere to the COUNTER Code of Practice include the following:[6]

- Data elements to be measured
- Definitions of these data elements

- Content and format of usage reports
- Requirements for data processing
- Requirements for auditing
- Guidelines to avoid duplicate counting, when intermediary gateways and aggregators are used

Analyzing the usage statistics can tell us how often users accessed a database, how many searches they performed, and most important, how often they downloaded the results. In the stewardship model, the cost of a database is also included in the analysis, and the usage versus cost calculation provides additional evaluative data. It is important to recognize that a cost analysis of database usage will not be uniform across broad disciplines–for example, it should be expected that databases for the biosciences would have a higher usage:cost ratio than databases for the humanities.

Procedure

At the KU Libraries, electronic usage statistics are gathered monthly from all vendors and disseminated in an easy-to-access format through the library's intranet. A student worker is assigned to download usage statistics from the vendors' Web sites.[7] Collection development staff will ensure the accuracy of the downloaded data, and then proceed to organize and upload the data to the intranet. The Electronic Resources Usage Reports Web site lists all databases alphabetically, and wherever appropriate, the COUNTER symbol is prominently displayed next to the database's name (Figure 3.2). This provides bibliographers instant information on how the vendor has extracted the usage statistics. Links to the COUNTER Web site are also provided, should bibliographers or other library staff require additional information. As database stewardship reports are completed, they too are linked by the database name on the Electronic Resources Usage Reports Web site, also making it easy for other staff to access all reports. Collection development staff also assists bibliographers with obtaining additional data from vendors–especially from vendors whose usage statistics are not COUNTER-compliant. Collecting usage statistics is not inexpensive, something often pointed out in the literature,[8] but utilizing well-trained student workers to perform routine downloads from publishers' sites reduces the cost significantly and provides higher paid staff and librarian with a data tool in their database evaluations.

FIGURE 3.2. From the University of Kansas Libraries Intranet, Collection Development, Electronic Resources Usage Reports. Reprinted with permission.

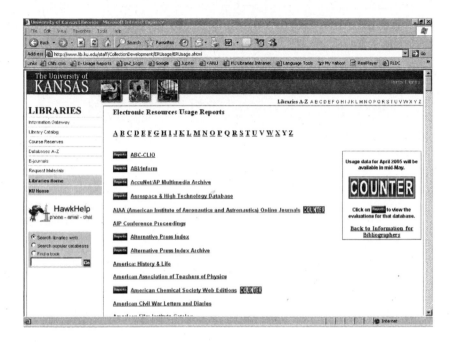

ALTERNATIVE PRODUCTS

Stewards also need to monitor the marketplace for alternatives to existing resources, utilizing professional literature, listservs, and publishers' information. Primarily, they will be looking for enhancements to content, and they will also be looking for alternative platforms that might be user-friendlier. Finally, price will also be an important component of any alternative product consideration. When alternative products are identified, the bibliographer coordinates trials with appropriate staff, publicizes the trial of the new format or database, and collects feedback on trials from library staff, faculty, and students, as appropriate. If the alternative product carries a higher price, the bibliographer will also need to coordinate the initial funding request for the resource.

FEEDBACK

Stewards are responsible for promoting their databases to users as well as to the library staff. In addition to providing orientations to colleagues on how to use particular databases, bibliographer stewards also provide assistance and instruction to students and faculty. Further, a steward may also monitor the status of the product's development and maintain awareness of problems, bugs, and other issues or concerns to be discussed with the vendor. A steward's review of a resource may result in a recommendation to cancel it outright, or to cancel and replace it with an alternative. Stewards are responsible for including interested bibliographers and other staff in the decision-making process–especially when they recommend cancellation of a multidisciplinary electronic resource.

One recent outcome of the implementation of the stewardship model revealed that one of KU's business-related databases was no longer as useful an information tool as it once had been. Not only did the bibliographer establish that the database's usage statistics had decreased over time, compared to similar databases, but he was also able to identify alternative databases with better scope and coverage. It was therefore an easier decision for the bibliographer to recommend the cancellation of the database and to request that the funds be diverted to the addition of two new databases, which would more clearly meet KU users' needs. The bibliographer was also able to use the analysis tool when discussing the recommended changes with the business faculty.

CONCLUSIONS

Electronic information will continue to be a substantial and growing part of any library's materials budget, and to ensure that the subscribed databases continue to meet users' needs, it is important that systematic and consistent evaluation tools are used to assess all databases. Databases constantly change, and tracking these changes can often be a daunting task. Though the database stewardship model is still relatively new at the KU Libraries, it is believed that we have developed a tool that will assist the KU Libraries in this process. By tracking details such as what is in the database (scope and coverage), how frequently a database is used (usage statistics), what other products may provide the same or similar information and in what interface (alternative product), and also what students, faculty, and other librarians tell us about a database (feedback), the KU Libraries have started a method of systematic data gathering and database evaluation, which, based on early results, looks very promising.

NOTES

1. Robert E. Dugan (2002) Information Technology Budgets and Costs: Do You Know What Your Information Technology Costs Each Year? *The Journal of Academic Librarianship* 28: 38-43.

2. Informal survey of sixteen libraries in the mid-west and west, April 2005.

3. Sheila S. Intner (2003) Implications for teaching collection development. *Technicalities* 23:1, 15-17; available from Wilson OmniFile http://www.vnweb. hwwilsonweb.com/hww (accessed 20 April 2005).

4. Julie C. Blake and Susan P. Schleper (2004) From Data to Decisions: Using Surveys and Statistics to Make Collection Management Decisions. *Library Collections, Acquisitions, & Technical Services* 28: 460-464.

5. "Launched in March 2002, COUNTER (Counting Online Usage of Networked Electronic Resources) is an international initiative designed to serve librarians, publishers, and intermediaries by facilitating the recording and exchange of online usage statistics. The use of online information resources has been growing exponentially, and it is widely agreed by producers and purchasers of information that the use of these resources should be measured in a more consistent way." http://www.projectcounter. org/about.html (accessed 20 April 2005).

6. Summary from http://www.projectcounter.org/ (accessed January 2005).

7. KU also maintains a spreadsheet of all vendor statistics that is updated monthly (as each database statistics are downloaded) and is maintained for the purpose reporting to the Association of Research Libraries (ARL). In this way, collecting the ARL annual electronic usage information has become as simple as reading the table summaries at the end of the reporting year.

8. Several articles have discussed the high cost of collecting electronic usage statistics as well as the methods used. For example, Tony Ferguson suggests a moderated approach to collecting statistics (Ferguson, Anthony W. (2003) Usage Statistics: Are They Worth It? *Against the Grain,* December 2002-January 2003: 93-94), and James Stemper and Janice Jaguszewski suggest that librarians combine internally generated data with data supplied by vendors (Stemper, James A., and Janice M. Jaguszewski (2003) Usage Statistics for Electronic Journals: An Analysis of Local and Vendor Counts. *Collection Management* 28: 3-22).

doi:10.1300/J123v53S09_04

Chapter 4

MaxData:
A Project to Help Librarians
Maximize E-Journal Usage Data

Carol Tenopir
Gayle Baker
Eleanor J. Read
Maribeth Manoff
Kitty McClanahan
David Nicholas
Donald W. King

INTRODUCTION

All libraries and librarians make substantial investments in digital collections, especially collections of digital serials. Librarians are also responsible for the justification of their expenditures and decisions about the best form and format for journal purchases. They must collect and interpret data about the use of print and electronic journal collections in a way that will help them to make good collection development decisions. These decisions should be based on knowledge of user needs, user preferences, and behavior patterns, in addition to the cost effective-

[Haworth co-indexing entry note]: "MaxData: A Project to Help Librarians Maximize E-Journal Usage Data." Tenopir, Carol et al. Co-published simultaneously in *The Serials Librarian* (The Haworth Information Press, an imprint of The Haworth Press, Inc.) Vol. 53, Supplement No. 9, 2007, pp. 55-77; and: *Usage Statistics of E-Serials* (ed: David C. Fowler) The Haworth Information Press, an imprint of The Haworth Press, Inc., 2007, pp. 55-77. Single or multiple copies of this article are available for a fee from The Haworth Document Delivery Service [1-800-HAWORTH, 9:00 a.m. - 5:00 p.m. (EST). E-mail address: docdelivery@haworthpress.com].

ness of the various online products. Gathering and interpreting reliable data on needs, preferences, and use patterns has become a necessary challenge for all libraries. Because there is a great need to justify the cost of investments and to provide the best resources for users, usage data of many types have become essential. It can, however, be difficult for librarians to know what data will provide them with the information they most need for their decision making.

The MaxData research project is sponsored by the United States Institute of Museum and Library Services (IMLS), in order to analyze and evaluate usage and survey data to determine the effectiveness of various types of usage data collection methods. The project proposes to assist librarians in their justifications and decision making by comparing different types of data collection and data analysis. The MaxData project will enable librarians to learn what conclusions can be drawn from each technique, the limitations and strengths of each one, how they complement one another, and what types of generalized conclusions can be drawn if only a single usage data technique must be chosen. A cost-benefit model for the best use of e-journal usage data will be developed in the project, which runs from 2005 through 2007.

Three types of usage data in academic libraries are being compared in both a single university library setting and in a large academic library consortium. Data collection and analysis are being done by researchers who are experts in the following techniques:

1. Deep log analysis of e-journal usage log data collected by the Ohio Library and Information Network (OhioLINK) library consortia,
2. Analysis of usage reports provided to the University of Tennessee Libraries by various vendors and usage data collected internally from various systems such as link resolvers and proxy servers, and
3. Surveys of faculty and students at the University of Tennessee and several Ohio universities that probe not only into the reading patterns of library users, but also their preferences, motivations, and outcomes of readings.

The broad aim of the MaxData project is to compare the costs and benefits of various methods of usage data collection and analysis in university libraries. The project also seeks to better understand user behavior, user preferences, and usage of these collections. While Max-Data focuses on academic libraries, the resulting recommendations and usage data model will be widely adaptable in all types of libraries that provide access to digital collections. Widespread dissemination of data through the project Web site, professional conferences, and the library literature will ensure that libraries receive the information they need about the project in order to adapt it to their own situation.

PARTICIPANTS

Participants in this research project include the University of Tennessee's School of Information Sciences and University Libraries; University College London and its Centre for Information Behaviour and the Evaluation of Research; and the OhioLINK consortium, which is providing usage data.

The University of Tennessee (UT) is the flagship research-extensive university in the state of Tennessee. The main campus is located in Knoxville with a student population of over 25,000 and with over 1,200 faculty members. The UT Libraries provide a collection of approximately three million items, including an extensive collection of e-journals, e-books, and databases. Metasearch capabilities are available, as well as individual searching by database or e-collection title. The SFX link resolver provides links to full-text articles from multiple sources. Remote access to IP-authenticated resources is provided through a proxy server.

The Centre for Information Behaviour and the Evaluation of Research (CIBER), headquartered at University College London, specializes in monitoring the rollouts of national services/systems and evaluating their impact, specifically for policy makers and senior managers. CIBER researchers have developed a technique for analyzing usage logs called deep log analysis, which provides insights into patterns of use of electronic resources.

OhioLINK is a consortium of Ohio academic libraries with a membership of seventeen public universities, twenty-three community/ technical colleges, forty-four private colleges, and the State Library of Ohio. It was one of the first attempts in the United States to create a statewide virtual library system. OhioLINK's goal is to provide easy access to information and rapid delivery of library materials throughout the state. It serves more than 600,000 students, faculty, and staff at eighty-five institutions via campus-based electronic library systems, the OhioLINK central site, and Internet resources. OhioLINK provides access to more than forty-four million library items statewide through its catalog.

BACKGROUND AND LITERATURE REVIEW

The move towards having electronic collections in libraries is nationwide (indeed, worldwide) and the results of this project will have significant national interest. According to the Association of Research Libraries (ARL), the percentage of spending on serials by ARL member libraries increased from under 2.5 million dollars in 1990 to over four million dollars by 2000, while spending on monographs held steady or decreased during the same period. King et al. (2004a) and Schonfeld et al. (2004) found similar trends in two recent cost studies of print and electronic resources.

Tenopir (2003) concluded in a recent report for the Council on Library and Information Resources that libraries and their users prefer digital collections because digital journals can be linked from and to indexing and abstracting databases; access can be from the user's home, office, or dormitory, whether or not the physical library is open; the library can get usage statistics that is not possible with print collections; and digital collections save space and are relatively easy to maintain. When total processing and space costs are taken into account, electronic collections may also result in some overall reductions in library costs (Montgomery and King, 2002).

By the academic year 2000-2001, research libraries were spending an average 16.3 percent of their budgets on electronic resources, compared to only 3.6 percent in 1992-1993. Some libraries reported spending over 20 percent of their total budget on electronic resources. Between 1992 and 2000, ARL libraries increased spending on electronic resources by 446.9 percent (with only a 49.4 percent increase for total library materials).

The price of serials (in either print or electronic form) has increased steadily, at a rate that far outpaces library budget increases. According to *Library Journal*'s 2005 Periodical Price Survey (van Orsdel and Born, 2005), the average yearly subscription price for scientific and technical journals published outside the United States (including the majority of commercial science, technical, and medical publishers) rose from $1,266 per year in 2001, to $1,732 per year in 2005.

At the same time, the number of peer-reviewed journals and the percentage of those available in digital form have also increased steadily.

According to *Ulrich's Guide to Periodicals,* in 2005, there were approximately 190,000 active serials being published, over 22,000 of which were peer-reviewed scholarly journals. Over half of the active peer-reviewed journals are available in digital form, with a higher percentage of science, technology, and medicine titles online. There are actually many more e-serials, when those that are not peer-reviewed are included. *Fulltext Sources Online* (2004) lists approximately 22,150 serial titles that are online from one or more online services. Many journals now provide access to their articles from multiple sources–directly from the publisher and through multiple aggregator services. For example, the full-text of journals such as *Chemical Week, The Economist, Library Journal,* and *Science* are each covered in multiple services such as EBSCOhost, ProQuest, and WilsonWeb, in addition to publisher Web sites.

Documenting the usage of electronic information sources, particularly journals, is an important issue for academic libraries, for a number of reasons that have been well elucidated in recent library and information science literature. Many authors note that in today's economic climate of shrinking library budgets, expenditures on e-journals must be supported by use data that indicate their value to library users. Duy (2004) has pointed out that usage data is important to librarians who make collection management decisions about electronic resources, including renewals and new product choices, as well as determine how to display access to particular resources on library Web sites. Pesch (2004) has noted that evidence of electronic resource use is often required by accreditation agencies. In light of all these facts, Jacsó (2004) actually termed this task of tracking journal usage as the "Holy Grail" for libraries.

Many studies have examined online journal usage from a user perspective, utilizing surveys to evaluate the use of online journals and databases (e.g., DeGroote and Dorsch, 2003; Franklin and Plum, 2003). These studies are useful in providing qualitative insights on the "why" questions about e-journal use. Libraries now have access to an increasing amount of systematic usage log use, which answers some questions on "what" their patrons are using.

Problems with inconsistency and interoperability of vendor-supplied data have been thoroughly discussed in the literature (e.g., Shim and McClure, 2002; Luther, 2000). Pesch (2004) has offered a table of very specific ways in which vendor-supplied data can vary, preventing accurate comparisons between vendors. Galbraith (2002) has decried the fact that some publisher data fails to differentiate between "hits" on a title and abstract, and a full-text article download. Hartland-Fox and Thebridge (2003) have noted a wide range of problems with vendor-supplied data, including incomparability between vendors, discrepant ways of measuring usage or "sessions," the potential for users being "invisible" when different access routes to a resource are used, irregular delivery schedules of vendor reports, and a lack of access to specific title data. Duy and Vaughan (2003) have even reported multiple instances of vendors sending usage data to the wrong library—a flaw that could conceivably result in decisions being made based on another library's data.

Publishers have even acknowledged the parsimonious nature of some vendor-supplied usage data and the economic disincentives to providing them to libraries. A publishing executive from a prominent medical journal noted that what it supplied to librarians was actually "download data" rather than "usage statistics," adding that "The rest, we consider 'customer information,' which we keep for ourselves" (Lichtenberg, 2004).

Dissatisfaction with vendor-supplied usage data has spawned a number of institution-specific systems for measuring e-resource use (e.g., Weintraub, 2003-2004). The title of Matthews' (2002) article is self-explanatory: "What's one to do when vendors, publishers, and aggregators do not meet your usage reporting needs? Do it yourself!" However, as Shim and McClure (2002) documented in their survey of academic libraries, the development of a "home-grown" system is not practical for many libraries, due to a lack of required resources, inadequate institutional support, or precluding situational factors.

Duy's (2004) book chapter, "Usage Data: Issues and Challenges for Electronic Resource Collection Management," gives a thorough discussion of the importance of obtaining e-resource usage data, as well as the complexities of doing so. In addition, many authors have noted the important contributions of Luther's (2000) seminal white paper to the professional dialogue about measuring e-journal use.

Although a substantial number of articles have documented the problems with existing vendor usage data, and a significant number of other articles have described examples of in-house systems to track e-resource usage, there have been less than a handful of empirical studies actually comparing "home-grown" data with vendor-supplied data. The first of these studies, conducted by Duy and Vaughan (2003), compared North Carolina State University Libraries' internal use data from its Web server logs to vendor-supplied use data for a twelve-month period. The data were compared using two separate analyses. The first used correlation analysis to examine whether the two data sets showed the same general pattern of high versus low resource use for each month of the year. The study found that data from 83 percent of the vendors were similar, in this general way, to the pattern for the in-house data. The second analysis investigated how close the actual data values were for the two groups for the same period, using a constructed ratio of local data over vendor data. On this more precise measure, the authors reported that data for fewer than half of the library's vendors were reasonably close to the in-house data. Of the rest of the vendors they studied, most vendors provided data that overstated resource use, vis à vis the in-house data. For the few vendors whose data showed lower usage than the in-house data, the authors suggested that this underreporting is an artifact of how logins are counted by Internet Protocol (IP) addresses, or by alternative ways to access a resource. The authors pointed out the need for standardization of session data across vendors, while defending local data collection as failsafe against the current flaws of vendor-supplied data.

Another empirical study of vendor versus in-house usage data was conducted by Stemper and Jaguszewski (2003), using the University of Minnesota–Twin Cities Libraries' e-journal counter data. The counter tracked user clicks on resource links in the online catalog, or on the library Web page, and these data were compared to data supplied by four major vendors. These authors were interested in more than just whether the two counts matched; they were also studying the importance of individual titles versus journal packages. With its emphasis on titles, this paper took a different statistical approach to quantifying "matching usage." Frequency data were used to rank journal titles from "high" to "low" levels of use, and the percentage of journals falling in each category was comparable for vendor data and for library data. The study also showed that the particular titles that fell into each category in the vendor data corresponded quite closely with those identified in the library data. These authors concluded by recognizing the value of the Project COUNTER (Counting Online Usage of NeTworked Electronic Resources) goal of standardizing vendor data, but felt that in-house metrics are currently needed, because COUNTER is still building the "critical mass" of compliant vendors needed to provide libraries with the quality of usage data they need.

A third empirical study, conducted by McDowell and Gorman (2004), compared the e-resource usage data requirements of academic librarians in New Zealand with the vendor-supplied data that was available to them. The librarians' needs were identified through a survey.

This study determined that although New Zealand librarians were using vendor-supplied data for collection development decisions, these vendor-supplied data suffered from both a lack of standardization and serving the vendors' objectives more than the librarians' needs. The authors noted that the definition of a "use" of a resource varied substantially from vendor to vendor, while librarians were quite consistent in their definition of what constituted a "use." The authors concluded that this discrepancy indicated that librarians were not necessarily interpreting vendor-supplied data accurately, a situation which has negative implications for collection development decisions based on these data. McDowell and Gorman proposed that the solution lies in standardization of vendor data through initiatives such as Project COUNTER.

King and Montgomery (2002) compared user survey data with log analysis at Drexel University. Drexel made the decision to discontinue print subscriptions to journals whenever possible, and has aggressively grown its electronic journal collections through both aggregated full-text databases and e-journal systems directly from publishers. Drexel's journal collection now includes over 9,000 titles. The log analysis of "hits" was about one-third higher than the amount of reading from a readership survey. A similar result was observed from a readership survey of faculty, staff, and students at the University of Pittsburgh (King et al., 2004b). Here the number of vendor-reported "hits" was about 40 percent above the estimated amount of reading from the survey. At the time of the survey, the University of Pittsburgh had about 16,000 electronic journals available and subscribed to about an equal number of print journals. The two surveys showed that most of the faculty's reading from the library collection was from electronic formats, whereas, most reading from personal subscriptions was from print versions.

Publishers and their funding sources also have a stake in accurate estimates of readership. King et al. (2006) point out weaknesses in counting electronic hits and downloads as indicators of amount of reading articles and journals. For many journals, personal subscriptions and some library collections (particularly current periodical collections) continue to be read in print. Some journals, such as *Pediatrics,* continue to be read largely in print (Tenopir et al., 2007). Thus, hits and/or downloads can present an incomplete picture of article and journal use. The article presents another approach to estimating amount of reading, which involves a survey of potential article and journal readers. The survey gives a recently published journal issue table-of-contents *(Pediatrics)* and respondents are asked which articles they read (and how much of the article was read). Other parts of the survey established the age of articles read and format of the articles. The survey yielded an estimate of amount of reading of articles (i.e., an average of 14,700 readings per article) and the journal (i.e., 2.1 million readings). Note that *Pediatrics* is a society journal, with the society having about 60,000 members, so the amount of reading is not typical of journals. However, examined from a cost and benefit perspective, it is estimated that the publishing cost per reading is $0.67 per reading. Readers pay about $27 per reading in terms of their time, so their determination of what they are willing to pay in terms of their time far outweighs the publishing cost and/or price paid. This would seem to be valuable information for the publisher and the society it represents. One cannot be assured of total reading without including reading from all sources and all formats.

METHODS AND CONCEPTS

General Comments

Tenopir (2003) emphasized that the method or methods used in a research study determine what type of conclusions can be drawn about the sampled participants and what findings can be generalized to the population as a whole. In an overview of methods for user behavioral research, Wang (2001) found that user studies for libraries generally used one or more of the following methods: surveying users; interviewing users (including focus groups); and observing users through experiments, natural settings, or log analysis.

Covey (2002) also categorized usage studies to help librarians design the most appropriate studies for the type of information they hoped to gather. Covey's categories of research studies were similar to Wang's and included surveys, questionnaires, focus groups, and user protocols such as experiments and observations. Other methods included heuristic evaluations, paper prototypes and scenarios, card-sorting tests, and transaction log analysis.

Each of these methods had some advantages and disadvantages. According to Covey, problems or concerns with surveys included the following: general surveys were time-consuming and expensive to prepare, conduct, and interpret; longitudinal analysis could track changing patterns of use, but surveys provided no baseline data unless follow-up work was conducted; people received many surveys, thus it was difficult to motivate them to complete and return them; usage information gathered in general surveys might better be gathered by transactional logs; specific surveys were more beneficial, but must be repeated over time; user satisfaction surveys may not provide enough information to solve the problem, and service "gap" surveys are more difficult to administer and analyze; and a survey was only as good as the wording of the questions and the response rate. Further, problems with transaction log analysis included the following: deciding on the correct and most useful usage statistics; collecting the correct usage statistics; getting the correct and consistent usage statistics from vendors; analyzing and interpreting data (possibly time-consuming and difficult); and presenting the resultant data in a meaningful way.

Deep Log Analysis

One purpose of the MaxData study is to identify what kinds of information could be most profitably extracted from a usage log file using the powerful, emerging methodology called deep log analysis. Usage log data will be provided by the multilibrary OhioLINK consortia. OhioLINK offers access to more than 100 electronic databases, 6,300 scholarly journal titles, and a variety of multimedia material, e-book titles, and theses and dissertations. Electronic journals are locally loaded on OhioLINK servers, and articles are searchable through a single, federated search engine maintained centrally by OhioLINK. The University College, London's Centre for Information Behaviour and the Evaluation of Research, the originators of deep log analysis software and techniques, will load and analyze the OhioLINK data.

All digital information platforms–the Internet, touchscreen kiosks, digital interactive television, and mobile devices–have a facility by which logs are generated that provide an automatic and real-time record of use by everyone who accesses information services on these platforms. The attraction of logs is that they provide abundant and fairly robust evidence of use. With log analysis, it is possible to monitor the use of a system by anyone who happens to engage with the system–there is no need to take a sample. The great advantages of the logs are not simply their size and reach, although the dividend here is indeed a rich and unparalleled one. Perhaps most important, they are a direct and immediately available record of what people have done–not what they say they might or would do; not what they were prompted to say, and not what they thought they did. The data are unfiltered, can stand alone, and provide a reality check that both represents the users and complements important contextual data obtained by engaging with real users and exploring their experiences and concerns.

Logs can also reveal much about users' searching styles. Search styles and approaches can be monitored in two ways: via the search expression typed into a search engine, which gets people to the Web site, and via the search expression used on the site's search engine. Search terms used in a search engine can sometimes be extracted from the referrer logs, where these are available. The referrer logs give the first and last pages viewed by the user, and where the user has used a search engine to find a site. The search engine used and often the search terms used are also reported. The server also stores the user's search expressions on this internal search engine. In addition, logs can tell us about the user's preference for either keyword searching or browsing.

Deep log analysis involves several steps. First, the assumptions on how the data are defined and recorded (for instance, who is a user, what is a hit, what represents online success, etc.) are questioned and realigned as necessary, and their statistical significance assessed. This is important, as skewed data are a problem that can result in incorrect, overinflated readings and give a false sense of achievement or progress and misalignment to organizational goals. The second step, if necessary, is to put in place the data collection mechanisms and then collect the data. Third, the usage logs are enriched by attaching user demographic data (e.g., age, gender, ethnicity, occupation, subject specialist, organizational affiliation, postal code) to them, with additional data obtained from either a subscriber database or online questionnaires. When available, outcome or impact data, regarding, for instance, research performance or promotions, may be related as well.

In addition to the general provision of use and user data, we have targeted a number of analyses as being especially beneficial to the library community:

- The decay in article usage
- Subnetwork analysis and usage
- Web navigation and searching approache
- The relationship between usage and citations

In the analysis of article use by age of article (decay), we will examine the analyses of IP addresses, in particular the information content of names and subnetwork labels of computers linking to the Web. This type of analysis is new, and has been found to be valuable. In terms of the analysis of navigation structure, OhioLINK presents an opportunity to look at usage implications as a result of the user using the search option, rather than a menu option. The analyses of navigation structure and the relationship between online usage and citations both add to and deepen the team's existing work into digital visibility. These analyses are not only valuable in their own right, but also provide the evidence to help formulate questions for questionnaires and focus groups.

Although log data are much trumpeted, (especially the "hits"), most people employ the term in a narrow and vague way, and its handling is problematical. Indeed, some commentators have questioned the appropriateness of the term "use." They have argued that use is not, in fact, being directly measured, and that it would be more accurate to claim that what is being measured are "accesses"–downloads, etc. Clearly, what actually constitutes "use" is open to question. There are difficulties in even determining whether use was intended or not in the surfing culture in which we find ourselves. Activity is clearly the defining characteristic of use, but what actually signifies it and whether all forms should be treated equally are the problem areas.

Deep log analysis challenges problems of definition by utilizing a number of metrics, which together present a larger picture of use and, in some cases, satisfaction. There is not just one metric to which you can ascribe use or success; there is a wide range, including time spent online, the number of visits, return visits, whether something is printed or not, and site preparation. If we can ascribe aggregated personal/ corporate characteristics (age, gender, occupation, institution, country) to the log data, then a data-rich picture emerges.

We employ the terms "items used, viewed, or requested" to describe use. In the case of OhioLINK, an item might be a list of journals ordered alphabetically or by subject, a list of journal issues, a content page of a journal issue, an abstract, or a full-text article. For Ohio-LINK, we have employed three "use" metrics–number of items viewed, number of sessions conducted, and amount of time spent online. In addition, we have employed a hybrid metric, site penetration, which is determined by counting the number of items viewed by a particular user during a visit to the site or service. This metric indicates how deep into the service users penetrate or burrow, and how much they take away with them.

To maximize the benefits of logs and to exercise our deep log analysis techniques to their full potential, we need to identify individual users and obtain some characteristics about them. This, however, is not easy. Web logs provide a user "trace," but not real user or individual identification. All we had to work with, in the case of OhioLINK, was the Internet

Protocol (IP) number, which provided us with the name of the institution to which the user belonged. The IP number could only be traced back to a machine, not to an individual. The use of proxy servers means that the IP address cannot be assumed to relate to use on a specific machine, and use might also relate to a group of users rather than an individual. In the case of OhioLINK, universities using a proxy server were identified by looking at the amount of use attributed to a single IP address; where this was high, the university was classified as having used a proxy server.

Furthermore, access to a site may be via multiple user machines, such as library machines, or the IP number might have been allocated temporarily to a client's machine using floating IP numbers. Hence, the IP number assigned to a machine in one period may not correspond to the IP number assigned in another period, making the identification of returning users especially difficult.

For OhioLINK, user IP numbers were analyzed and a reverse DNS (Domain Name System) lookup was carried out. Five groupings were identified: the online node name allocated to the computer, the subnetwork name, the host organization name, the organization type, and the organization location. On inspection of the data related to participating OhioLINK universities, it was found that the subnetwork names could be identified with academic department names, in the case of Ohio State University. That is, there was a matching of subnetwork label and physical location of the used computer. Subnetwork analysis was restricted to Ohio State University.

Equipped with a detailed picture of the digital environment, much will have to be explained and a whole range of questions will have to be asked through survey and qualitative work–questions about personal experiences, satisfaction, outcomes, and impacts. Observation often plays an important part in the analysis also, as issues concerned with usability, engagement, and exploitation of materials may be examined. Thus, logs alone are not the magic bullet, but they are the essential methodological first step. Logs map the digital environment and raise questions that *really* need to be asked by questionnaire and interview (so obtaining powerful triangulation). Clearly, if information-providers are to obtain rich and accurate data from log files, which will inform both them and their paymasters, they will have to go beyond proprietary logging software and start triangulating the data with other datasets and social survey collection methods.

Vendor Reports and Internal Log Data

The University of Tennessee (UT) leases access to more than 200 electronic resources, providing access to over 12,500 e-journal titles. UT provides linked access to e-journals through its library catalog and an e-journal list, with the library Web site acting as a gateway to multiple online systems. Unlike OhioLINK, UT does not locally load e-journals or databases; the data that can be collected, collated, and analyzed in this type of environment are usage reports from vendors and internal logs from different sources.

Vendor-supplied reports may be the only source of information about e-resource use that a library has. The reports vary, from vendor to vendor, in delivery method, time period covered, format, definitions of terms, and level of detail, among other things. The main source of vendor-supplied usage data in the future will be reports that are compliant with international standards promulgated by Project COUNTER, an international cooperative initiative of librarians, publishers, and professional organizations, which has developed standards for the delivery of usage data about online products to library customers.

In Release 1 of the COUNTER Code of Practice, there are two levels of COUNTER-compliant usage reports, with Level 1 being required for minimal compliance to the COUNTER Code. The levels and reports are as follows:

- Level 1
  —Journal Report 1: Number of Successful Full-Text Article Requests by Month and Journal
  —Journal Report 2: Turnaways by Month and Journal
  —Database Report 1: Total Searches and Sessions by Month and Database
  —Database Report 2: Turnaways by Month and Database
  —Database Report 3: Total Searches and Sessions by Month
- Level 2
  —Journal Report 3: Number of Successful Item Requests and Turnaways by Month, Journal, and Page Type
  —Journal Report 4: Total Searches Run by Month and Service

As of August 2005, the Register of Vendors providing COUNTER-compliant usage reports for databases and e-journals (http://www.projectcounter.org/articles.html) listed forty-five vendors, products, or services providing one or more compliant reports. COUNTER-compliant services include a number of major electronic services and provide libraries with somewhat consistent usage log data. Current COUNTER-compliant reports do not satisfy all of the libraries' information needs, however, because they provide fairly superficial usage log data about each system separately, and the aggregation across systems and interpretation is left up to the individual libraries.

Release 2 of the COUNTER Code of Practice for Journals and Databases became operational in January 2006. One of the changes involves reporting PDF and HTML full-text requests separately. Another change is the addition of publisher and platform columns to the reports to facilitate aggregation of data from different systems.

Many libraries have internal sources of aggregated log data, which may help provide information about usage of their e-resources. Data gathered from link resolvers, federated search engines, or proxy servers may be of use and have the advantage of being able to cut across vendor systems. In addition, libraries may have devised local systems to gather usage data from, for example, links from database-driven Web pages.

In 1999, the University of Tennessee Libraries implemented a system to record use of its databases. A locally developed Perl script writes to a MySQL database each time a user clicks on a link from one of the database menu pages. The data, collected monthly in tab-delimited format, include date and time, domain name (e.g., lib.utk .edu, comcast.net), database number, referring URL, and browser. For the past several years, analysis of these data using SAS software has helped to fill in gaps where vendor-supplied data on database use were incomplete or missing altogether, and has informed collection development decisions, such as changing the number of simultaneous users needed for database subscriptions. Note that these data elements provide information only as to whether a user attempted to begin a session in a particular database. They do not reflect whether the user successfully got into the database, how long they stayed, or what searching, viewing, or downloading activity took place.

Link resolver software providers have been developing and improving statistical modules in the past several years. The data collected in these modules show great promise for providing valuable information about usage at the level of individual electronic journal. At the UT Libraries, the SFX link resolver records data for each request made to the software. These requests occur at a number of access points: in SFX-enabled databases, when the user clicks on the FindText (SFX) button; on the e-journals Web page, where almost all e-journals are linked via SFX; and in the catalog, where the URLs for an increasing number of e-journals are being directed through the SFX server. The data from the requests (containing elements such as the journal being accessed and what package it is part of) are compiled into reports. For example, one might look at the number of requests for various full-text sources, the most popular titles in different full-text sources, or available journal titles that are not being requested at all. The SFX reports also provide use data for linked Open Access journals and some back files for which there may be no vendor-supplied data.

Many libraries are implementing federated search systems that have further implications for e-resource use data. In the case of database use, the searches generated via a federated search engine may or may not be included in vendor-supplied statistics. Some federated search software records users' search strategies, providing a level of detail that is seldom provided by vendors. The project team will investigate the utility of the statistics generated from one of these systems, MetaLib from Ex Libris.

Another common development in libraries is the implementation of proxy servers to facilitate remote access to IP-authenticated resources. Proxy servers such as the URL-rewriting software EZProxy, generate logs that can be analyzed. Some libraries direct links to their e-resources through such proxy servers for both local and remote users in order to collect usage statistics on all e-resource use. EZProxy logs at the UT Libraries will be examined for useful data elements that cannot be found in vendor-supplied or other reports.

Currently, there is no one source of usage data that fulfills the needs of library collection managers, or that gives a comprehensive picture of the use of e-resources. The data-producing systems described in the preceding sections provide information on use and user behavior and preferences in new and interesting ways. The ability to make efficient use of these systems involves not just collecting or capturing the data elements, but also having the means to convert it into useable form, as well as to analyze and interpret it. This is no small task and may require programming skills and specialized tools, such as statistical packages and Web log analysis software, as well as storage and computing capacity to handle very large files. The data collected from UT's internal systems and the vendor-supplied usage reports (both COUNTER-compliant and noncompliant) will be examined individually and in combination to discover their usefulness as wel as determine the resources and effort required to use them, in order to effectively make decisions on managing e-resources.

Readership Surveys

Log data and vendor reports provide much information on what people are using in a library's electronic collections, but they provide only part of the usage pattern picture. UT will conduct user surveys of faculty and students in four academic libraries in Ohio and at the University of Tennessee to correspond to the main user groups represented in the usage log data. Surveys will replicate those conducted by Carol Tenopir and Donald W. King of more than 100 organizations over thirty years (Tenopir and King, 2000). Questions will focus on the user's last article reading, providing information on readings from the library electronic collections, library print collections, and other sources. The survey results on readings from library-provided electronic sources will be compared to the log reports and deep log analysis from the same universities, while other questions will provide a more complete picture of reading behavior.

We will use three types of questions in readership questionnaires: (1) demographic, (2) general factual (e.g., how many articles did you read last month), and (3) critical incident questions, with the results from these questions compared and applied to reading behavior.

Demographic questions include such things as status of the respondent (e.g., undergraduate, graduate student, or faculty member), academic discipline, age, and gender. In past studies, academic discipline and status have been important differentiators of the amount and patterns of reading, with age and gender being less important. In addition, specialized demographic factors for faculty, such as number of articles published and awards won within the last two years, have been significant differentiators in patterns and amounts of reading.

General factual questions will be kept to a minimum, because peoples' recollections of past general events can be faulty. We do ask how many journal articles in total a respondent has read in the past four weeks to get an overall picture of reading amounts. Both demographic and general factual questions can be used as independent variables to segment users by amount of reading, productivity (authorship), award winners, etc., in addition to more common segments by age, discipline, and gender.

Finally, a "last reading" variation of the critical incident technique, used for three decades of research by Tenopir and King, asks respondents to focus on the specific article read most recently to uncover details about this reading. Such details include how the reader first learned about the article; where the article was obtained; the time spent obtaining and reading the article; the format of the article when last read; age of the article; and the consequences of having read the article.

The power of this variation of critical incident technique lies in the fact that every reading is different. Detailed patterns of information-seeking and reading can be determined, such as how older articles are identified, where they are obtained, what proportion of readings are from personal subscriptions or from library collections that are in electronic format, and so on. Such details about a specific reading are more likely to be recalled accurately by the respondent than details about general usage. With details of information relating to one reading, researchers can explore hundreds of combinations of information-seeking and reading patterns.

The critical incident method has also had a further advantage in that Tenopir, King, and colleagues were able to observe trends in the detailed patterns of information seeking and reading over a twenty-five-year period. For example, the amount of faculty reading increased by about sixty readings per year, which reflected an increase by the same amount from academic libraries. The trends also showed that reading from personal subscriptions decreased, articles identified by online searches increased dramatically, and the number of journals read by individual scientists nearly doubled, partly due to the access to expanded electronic library collections (King et al., 2003). They were also able to show how advances in technologies had a significant impact on information-seeking patterns (Tenopir et al., 2003, 2005).

The critical incident technique has been used for over a half century to analyze reports of human behavior. For information-related studies, there are basically two ways for which the critical incident technique has been applied. One approach is to identify an "incident" in which information may be needed, perhaps to solve a personal problem. Sometimes the incident is particularly noteworthy, such as a physician's diagnosing or treating an illness. Once an incident is identified, the research establishes the information-seeking behavior of the physician in addressing the problem. Another approach is to identify an information service incident or event such as an online bibliographic search or a reading of an article.

The critical incident technique emphasizes an occurrence, rather than opinion, by asking users to identify a specific event they experienced, such as the reading of an article that had an effect on the outcome of their information need or problem. Because heavy readers may be different from light readers, we often post-stratify in order to obtain a better understanding of the differences between the two groups.

Schedule

The first year of the project concerns project design and structure. Usage log data from OhioLINK libraries will be received, loaded, encoded, and processed; test data analyses will be run. A portion of the usage logs will be selected, isolated, collected internally, encoded, and setup for data analysis. Vendor usage reports for UT will be analyzed and described, while local database log data will be analyzed as usual. Other sources of log data from systems associated with access to e-resources (link resolver, metasearch engine, proxy server) will be reviewed for their utility. Questionnaires for faculty and students will be developed, with pilot tests run. Samples will be drawn from the user populations for distribution to four Ohio universities and the University of Tennessee.

The second year involves intensive data analysis. Deep log analysis will be used to examine data using standard data analysis techniques. Vendor reports and locally collected data will continue to be analyzed and compared, with attention paid to changes brought by Release 2 of the COUNTER Code of Practice. Data from the returned questionnaires will be analyzed and compared. Internal reports will be drafted to be shared with all members of the team.

During the third year, data analysis refinements and comparison and dissemination of results will be completed. Results and data analysis techniques will be compared by all team members, necessary refinements in data analysis techniques or extensions of analysis will be made, reports will be prepared, and results will be disseminated widely by all project participants.

CONCLUSIONS

The MaxData project seeks to determine how to engineer a system that adequately measures the effectiveness of the library's e-resources. In a sense, this research project is in itself an evaluation–the testing and evaluation of various methods of usage data collection and analysis–so the evaluation will be of the project methods to ensure validity and reliability of results. In the long term, the beneficiaries of the results for this project will be the users of library e-resources, who will benefit from the best choice of appropriate formats, collections, and user-centered systems. Both long- and short-term beneficiaries will be librarians, who will have the information they need to collect and analyze the most appropriate and effective usage data for their collections and decision making.

REFERENCES

Association of Research Libraries. "Monograph and Serial Costs in ARL Libraries, 1986-1999, 2020." Available at: http://www.arl.org/newsltr/210/coststbl.html

Centre for Information Behaviour and the Evaluation of Research (CIBER) Web site. http://www.ucl.ac.uk/ciber/ciber.php

Covey, Denise Troll. *Usage and Usability Assessment: Library Practices and Concerns.* Washington, D.C.: Digital Library Federation and Council on Library and Information Resources, 2002. Available at: http://www.clir.org/pubs/reports/ pub105/contents.html

DeGroote, Sandra L., and Josephine L. Dorsch. "Measuring Use Patterns of Online Journals and Databases." *Journal of the Medical Library Association* 91, no. 2 (2003): 231-240.

Duy, Joanna. "Usage Data: Issues and Challenges for Electronic Resource Collection Management." In ed. David C. Fowler, E-serials Collection Management: Transitions, Trends, and Technicalities, 111-138. Binghatmon, NY: Haworth Information Press, 2004.

Duy, Joanna, and Liwen Vaughan. "Usage Data for Electronic Resources: A Comparison between Locally Collected and Vendor-Provided Statistics." *Journal of Academic Librarianship* 29, no. 1 (2003): 16-22.

Franklin, Brinley, and Terry Plum. "Documenting Usage Patterns of Networked Electronic Services." *Association of Research Libraries* 230/231 (October-December 2003): 20-21.

Fulltext Sources Online. Medford, N.J.: Information Today, January 2004.

Galbraith, Betty. "Journal Retention Decisions Incorporating Use-Statistics as a Measure of Value." *Collection Management* 27, no. 1 (2002): 79-90.

Hartland-Fox, Rebecca, and Stella Thebridge. "Electronic Information Services Evaluation: Current Activity and Issues in UK Academic Libraries." *Serials* 16, no. 1 (2003): 63-68.

Jacsó, Peter. "The COUNTER Project." *Information Today* 21, no. 5 (2004): 17, 19.

King, Donald W., and Carol Hansen Montgomery. "After Migration to an Electronic Journals Collection: Impact on Faculty and Students." *D-Lib Magazine* 8 (December 2002). Available at: http://www.dlib.org/dlib/december02/king/12king .html.

King, Donald W., Carol Tenopir, Carol Hansen Montgomery, and Sarah E. Aerni. "Patterns of Journal Use by Faculty at Three Diverse Universities." *D-Lib Magazine* 9 (October 2003). Available at: http://www.dlib.org/dlib/october03/king/10king.html.

King, Donald W., Carol Tenopir, and Michael Clarke. "Measuring Total Reading of Journal Articles." *D-Lib Magazine* 12 (October 2006). Available at: http://www.dlib.org/dlib/october06/king/10king.htm.

King, Donald W., Sarah Aerni, Fern Brody, Matt Herbison, and Paul Kohberger. *Comparative Cost of the University of Pittsburgh Electronic and Print Library Collections.* Pittsburgh, PA: Sara Fine Institute, University of Pittsburgh, 2004a. Available at: http://www.crash.exp.sis.pitt.edu/sfi/documents/sfi-pub20040405a.pdf.

King, Donald W., Sarah Aerni, Fern Brody, Matt Herbison, and Amy Knapp. *The Use and Outcomes of University Library Print and Electronic Collections.* Pittsburgh,

PA: Sara Fine Institute, University of Pittsburgh, 2004b. Available at: http://www. crash.exp.sis.pitt.edu/sfi/documents/sfi-pub20040405b.pdf.

Lichtenberg, James. "Industry Investigating How to Use 'Usage Statistics'." *Publishers Weekly* 251, no. 1 (2004): 12.

Luther, Judy. *White Paper on Electronic Journal Usage Statistics.* Washington, D.C.: Council on Library and Information Resources, 2000. Available at: http:// www.press.umich.edu/jep/06-03/luther.html.

Matthews, Karen. "What's One To Do When Vendors, Publishers, and Aggregators Do Not Meet Your Usage Reporting Needs? Do It Yourself!" *The Serials Librarian* 42, no. 3/4 (2002): 223-228.

McDowell, Nicola, and G. E. Gorman. "The Relevance of Vendors' Usage Statistics in Academic Library E-resource Management: A New Zealand Study." *Australian Academic and Research Libraries* 35, no. 4 (2004): 322-343.

Montgomery, Carol Hansen, and Donald W. King. "Comparing Library and User Related Costs of Print and Electronic Journal Collections: A First Step Towards a Comprehensive Analysis." *D-Lib Magazine* 8 (October 2002). Available at: http://www.dlib.org/dlib/october02/montgomery/10montgomery.html.

Pesch, Oliver. "Usage Statistics: Taking E-metrics to the Next Level." *The Serials Librarian* 46, no.1/2 (2004): 143-154.

Project COUNTER Web site. http://www.projectcounter.org.

Schonfeld, Roger C., Donald W. King, Ann Okerson, and Eileen Gifford Fenton. *The Nonsubscription Side of Periodicals: Changes in Library Operations and Costs between Print and Electronic Formats.* Washington, DC: Council on Library and Information Resources, 2004. Available at: http://www.clir.org/pubs/reports/pub127/pub127.pdf.

Shim, Wonsik, and Charles R. McClure. "Data Needs and Use of Electronic Resources and Services at Academic Research Libraries." *Portal* 2, no. 2 (2002): 217-236.

Stemper, James A., and Janice M. Jaguszewski. "Usage Statistics for Electronic Journals: An Analysis of Local and Vendor Counts." *Collection Management* 28, no. 4 (2003): 3-22.

Tenopir, Carol. *Use and Users of Electronic Library Resources: An Overview and Analysis of Recent Research Studies.* Washington, DC: Council on Library and Information Resources, 2003. Available at: http://www.clir.org/pubs/abstract/pub120abst.html.

Tenopir, Carol, and Donald W. King. *Towards Electronic Journals: Realities for Scientists, Librarians, and Publishers.* Washington, DC: Special Libraries Association, 2000.

Tenopir, Carol, Donald W. King, Peter Boyce, Matt Grayson, and Keri-Lynn Paulson. "Relying on Electronic Journals: Reading Patterns of Astronomers." *Journal of the American Society for Information Science and Technology* 56 (June 2005): 786-802.

Tenopir, Carol, Donald W. King, Peter Boyce, Matt Grayson, Yan Zhang, and Mercy Ebuen. "Patterns of Journal Use by Scientists through Three Evolutionary Phases." *D-Lib Magazine* 9 (May 2003). Available at: http://www.dlib.org/dlib/may03/king/05king.html.

Van Orsdel, Lee C., and Kathleen Born. "Choosing Sides." *Library Journal* 130 (April 15, 2005): 43-48.

Wang, Peiling. "Methodologies and Methods for User Behavioral Research." In *Annual Review of Information Science and Technology*, vol. 34, edited by Martha E. Williams, 53-99. Medford, N.J.: Information Today, 2001.

Weintraub, Jennifer. "Usage Statistics at Yale University Library." *Against the Grain* 15 (December 2003-January 2004): 32, 34.

Related Readings and Selected CIBER Research Projects

Blecic, Deborah, Joan Fiscella, and Stephen Wiberley, Jr. "The Measurement of Use of Web-based Information Resources: An Early Look at Vendor-Supplied Data." *College and Research Libraries* 62, no. 5 (2001): 434-453.

Blixrud, Julia C., and Martha Kyrillidou. "E-metrics: Next Steps for Measuring Electronic Resources." *Association of Research Libraries* 230/231 (October-December 2003): 11-13.

Borghuis, Marthyn G.M. "Getting the Best Out of It! Usage Analysis from the Publishing Perspective." *Against the Grain* 15 (December 2003-January 2004): 34, 36.

CIBER Research Project. "The Changing Information Environment: The Impact of the Internet on Information Seeking." British Library, 1997-1998.

CIBER Research Project. "Digital Journals–Site Licensing, Library Consortia Deals, and Journal Use Statistics." The Ingenta Institute, 2002.

CIBER Research Project. "The Virtual Scholar Research Program–Use and Impact of Digital Libraries in Academe." Blackwell/Emerald/British Library/ Elsevier, 2003-2004.

Hahn, Karla L., and Lila A. Faulkner. "Evaluative Usage-Based Metrics for the Selection of E-journals." *College and Research Libraries* 63, no. 3 (2002): 215-227.

King, Donald W., and Carol Tenopir. "Using and Reading Scholarly Literature." In *Annual Review of Information Science and Technology*, vol. 34, edited by Martha E. Williams, 423-477. Medford, N.J.: Information Today, 2001.

King, Donald W., Peter B. Boyce, Carol Hansen Montgomery, and Carol Tenopir. "Library Economic Metrics: Examples of the Comparison of Electronic and Print Journal Collections and Collection Services." *Library Trends* 51 (Winter 2003): 376-400.

Molyneux, Robert. "Devil's Advocate: COUNTER, XML, and Online Serials Management." *Against the Grain* 15 (December 2003-January 2004): 92-94.

Molyneux, Robert. "Making Haste Slowly: E-metrics, Where Are We Now, and What Can We Expect?" *Against the Grain* 15 (December 2003-January 2004): 18, 20.

Nicholas, David and Paul Huntington. "Micro-mining and Segmented Log File Analysis: A Method for Enriching the Data Yield from Internet Log Files." *Journal of Information Science* 29, no. 5 (2003): 391-404.

Nicholas, David, Paul Huntington, and Anthony Watkinson. "Digital Journals, Big Deals and Online Searching Behaviour: A Pilot Study." *Aslib Proceedings* 55, no. 1/2 (2003): 84-109.

Nicholas, David, Paul Huntington, Ian Rowlands, Bill Russell, and Jill Cousins. "Opening Up the Digital Box: What Deep Log Analysis Can Tell Us about Our Digital Journal Users." In *Charleston Conference Proceedings, 2003*, edited by Rosann Bazirjian and Vicky Speck, 118-138. Westport, CT: Libraries Unlimited, 2004.

Nicholas, David, Paul Huntington, Peter Williams, and Barrie Gunter. "'Search-disclosure': Understanding Digital Information Platform Preference and Location in a Health Environment." *Journal of Documentation* 59 (September 2003): 523-539.

Nicholas, David, Paul Huntington, Peter Williams, and Tom Dobrowolski. "Re-appraising Information Seeking Behaviour in a Digital Environment: Bouncers, Checkers, Returnees, and the Like." *Journal of Documentation* 60 (January-February 2004): 24-43.

Sack, John. "The Beginning of Value Assessment: Usage Information in the E-journal Age." *Against the Grain* 15 (December 2003-January 2004): 36, 38, 40.

Shepherd, Peter T. "The COUNTER Code of Practice: Implementation and Adoption." *SCONUL Newsletter* 29 (Summer/Autumn 2003): 22-26.

Shepherd, Peter T. "COUNTER: Progress Through Cooperation." *Against the Grain* 15 (December 2003-January 2004): 44, 46, 50.

Shepherd, Peter T. "Keeping Count: Project COUNTER, Measuring Usage of Online Resources and Establishing Standards for Data Transmission." *Library Journal* 128, no. 2 (2003): 46-48.

Shepherd, Peter T., and Denise M. Davis. "Electronic Metrics, Performance Measures, and Statistics for Publishers and Libraries: Building Common Ground and Standards." *Portal* 2, no. 4 (2002): 659-663.

Tenopir, Carol, and Donald W. King. *Communication Patterns of Engineers*. New York: IEEE/Wiley InterScience, 2004.

Tenopir, Carol, and Donald W. King. "Lessons for the Future of Journals." *Nature* 18 (October 2001): 672-674.

Tenopir, Carol, and Donald W. King. "The Use and Value of Scientific Journals: Past, Present and Future." *Serials* 14 (July 2001): 113-120.

doi:10.1300/J123v53S09_05

Chapter 5

E-Resource Management in Connecticut Academic Libraries: 2005 CCALD Survey Results

Carol Abatelli

INTRODUCTION

Speaking at the Connecticut Library Association's 2005 annual conference on the new role of technical services in libraries, William M. Wakeling, associate dean of Collections and Technical Services at Northeastern University, noted that the management of e-resources is challenging technical services departments to alter workflows and job responsibilities in order to adapt to a new paradigm. In her report of this conference program for *Connecticut Libraries,* Hing Wu of Southern Connecticut State University, summarized Wakeling's remarks thusly:

As library holdings rapidly evolve into a hybrid print/non-print collection, the bibliographic control and acquisition activities of

---

The author gratefully acknowledges the editorial assistance of Patricia Banach, Director of Library Services at J. Eugene Smith Library, Eastern Connecticut State University, and of her husband, Frank Davis, who has many years of experience as a technical writer.

[Haworth co-indexing entry note]: "E-Resource Management in Connecticut Academic Libraries: 2005 CCALD Survey Results." Abatelli, Carol. Co-published simultaneously in *The Serials Librarian* (The Haworth Information Press, an imprint of The Haworth Press, Inc.) Vol. 53, Supplement No. 9, 2007, pp. 79-109; and: *Usage Statistics of E-Serials* (ed: David C. Fowler) The Haworth Information Press, an imprint of The Haworth Press, Inc., 2007, pp. 79-109. Single or multiple copies of this article are available for a fee from The Haworth Document Delivery Service [1-800-HAWORTH, 9:00 a.m. - 5:00 p.m. (EST). E-mail address: docdelivery@haworthpress.com].

Available online at http://ser.haworthpress.com
doi:10.1300/J123v53S09_06

TS (technical services) are steadily replaced by the managing of electronic resources. Now is the moment to shed the "library housekeeping" image, Mr. Wakeling declared; instead, TS professionals should take on the challenges of electronic resources management and the efficient delivery of e-resources.[1]

In closing her report, however, Wu added her own perspective on Wakeling's call for the reorganization of library technical services to better manage e-resources, remarking, "Those who have the administrative support and resources will no doubt be inspired to take a great leap forward."[2]

Are Connecticut's academic libraries poised to take this "great leap" into the challenging new world of efficient e-resource management that Wakeling and Wu foresee? Wakeling's conference presentation was timely, because a number of those involved with e-resources in Connecticut libraries have recently begun to look at how their institutions are handling the management of these resources, and to ask how other institutions within the state are coping with the challenges that e-resources have created. Library directors, technical services librarians, and others involved with e-resource collections are asking such questions as: What are the other academic libraries around the state spending on e-resources? What staff positions are managing the various aspects of e-resource acquisition and provision? How much time is being spent on managing e-resources collections? Finally, what usage statistics, if any, are libraries tracking?

In an effort to get some idea of the answers to these and related questions, the author developed an e-resource management survey and sent it to members of the Council of Connecticut Academic Library Directors (CCALD) in March 2005 (Appendix). CCALD is a statewide, nonprofit library consortium whose members represent all types of academic libraries, including those serving community colleges (and others that offer associate degrees), four-year colleges, and several universities.[3] The author chose to survey the CCALD libraries because it was believed that a reasonably good response from this group would provide a "snapshot" of e-resource management at academic libraries statewide.

The survey was initially posted to the CCALD LISTSERV on March 13, 2005. Ten responses were received to the LISTSERV posting. Two weeks later, paper copies of the survey were mailed to CCALD libraries that had not responded to the LISTSERV version. Twenty responses were received to the postal mailing. Including the author's library, the total survey responses thus came to thirty-one. With forty-three

CCALD libraries eligible to respond,[4] the response rate is calculated to be approximately 72 percent.

DISCUSSION OF SURVEY RESULTS

This section is divided into two parts. Following a brief review of recent library surveys on e-resource management, Part 1 covers Questions 1-6 of the survey, which asked for information about library type, e-resource budget size, and staffing. Part 2 covers Questions 7-14, which dealt mainly with the CCALD libraries' collection and usage of e-resource statistics.

PART 1:
LIBRARY TYPE, E-RESOURCE BUDGET SIZE, AND STAFFING

Over the past five years, several authors have published the results of surveys that were focused on library e-resource acquisition and management and on staffing for these functions. Generally, the results of these surveys tend to confirm the hypothesis that the management of e-resource collections has affected library staffing in one or more ways. In 2001, Susan Gardner wrote an article for *Serials Review,* in which she simultaneously published the results of her survey of Association of Research Libraries (ARL) libraries on how e-serials management had affected staffing and workflow, as well as a critique of her own survey methodology.[5] Despite its design flaws, Gardner's survey results did tend to suggest that more library departments might be involved in handling e-serials than had been involved in handling print journals and indexes.[6] (At the 2002 conference of the North American Serials Interest Group (NASIG), Gardner provided a workshop on conducting serials surveys, in which she offered "lessons learned," based on her experience conducting the ARL survey.)[7]

In 2002, Ellen Finnie Duranceau and Cindy Hepfer presented the results of a small survey (fifteen U.S. academic libraries) of library staffing trends in e-resource management.[8] Duranceau and Hepfer found that staffing for e-resource management was generally inadequate among their survey respondents, and also that libraries were tending to redistribute e-resources work among existing staff, rather than hiring additional staff to cope with the increased workload created by e-resource collections.[9]

In late 2003 and early 2004, Sandhya Srivastava and Paolina Taglienti surveyed small and medium-sized libraries on e-journal management.[10] Their survey asked some general questions about the funding and size of libraries' print and electronic serials collections, but it mainly focused on what tools libraries were using to manage e-journals and the role of integrated library systems in relation to e-journal management programs such as Serials Solutions or EBSCO's A-Z. Srivastava and Taglienti's survey also asked the question "Who in your Library maintains the electronic journal data?"[11] The answers received (from 130 respondents) indicated that electronic resources librarians, reference librarians, administrators, systems librarians, serials librarians, and many others have all become involved in tracking e-journal data, and that, in many cases, more than one type of librarian at the same institution is involved in maintaining this data.[12]

Turning our attention to the present survey, the first question asked of each respondent was to identify his or her library as serving a community college, a four-year college with mainly baccalaureate degree programs (hereafter, "Type 1" colleges), a four-year college with a substantial number of master's degree programs (hereafter, "Type 2" colleges), or a doctoral degree-granting university (Figure 5.1). Ten respondents (32 percent) identified their institutions as community college libraries, seven (23 percent) identified their institutions as libraries serving "Type 1" colleges, ten (32 percent) identified their institutions as libraries serving "Type 2" colleges, and four (13 percent) identified their institutions as university libraries.[13]

Thus, all types of academic libraries within the state were represented to some extent by the survey results. (Wherever practical, survey results are broken out by library type throughout this report.)

FIGURE 5.1. Type of institution.

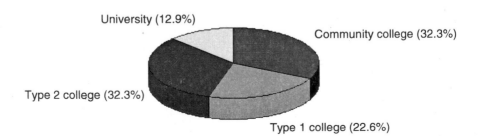

University (12.9%)

Community college (32.3%)

Type 2 college (32.3%)

Type 1 college (22.6%)

The second survey question asked each respondent to select a range for his or her library's annual electronic resources budget (Figure 5.2). Eight of the ten (80 percent) community college libraries were in the $25,000 or less range; one (10 percent) was in the $25,000-$50,000 range; one (10 percent) was in the $50,000-$100,000 range.

In contrast to the community college libraries, both "Type 1" and "Type 2" college libraries showed wide variation in e-resource budgets (Figures 5.3 and 5.4).

Libraries in the "Type 1" group (seven libraries) reported:

- One (14 percent) in the $25,000-$50,000 range
- Two (29 percent) in the $50,000-$100,000 range
- One (14 percent) in the $100,000-$200,000 range
- Two (29 percent) in the $200,000-$300,000 range
- One (14 percent) in the over $400,000 range

Libraries in the "Type 2" group (ten libraries) reported:

- Three (30 percent) in the $25,000 or less range
- One (10 percent) in the $25,000-$50,000 range
- One (10 percent) in the $50,000-$100,000 range
- Four (40 percent) in the $100,000-$200,000 range
- One (10 percent) in the $200,000-$300,000 range

Four university libraries reported (Figure 5.5), two (50 percent) were in the $200,000-$300,000 range and two (50 percent) were in the over $400,000 range.

FIGURE 5.2. E-R Budget–Community colleges.

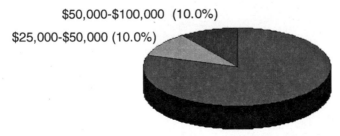

$50,000-$100,000 (10.0%)

$25,000-$50,000 (10.0%)

$25,000 or Less (80.0%)

Out of thirty-one total responding libraries, there were:

- Eleven (35 percent) in the $25,000 or less range
- Three (10 percent) in the $25,000-$50,000 range
- Four (13 percent) in the $50,000-$100,000 range
- Five (16 percent) in the $100,000-$200,000 range
- Five (16 percent) in the $200,000-$300,000 range
- Three (10 percent) in the over $400,000 range

Interestingly, there were no libraries of any type in the $300,000-$400,000 range (Figure 5.6).

The small e-resource budgets reported by the community college libraries (80 percent in the $25,000 or under range) should be explained, lest readers outside Connecticut form the impression that these libraries are not offering adequate e-resources to students at their institutions. In fact, all of Connecticut's academic libraries have access to a core collection of online databases offered at state expense by the Connecticut Digital Library (iCONN.org). iCONN is a joint project of the Connecticut State Library and the state Department of Higher Education that provides access to standard academic databases such as LexisNexis Academic Universe, Business & Company Resource Center, Expanded Academic ASAP, General Reference Center Gold, Professional Collection, and PsycINFO, among others. Community college and other academic libraries in Connecticut have been able to rely upon the iCONN group of databases to supplement their e-resource collections.

The third survey question asked respondents to indicate whether there was a Master of Library Science (MLS)-level librarian position devoted to the management of e-resources at their institutions. Among responding libraries, over all, the numbers were about evenly divided with fourteen (45 percent) answering "yes," sixteen (52 percent) answering "no," and one library (3 percent) answering that it was planning to staff such a position in the near future. However, when broken down by library type, the picture is different. Among the ten community college libraries, only three (30 percent) answered this question affirmatively, with one respondent who did so commenting: "the director." Four of the seven "Type 1" college libraries (57 percent) and five of the ten "Type 2" college libraries (50 percent) answered "yes" to this question. Among the four university libraries, the proportion was similar, with two clear "yes" answers, one "no," and one answer that was "no, but we are planning to staff this position in the near future." However, one respondent pointed out that, although her institution has an e-resources librarian, this person also has other duties aside from e-resource management, something that is true in the author's case as well. Greater specificity with regard to the percentage of time actually spent on e-resource management by those with responsibilities in this area might have improved the quality of the responses to this question.

FIGURE 5.3. E-R Budget–Type 1 colleges.

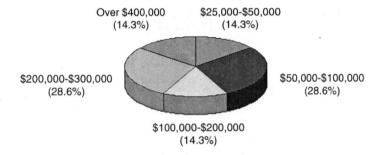

FIGURE 5.4. E-R Budget–Type 2 colleges.

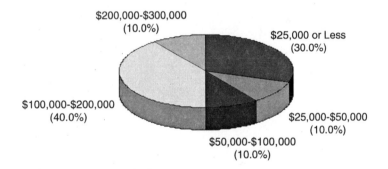

FIGURE 5.5. E-R Budget–Universities.

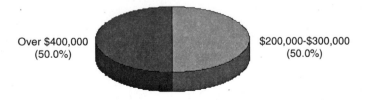

FIGURE 5.6. Budget–All colleges.

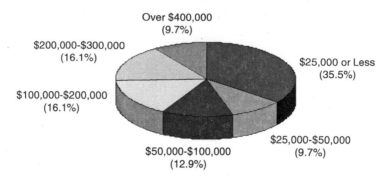

Over $400,000
(9.7%)

$200,000-$300,000
(16.1%)

$100,000-$200,000
(16.1%)

$25,000 or Less
(35.5%)

$50,000-$100,000
(12.9%)

$25,000-$50,000
(9.7%)

The author attempted to get some idea about the time being spent on e-resource management in Connecticut libraries with Question 4, which asked respondents to estimate the average number of hours per week devoted to e-resource management by MLS-level staff (including the library director), systems staff, and paraprofessional staff. Again, a problem arose concerning interpretation of the question. One respondent at a "Type 2" college library, noting that the systems librarian there had an MLS, assigned that individual's time to the MLS category, while a respondent at a "Type 1" college assigned the weekly hours of the systems librarian, who also had an MLS, to the systems category. To get around this discrepancy, the author decided to combine the MLS and systems categories together as "professional staff" in discussing the responses to Question 4, but to show the responses as was received for those who are interested in Table 5.1.

Using the two category distinctions (professional and paraprofessional), nine community college libraries reported a total of 52.5 professional hours per week and 11 paraprofessional hours per week. (One library's response was interpreted as "unknown.")[14] This worked out to be an average of 5.83 hours per week of professional time, and 1.22 hours per week of paraprofessional time. Six "Type 1" college libraries reported a total of 131 professional and 6.5 paraprofessional hours per week, with one "unknown" response. This worked out to an average of 21.83 hours per week of professional time and 1.08 hours of paraprofessional time. Eight "Type 2" college libraries reported a total of 89.5 professional and 16.75 paraprofessional hours per week, with two "unknown" responses.[15] This worked out to an average of 11.19

TABLE 5.1. Total number of hours per week devoted to e-resource management for three staff categories as reported. Number of libraries that answered Question 4 is shown in parenthesis.

	Hours	Average (hours)
Community college libraries (9)		
MLS Staff/Director	38.5	4.28
Systems	14	1.56
Paraprofessional	11	1.22
Total	63.5	7.06
Type 1 college libraries (6)		
MLS Staff/Director	115	19.17
Systems	16	2.67
Paraprofessional	6.5	1.08
Total	137.5	22.92
Type 2 college libraries (8)		
MLS Staff/Director	77.75	9.72
Systems	11.75	1.47
Paraprofessional	16.75	2.09
Total	106.25	13.28
University libraries (4)		
MLS Staff/Director	380	95
Systems	55	13.75
Paraprofessional	136	34
Total	571	142.75
All libraries (27)		
MLS Staff/Director	611.25	22.64
Systems	96.75	3.58
Paraprofessional	170.25	6.31
Total	878.25	32.53

hours per week of professional time and 2.09 hours per week of paraprofessional time.

The responses of the university libraries are not averaged, as one library listed 350 MLS hours, 30 systems hours, and 100 paraprofessional hours, skewing any attempt to calculate a meaningful average number of hours in either the professional or paraprofessional categories for university libraries (Table 5.1).

That the community college libraries were expending only an average of 5.83 hours per week of professional time and 1.22 hours per week of paraprofessional time on e-resource management makes sense, given their relatively small budgets, and the likelihood that some are providing only the iCONN package supplied by the state. However, the fact that the "Type 1" college libraries reported spending nearly double the number of professional staff hours on e-resource management to that reported by the "Type 2" institutions (21.83 versus 11.19 hours) is more difficult to understand. It is possible that circumstances unique to the individual libraries in this group, such as e-journal cataloging projects, chronic network problems, or particularly stringent administrative oversight of e-resource licensing, might have bumped up the number of hours expended by librarians and systems staff at these institutions.

Question 5 (Figure 5.7) asked how the number of staff hours working on e-resource management functions changed in the past two years. Overall, thirteen libraries (eight of which were in the community college category) or 42 percent, reported that the number of hours stayed the same, eight (26 percent) reported that hours had increased by one-half of a full-time equivalent (FTE) employee or less, nine (29 percent) reported that hours had increased by more than one-half of an FTE employee, and one (3 percent) reported "don't know."

These findings differ from those of Duranceau and Hepfer, whose previously cited survey found that "eight of fourteen respondents (57 percent) reported staff growth for e-resource support hovering around the 100- to 200-percent range."[16] However, as might have been anticipated, no CCALD library reported any decrease in staff hours spent on e-resource management over the past two years (Table 5.2).

Question 6 asked respondents to indicate which staff members are responsible for eleven specific e-resource management functions:

FIGURE 5.7. E-R Staffing change in past two years.

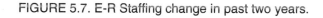
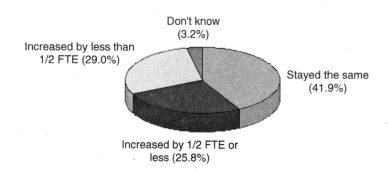

TABLE 5.2. Change in staff hours spent on e-resource activities by staff category over past two years.

Our e-resource staff hours have:	CC (10)	%	Type 1 (7)	%	Type 2 (10)	%	Univ (4)	%	All (31)	%
Stayed the same	8	80	2	29	3	30	0	0	13	42
Increased by ½ FTE or less	1	10	1	14	5	50	1	25	8	26
Increased by more than ½ FTE	1	10	3	43	2	20	3	75	9	29
Decreased by ½ FTE or less	0	0	0	0	0	0	0	0	0	0
Decreased by more than ½ FTE	0	0	0	0	0	0	0	0	0	0
Don't know	0	0	1	14	0	0	0	0	1	3
Total	10	100	7	100	10	100	0	100	31	100

selection, vendor contact, license review, license signing, e-resource ordering, e-journal activation, cataloging, A-Z listing, troubleshooting access problems, collecting usage statistics, and budget monitoring. Although seemingly complex, this question was actually intended to get a "quick take" on two broad and related trends that have been discussed in the literature: (1) that responsibility for various e-resource functions is being distributed between a large number of library departments[17] and (2) that library workers from different departments are sharing responsibilities for the same function (Table 5.3).[18]

One noteworthy difference among the four types of libraries that deserves mention, however, is that community college library directors are often more directly involved in e-resource management than are directors of other types of libraries (Table 5.4).

This would seem to indicate that e-resource management is considered a key aspect of collection development at these institutions. (Please note that in discussing results for this question, the term "library director" also includes associate and assistant library directors.)

Further review of the responses shown in Table 5.3 indicate that across all types of libraries MLS-level librarians and other library workers from many different library departments are involved in various aspects of e-resource management, as noted by both Gardner and Duranceau and Hepfer.[19] This is hardly surprising for a function such as e-resource selection, as many libraries, particularly small libraries, traditionally divide collection development responsibilities among

TABLE 5.3. Type of staff assigned to e-resource functions: responses from all libraries. (Libraries can have more than one staff member for the same function.)

Function	ACQ	CAT	CD	E-R	PS	REF	SER	SYS	TS	DIR	SEC	PAR	OUT	DON'T DO	DON'T KNOW
Selection	2		9	3	1	14	1			16					
Vendor contact	9		2	4		6	2	4		14	3				
License review . . .	6		2	3		1	2	1		23			4		
License signatory				1			1			27			2		
Ordering	12		2	3	1	2	2	3	1	9	3	3			
Activation . . .	6	1	2	3	1	2	6	12	1	3		1		2	2
Cataloging	1	22			1	1	3	2	1	3		2	1	3	2
A-Z listing . . .	3	3	1	3	1	3	8	8		3		3		1	
Troubleshooting . . .	3		2	4	1	8	3	16	2	7	1	1			2
Collecting stats	4		1	4	1	9	3	7	1	7	1	4			
Budget . . .	5		4	3		2	2		1	23	2				

ACQ: Acquisitions; CAT: Cataloging; CD: Collection Development; E-R: E-Resources; PS: Public Services; REF: Reference; SER: Serials; SYS: Systems; TS: Technical Services; DIR: Library Director or Assistant Director; SEC: Library Secretary; PAR: Library paraprofessional; OUT: Outside unit (e.g., Legal); DON'T DO: Don't perform this function; DON'T KNOW: Don't Know.

TABLE 5.4. Percentage of community college library directors directly involved in e-resource management functions versus percentage of all other directors involved in these functions.

Function	CC directors	Percent of CC libraries (10)	All other directors	Percent of all other libraries (21)
Selection	8	80	8	38
Vendor contact	6	60	8	38
License review . . .	10	100	13	62
License signatory	10	100	17	81
Ordering	6	60	3	15
Activation . . .	2	20	1	5
Cataloging	2	20	1	5
A-Z listing . . .	2	20	1	5
Troubleshooting . . .	4	40	3	15
Collecting stats	4	40	3	15
Budget . . .	10	100	13	62

various staff. However, a look at responses to the question of who bears responsibility for another traditional library function, ordering, suggests that more types of staff have become involved in e-resource acquisition than were previously involved in ordering print materials. Subscriptions to paper serials, for example, are still typically ordered by serials, acquisitions, or technical services departments, depending on library size. Among the CCALD libraries surveyed, however, the ordering of e-resources is being handled by the following departments and staff:

- Acquisitions: twelve cases
- Collection Development: two cases
- E-Resources: three cases
- Public Services: one case
- Reference: two cases
- Serials: two cases
- Systems: three cases
- Technical Services: one case
- Library Director: nine cases
- Library Secretary: three cases
- Paraprofessional staff (from any dept.): three cases

The acquisition of library materials by Public Services, Reference, and Systems, even though the number of cases is small, appears to represent some change in the role of these positions. It is also worth noting the large number of cases (twelve) where the library director or the director's secretary was involved in ordering e-resources, because this suggests that these resources were receiving special handling (i.e., they were not being ordered by the same staff who order other types of library materials).

Another e-resource function that illustrates how e-resource management is being handled by numerous library departments, and one especially relevant to the subject of this volume, is the collection of usage statistics. The answers to this part of Question 6 indicate that, with the exception of cataloging, every type of library department or staff type listed in the survey received at least one response.

- Acquisitions: four cases
- Collection Development: one case
- E-Resources: four cases
- Public Services: one case
- Reference: nine cases
- Serials: three cases
- Systems: seven cases
- Technical Services: one case
- Library Director: seven cases
- Library Secretary: one case
- Paraprofessional staff (from any dept.): four cases

The fact that there are more than the thirty-one responses for both ordering and collecting usage statistics indicates that, at some libraries, these e-resource functions are handled by more than one staff member. This finding agrees with Srivastava and Taglienti's observation that responsibility for maintaining electronic journal data was often shared by more than one staff member at the libraries in their survey.[20] That this distribution of labor is not necessarily within a single department, but rather across two or more departments, is suggested by the fact that in both examples, the number of responses remains higher than the number of libraries, even after the "library secretary" and "library paraprofessional staff" cases are discounted: thirty-five cases for ordering and thirty-seven for collecting usage statistics. (Paraprofessionals were discounted in this example, because they could be assigned to one of the listed departments; that is, a respondent could have indicated both "Cataloging" and paraprofessional staff catalog e-resources. However, it should be borne in mind that this is not necessarily the case: a paraprofessional from the cataloging department and another from "Systems" might both be collecting usage statistics.)

Further evidence that library workers from different departments are sharing responsibilities for the same function is provided by Table 5.5, which shows the number of cases where more than one department or staff member is involved in e-resources management functions (including the library secretary and paraprofessional staff).

The three highest categories where this was reported were, "Troubleshooting access problems" (48 percent of libraries surveyed); "Selection" (35 percent of libraries surveyed); and "Collecting usage statistics" (32 percent of libraries surveyed).

A final point about Question 6 is that responses received from libraries in both the "Type 1" and "Type 2" categories indicate that libraries of similar type and size may distribute e-resource management functions quite differently. Table 5.6 illustrates this observation by comparing two libraries of the same type, which reported similar budgets (additional information has been withheld to protect confidentiality).

TABLE 5.5. Cases where two or more staff or library depts. work on the same e-resource function.

Function	CC	Type 1	Type 2	University	Total	Percent of all libraries
Selection	3	4	3	1	11	35
Vendor contact	3	1	2	2	8	26
License review . . .	1	3	3	1	7	23
License signatory	0	1	0	0	1	3
Ordering	4	1	0	1	6	19
Activation . . .	1	1	2	2	6	19
Cataloging	4	1	1	2	8	26
A-Z listing . . .	1	2	0	3	6	19
Troubleshooting . . .	3	4	5	3	15	48
Collecting usage stats	2	1	5	2	10	32
Budget monitoring	1	3	2	2	8	26

TABLE 5.6. Responses to Question 6 from comparable libraries. (Answers are listed in order received.)

Function	Library 1	Library 2
Selection	Collection Development, Electronic Resources, Reference, Serials	Reference
Vendor contact	Library Director or Assistant Director, Acquisitions, Electronic Resources	Library Director or Assistant Director, Acquisitions, Reference
License review . . .	Library Director or Assistant Director, Acquisitions	Library Director or Assistant Director, Outside unit
License signatory	Library Director or Assistant Director	Library Director or Assistant Director
Ordering	Acquisitions	Acquisitions
Activation . . .	Electronic Resources	Acquisitions, Serials, Systems
Cataloging	Cataloging	Cataloging, Outside unit
A-Z listing . . .	Electronic Resources	Systems
Troubleshooting . . .	Electronic Resources, Systems	Reference, Systems
Collecting stats	Electronic Resources, Systems	Reference, Library paraprofessional
Budget . . .	Library Director or Assistant Director, Acquisitions	Technical Services

PART 2:
CCALD LIBRARIES' COLLECTION
AND USAGE OF E-RESOURCE STATISTICS

The remaining survey questions were designed to provide insight into how the various types of academic libraries within Connecticut are collecting and using statistics for electronic databases and journals. In a previous volume in this series, Joanna Duy discussed at length many of the issues surrounding the collection and interpretation of e-resource usage statistics, and the author is indebted to Duy for raising questions that the present survey attempts to address.[21] For example, in her discussion of the various statistical measures provided by vendors, Duy asks: "Which of the measures outlined . . . are the most useful for librarians interested in knowing how their electronic journals are being used?"[22] To learn what types of statistics, the CCALD libraries consider most useful, Question 7 asked respondents to provide information about the type of vendor-statistics collected (if any) by their libraries for each of the three types of e-resources: aggregated databases, e-journal collections, and individual e-journals.

Almost all of the libraries surveyed responded that they collected information about the number of searches performed on their aggregated databases. Nine of the ten community college libraries (90 percent) collected information about the number of searches, as did all seven "Type 1" college libraries (100 percent), nine out of the ten "Type 2" college libraries (90 percent), and two of the four university libraries (50 percent). In all, twenty-seven of the thirty-one libraries surveyed (87 percent) tracked the number of searches performed on their aggregated databases. Of the four remaining libraries, respondents for one community college library and one university library answered: "Don't collect," and respondents for one "Type 2" college library and another university library answered: "Don't know." Therefore, despite cautions in the literature about relying on search statistics to measure database use due to lack of standardization among vendors in search definition and other problems,[23] it seems clear that Connecticut libraries consider the number of searches performed on their databases to be an important measure of use.

After searches, the next most collected statistical measure for aggregated databases was the number of sessions, with six of the ten community college libraries (60 percent), one of the seven "Type 1" college libraries (14 percent), seven of the ten "Type 2" college libraries (70 percent), and two of the four university libraries (50 percent)–52 percent of all respondents–keeping track of session data. Other statistics kept for aggregated databases by the various types of libraries included: page views (by one "Type 2" college library and, "selectively," by one university library); article downloads (by three community college libraries, one "Type 1" college library, three "Type 2" college libraries, and two university libraries, albeit, "selectively" in one case); and turnaways (by one community college library, two "Type 1" college libraries, and one university library). The "Type 2" college libraries also responded with the "other" survey choice in five cases, with specific mention of "times used" and "full-text and abstracts viewed."

Usage statistics for e-journal collections and individual e-journals were much less frequently collected than for the aggregated databases: eight out of the ten community college libraries surveyed (80 percent) reported collecting neither. Two of these libraries did report collecting search statistics for e-journal collections; one of the two also collected search statistics for individual e-journals. (The other answered, "Don't know" regarding collection of statistics for individual e-journals). In few cases, respondents from community college libraries noted that these parts of Question 7 were not applicable to their libraries, presumably because their libraries did not subscribe to e-journal collections or to individual e-journals.

Six of the seven "Type 1" college libraries (86 percent) reported keeping data on the number of searches for their e-journal collections; one did not collect data of any type for this category of material. No "Type 1" college library reported collecting any type of usage data for individual e-journals. (Five responded that they did not collect usage data and two did not know.)

The "Type 2" college libraries collected the most usage data about e-journal collections and individual e-journals, although even this group collected much less usage data for these e-resource categories than for aggregated databases. For e-journal collections, six of the ten libraries in this group (60 percent) reported collecting some form of usage data: four collect the number of searches; four collect the number of sessions; one collects the number of page views; one collects the number of articles downloaded; two collect other statistics. (Three "Type 2" college libraries did not collect any statistics for e-journal collections; one responded, "don't know.")

For individual e-journals, only three out of the ten "Type 2" college libraries (30 percent) reported collecting any data: all three collected the number of searches; two collected the number of sessions and the number of articles downloaded; one collected other statistics ("times used"). (Six "Type 2" college libraries responded that they did not collect statistics for e-journals; one did not know.) In looking over this data, the author found it puzzling, that so few of the "Type 2" college libraries that collected usage data either for e-journal collections or for individual e-journals, reported collecting statistics for the number of articles downloaded. (Only one collected the number of articles downloaded from e-journal collections, and only two collected this data for individual e-journals.) For these types of e-resources, the number of articles downloaded would appear to be a key measure of use.[24]

Of the four university libraries included in the survey, one reported collecting search, session, and article downloads for e-journal collections; this library also collected some usage information, which varied by title, for individual e-journals. Another university library collected the number of article downloads for both its e-journal collections and its individual e-journals. (One university library did not collect usage data for either e-journal collections or individual e-journals; one responded,

"Don't know" to both parts of this question.) Table 5.7 summarizes data for all three parts of Question 7.

The next survey question (Question 8) asked libraries to record the most frequent interval they collected vendor-supplied usage statistics for each category of e-resource they tracked. Survey responses revealed that across the majority of library types and categories, collection most often took place on a monthly basis, with annual collection being the next most common interval. For aggregated databases–the e-resource type, for which the CCALD libraries most often reported keeping usage statistics–five of ten community college libraries (50 percent) collected monthly and two (20 percent) collected annually; four of seven "Type 1" college libraries (57 percent) collected monthly and two (29 percent) collected annually; seven of ten "Type 2" college libraries (70 percent) collected monthly and two (20 percent) collected annually; two of four university libraries (50 percent) collected monthly.

To summarize, eighteen of the thirty-one libraries surveyed (58 percent) reported collecting statistics for their aggregated databases monthly and another six (19 percent) reported collecting these statistics annually. For other e-resource categories, nine of the thirty-one libraries (29 percent) reported collecting statistics on e-journal collection usage monthly, and five (16 percent) reported collecting these statistics annually; three libraries (10 percent) reported collecting statistics on the usage of individual e-journals monthly and two (6 percent) reported collecting these statistics annually. A few libraries reported collecting statistics by semester, biannually, or at some other interval.

Question 9 asked whether the libraries participating in the survey collected e-resource usage statistics from their own servers, a practice that Duy recommended "to verify that the numbers provided by vendors are correct," among other reasons.[25] However, survey responses revealed that across all library types, only ten libraries (32 percent) reported collecting data from their own servers for aggregated databases, seven (23 percent) reported collecting them for e-journal collections, and three (10 percent) reported collecting them for individual e-journals. Interestingly, one university library, which did not report collecting vendor-supplied usage statistics, reported collecting its own usage statistics.

Question 10 asked simply, what method did libraries use to record their usage data? With the exception of the university libraries, the majority of libraries surveyed recorded usage data in a spreadsheet, a finding that is hardly surprising. For university libraries, two libraries (50 percent) used a database to record usage statistics, one used a spreadsheet (25 percent), and one did not record statistics at all. Altogether,

TABLE 5.7. Percentage of libraries (by library type) that collect different kinds of vendor statistics for three types of e-resources: Aggregated databases, e-journal collections, and individual e-journals.

Statistic type	CC (10)	% CC	Type 1 (7)	% Type 1	Type 2 (10)	% Type 2	University (4)	% University	All (31)	% All
Aggregated databases										
Searches	9	90	7	100	9	90	2	50	27	87
Sessions	6	60	1	14	7	70	2	50	16	52
Page views	0	0	0	0	1	10	1	25	2	6
Downloads	3	30	1	14	3	30	2	50	9	29
Don't collect	1	10	0	0	0	0	1	25	2	6
Don't know	0	0	0	0	1	10	1	25	2	6
Other	1	10	2	29	5	50	1	25	9	29
E-Journal collections										
Searches	2	20	6	86	4	40	1	25	13	42
Sessions	0	0	1	14	4	40	1	25	6	19
Page views	0	0	0	0	1	10	0	0	1	3
Downloads	0	0	3	43	1	10	2	50	6	19
Don't collect	8	80	1	14	3	30	1	25	13	42
Don't know	0	0	0	0	1	10	1	25	2	6
Other	0	0	0	0	2	20	0	0	2	6
E-Journals										
Searches	1	10	0	0	3	30	0	0	4	13
Sessions	0	0	0	0	2	20	0	0	2	6
Page views	0	0	0	0	0	0	0	0	0	0
Downloads	0	0	0	0	2	20	1	25	3	10
Don't collect	8	80	5	71	6	60	1	25	20	65
Don't know	1	10	2	29	1	10	1	25	5	16
Other	0	0	0	0	1	10	1	25	2	6

sixteen libraries (52 percent) reported using a spreadsheet, six (19 percent) reported keeping paper records, four (13 percent) reported using a database, and two (6 percent) reported using a word processor to record their statistics. (Of the four who used a database, one respondent from a "Type 2" institution reported also using a spreadsheet as a supplementary resource.) In addition, one library reported keeping e-mailed reports from vendors, and two reported that they did not keep any records.

Data for Question 11, which asked how much time each library spent on recording all types of e-resource statistics per collection period, are presented in connection with Question 8, which asked for the collection interval for vendor usage statistics, and Question 9, which asked whether additional statistics were recorded.

Although, Question 8 asked respondents to record the most frequent interval their libraries collected vendor-supplied usage statistics for each category of e-resource being tracked, all but one reported recording all usage data at the same interval, making it possible to correlate this data with the time spent recording it (Table 5.8). As those libraries that tracked usage data from their own servers might also record such data during the reported interval, a column was added to indicate whether a library recorded its own usage data (i.e., data obtained from the institution's own servers).

As was previously noted, survey responses revealed that across the majority of library types, statistics collection most often takes place on a monthly basis, with annual collection being the next most common interval. Of the eighteen libraries that performed monthly collection of usage data, exactly half (nine libraries or about 29 percent of the thirty-one libraries surveyed) spent less than two hours doing so each month. Of the remaining nine that perform monthly collection of their usage statistics, four spent two to four hours a month on this task, two spent four to eight hours a month, and three spent over eight hours monthly. It is possibly worth noting that, the last three were either university or "Type 2" college libraries, each of which also reported collecting data from institutional servers.

Question 12 provided a list of potential uses for e-resource statistics and asked libraries to check any that applied to their libraries. As the responses received did not fall into any pattern by library type, they are presented in a summary. Not surprisingly, the most frequently cited use of e-resource statistics was to "Decide whether to retain or drop a particular e-resource" (twenty-two times). The next two most cited uses were, "Prioritize e-resource purchasing decisions" (sixteen times) and "Justify the e-resources budget in administrative reports" (fifteen times). Five respondents also checked "Analyze faculty requests." Two respondents, one from a "Type 2" college library and one from a university library, checked "Don't use statistics effectively," but neither explained why this is the case. One respondent from a community college library noted that statistics were used to "demonstrate that there is some use of iCONN provided databases." Another respondent, who worked at a "Type 2" college library, wrote, "We only use iCONN, Statistics will be useful for future purchase decisions."

Question 13 asked respondents to state how e-resource usage had changed at their institutions in the past two years. Among the community colleges (Figure 5.8), three respondents believed that usage had increased by 25 percent or less in the past two years, six believed that it had increased by more than 25 percent, and one did not know whether usage had changed. Among the "Type 1" college libraries, three believed that e-resource usage had increased by 25 percent or less, and four believed that usage had increased by 25 percent or more. Among the "Type 2" college libraries, three believed that e-resource had increased by 25 percent or less, five believed that usage had increased by more than 25 percent, and two did not know whether usage had changed. Among the university libraries, one believed that e-resource usage had increased by more than 25 percent; two did not know whether usage had changed, and one did not answer.

To summarize the answers to Question 13, nine respondents (29 percent) believed that e-resource usage had increased by less than 25 percent over the past two years; sixteen respondents (52 percent) believed that usage had increased by more than 25 percent over the same time period; and six respondents (19 percent) did not know whether e-resource usage had changed, or simply did not answer this question. No respondent reported believing that e-resource usage had decreased at his or her library over the past two years.

The last survey question (Question 14), asked whether a library used an e-resource management system. Respondents for one community college library, one "Type 1" college library, two "Type 2" college libraries, and two university libraries (six libraries or 19 percent of all respondents) answered affirmatively; respondents for nine community college libraries, six "Type 1" college libraries, and eight "Type 2" college libraries (twenty-three libraries or 74 percent) said "no"; respondents for two university libraries (6 percent) reported that their libraries planned to implement such a system in the near future.

TABLE 5.8. Time spent recording vendor usage statistics, collection interval, and whether or not other usage statistics are collected, by library.

Libraries	Collection interval for all usage statistics	Time spent recording all usage statistics	Also collects own statistics (Yes or No)
Community colleges	Once a month	< 2 hours	No
	Once a month	< 2 hours	No
	Once a month	< 2 hours	No
	Once a month	< 2 hours	Yes
	Once a month	2-4 hours	No
	Each semester	Left blank (didn't know?)	No
	Twice a year	2-4 hours	Yes
	Once a year	4-8 hours	No
	Once a year	Don't know	No
	Don't collect	Don't record	No
Type 1 college libraries	Once a month	< 2 hours	No
	Once a month	2-4 hours	No
	Once a month	4-8 hours	No
	Once a month	4-8 hours	No
	Once a year	2-4 hours	No
	Once a year	Don't know	No
	Other interval	> 8 hours	Yes
Type 2 college libraries	Once a month	< 2 hours	No
	Once a month	< 2 hours	No
	Once a month[1]	< 2 hours	No
	Once a month	< 2 hours	Yes
	Once a month	2-4 hours	Yes
	Once a month	2-4 hours	Yes
	Once a month	> 8 hours	Yes
	Once a year	4-8 hours	No
	Once a year	Don't know	Don't know
	Don't know	< 2 hours (?)	Don't know
University libraries	Once a month	> 8 hours	Yes
	Once a month	> 8 hours	Yes
	Don't collect	Don't record	No
	Don't know	< 2 hours (?)	Yes

[1]Library indicated that it also collects some statistics twice a year.

FIGURE 5.8. E-R Usage change in past two years.

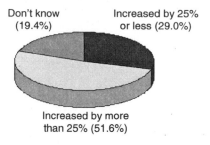

Don't know (19.4%)

Increased by 25% or less (29.0%)

Increased by more than 25% (51.6%)

CONCLUSIONS

This survey of thirty-one member libraries of the (CCALD) requested information about how these libraries were managing their e-resource collections, including information about library type, e-resource budget size, staffing, and the collection of e-resource usage statistics. In general, the survey results revealed that most Connecticut academic libraries were coping with e-resource management by distributing e-resource activities among various library departments including, in some cases, non-technical services units such as public services and reference. While the survey results did show that some libraries were expending more staff hours on managing their e-resource collections than in the past, it did not uncover evidence that Connecticut's academic libraries were experiencing great difficulty in managing these collections. Whether these libraries will need to reorganize their technical services departments and personnel to cope with e-resource growth in the future, as William Wakeling suggested in his Connecticut Library Association (CLA) conference program in 2005, remains an open question.

That CCALD libraries are able to manage their e-resource collections, at least for the present, is suggested by the fact that while over four-fifths of the respondents surveyed believe that e-resource usage had increased in the past two years, only a little over one-half of them reported that the number of staff hours working on e-resource management functions had increased over the same period. Furthermore, although just less than one-half of the libraries surveyed reported they have an MLS-level position devoted to e-resource management, in some cases, it was indicated that this librarian has other duties as well.

These findings, taken together with those showing that, excluding the university libraries (and the few that did not answer Question 4), the CCALD libraries spent approximately twelve hours of professional time per week on e-resource management activities, did not suggest that Connecticut libraries are "in dire need of more staff to support the acquisition and ongoing management of digital resources," as Duranceau and Hepfer concluded of the libraries they surveyed.[26]

Rather, as noted previously and reported by the libraries in Duranceau and Hepfer's survey and others discussed in the literature, Connecticut libraries do appear to be accommodating their growing e-resource collections, primarily by dividing responsibility for e-resource management functions among existing staff from all library departments. However, because so many library departments have become involved in e-resource management functions, and because a single function is sometimes handled by more than one staff member, it is possible that increments of time spent on e-resource management activities went unreported, and that the total number of hours spent engaged in e-resource management is somewhat higher than the survey indicated. Also, as so few CCALD libraries reported tracking usage of individual e-journals, it is possible that these e-resources are not yet being collected, or are not being managed in an optimal way.

In addition to revealing staffing trends across library types, the survey did uncover a few differences in the way e-resources are being handled at the different types of academic libraries within the state. Based on the survey findings, it appeared that most of Connecticut's community college libraries, along with some four-year institutions, relied upon the state-funded iCONN databases to provide a major portion of their e-resource collections. The survey also found that directors of community college libraries were more likely to be directly involved in e-resource management than were directors at other types of academic libraries.

One survey finding the author cannot explain is the greater number of professional staff hours spent on e-resource management by libraries serving smaller four-year colleges than those associated with master's degree-level colleges. It would be interesting to learn whether this finding is consistent with any others.

In closing, the author wishes to thank those CCALD libraries that participated in the survey and to express the hope that similar surveys might be undertaken in other states, so that a more complete understanding of e-resource management practices at various types of academic libraries, particularly those serving small and medium-sized institutions, can be obtained.

NOTES

1. Hing Wu, "New Role of Technical Services." *Connecticut Library Association Conference Proceedings*. 114th CLA annual conference, New Haven, April 11-13, 2005. Proceedings available online at: http://www.cla.uconn.edu/proceedings/techserv. html (accessed May 8, 2005); report summary published in *Connecticut Libraries,* May 2005: 2-3. Reprinted with permission. (This issue is also available online at http://www.cla.uconn.edu/ under Connecticut Libraries Newsletter Archives.)

2. Ibid., 3 (of report summary in *CL*).

3. http://www.faculty.quinnipiac.edu/ccald/ (accessed May 8, 2005).

4. There are discrepancies between the CCALD member list and the CCALD contact list; for example, the contact list includes the names of individual libraries that are shown as one membership on the member list. Also, both lists include research libraries that are not associated with academic institutions or other special cases. These were not counted for the purposes of the survey.

5. Susan Gardner, "The Impact of Electronic Journals on Library Staff at ARL Member Institutions: A Survey and a Critique of the Survey Methodology," *Serials Review* 27, no. 3/4 (2001): 17-32.

6. Ibid., 19.

7. Susan, Gardner and Susan B. Markley, "Conducting Serials Surveys: Common Mistakes and Recommended Approaches," in Susan L. Scheiberg and Shelley Neville, Eds., *Transforming Serials: The Revolution Continues*. Proceedings of the North American Serials Interest Group, Inc. (NASIG) 17th Annual Conference, June 20-23, 2002. (New York: The Haworth Information Press, 2003): 163-170.

8. Ellen Finnie Duranceau and Cindy Hepfer, "Staffing for Electronic Resource Management: The Results of a Survey," *Serials Review* 28, no. 4 (2002): 316-320.

9. Ibid., 317, 320.

10. Sandhya Srivastava and Paolina Taglienti, "E-Journal Management: An Online Survey Evaluation," *Serials Review* 31, no. 4 (2005): 28-38.

11. Ibid., 33-34.

12. Ibid., 29-30.

13. In two cases, categorization of the library type proved problematic. In one case, the parent institution offers a small number of baccalaureate degrees, in addition to a much larger number of associate degrees and certificate programs; the library serving this institution was assigned to the community college group for the purposes of the survey. In a second case, the parent institution was described as offering "graduate programs." The library serving this institution was assigned to the group of libraries serving four-year colleges with substantial numbers of masters programs. The author apologizes, if these categories were not the correct choices.

14. If a respondent entered figures for one or two staff categories and left one or two blank, any blank was assumed to be zero. However, if all three categories were left blank, the response was considered "unknown."

15. One respondent for a library in the type 2 college category entered the answer "< 1 hr." for each of the three staff categories. The author counted this response as seventy-five hour per week in each category.

16. Duranceau and Hepfer, "Staffing for Electronic Resource Management," 317.

17. Gardner, "The Impact of Electronic Journals on Library Staff at ARL Member Institutions," 17, 19; see also Duranceau and Hepfer, 317-318.

18. Srivastava and Taglienti, "E-Journal Management: An Online Survey Evaluation," 29-30.

19. Gardner, 17, 19; see also Duranceau and Hepfer, 317-318.

20. Srivastava and Taglienti, "E-Journal Management: An Online Survey Evaluation," 29-30.

21. Joanna Duy, "Usage Data: Issues and Challenges for Electronic Resource Collection Management," in David C. Fowler, Ed., *E-Serials Collection Management: Transitions, Trends, and Technicalities* (New York: The Haworth Information Press, 2004): 111-138.

22. Ibid., 123.

23. Ibid., 113.

24. Ibid., 124

25. Ibid., 119-120.

26. Duranceau and Hepfer, "Staffing for Electronic Resource Management," 320.

doi:10.1300/J123v53S09_06

APPENDIX
CCALD E-Resource Management Survey

Carol Abatelli, Head of Collections and E-Resources Management
ECSU Smith Library
Phone: (860) 465-5562; Fax: (860) 465-5517
abatellic@easternct.edu

1. What type of academic institution does your library serve?
    (Please check the box that best describes your institution.)
    ☐ Community college
    ☐ College with mainly baccalaureate programs (can include a few
       masters programs)
    ☐ College with a substantial number of masters programs
       (can include a few doctoral programs)
    ☐ University with a full range of graduate programs,
       ncluding many doctoral programs

2. Our library's current annual e-resources budget is approximately:

    ☐ $25,000 or less   ☐ $200,000-$300,00

    ☐ $25,000-$50,000   ☐ $300,000-$400,00

    ☐ $50,000-$100,000   ☐ Over $400,000

    ☐ $100,000-$200,000   ☐ Don't know

3. Does your library currently have an MLS librarian position devoted to the
    management of electronic resources?

    ☐ Yes
    ☐ No
    ☐ No, but we are planning to staff this position in the near future
    ☐ Don't know

4. For each of the three staff categories below, please estimate the average
    number of hours per week devoted to any aspect of e-resource management.

    Professional (MLS) Staff/Library Director   ___ Hours per week
    Systems/Technology Staff   ___ Hours per week
    Paraprofessional/Administrative Staff   ___ Hours per week

5. To the best of your knowledge, how has the number of staff hours work-
    ing on e-resource management functions at your library changed in the
    past two years? Please check the box that best describes your total (pro-
    fessional, technical, and paraprofessional) staffing change.

Our e-resource staff hours have:

☐ Stayed the same
☐ Increased by ½ FTE or less
☐ Increased by more than ½ FTE
☐ Decreased by ½ FTE or less
☐ Decreased by more than ½ FTE
☐ Don't know

6. Who is currently responsible for each of the following e-resource acquisition and management functions (listed on the left below)? For each function, please choose the number from the right hand column that best describes who performs this function and write it in the space provided. If two or more staff from different areas perform a function, please record more than one number.

E-Resource Function

____ Selection
____ Vendor contact
____ License review/negotiation
____ License signatory
____ Ordering

____ Activation (e-journals)
____ Cataloging
____ A-Z Listing or entry into journal manager
____ Troubleshooting access problems
____ Collecting usage statistics
____ Budget monitoring

Staff Person(s) Responsible
MLS Librarian(s)
1-Acquisitions
2-Cataloging
3-Collection Development
4-Electronic Resources
5-Public Services (other than Reference)
6-Reference
7-Serials
8-Systems
9-Technical Services
Other Staff
10-Library Director or Assistant Director
11-Library Secretary
12-Library paraprofessional staff (any)
13-Outside unit (e.g., Legal)
14-Don't perform this function
15-Don't know

7. For each of the e-resource categories listed below, please check the type of vendor statistics that your library collects. (Check all that apply.) If you collect other types of vendor statistics, please explain in the space provided.

Aggregated Databases (Examples: Academic Search, MLA, Psyc-INFO, etc.)

☐ Searches   ☐ Sessions   ☐ Page views
☐ Article downloads   ☐ Don't collect   ☐ Don't know
☐ Other type of statistics:

E-journal Collections (Examples: JSTOR, Project Muse, etc.)

☐ Searches   ☐ Sessions   ☐ Page views
☐ Article downloads   ☐ Don't collect   ☐ Don't know
☐ Other type of statistics:

Individual e-journals (Examples: Adult Education Quarterly, Current History, etc.)

☐ Searches   ☐ Sessions   ☐ Page views
☐ Article downloads   ☐ Don't collect   ☐ Don't know
☐ Other type of statistics:

8. For each e-resource category listed at left below, please write the number that best describes how often your library records vendor usage statistics for the category. (Use the number that represents the most frequent interval in which you record statistics.)

E-Resource   Frequency
___ Aggregated databases   1-Once a month   6-Don't collect
___ E-journal collections   2-Each semester   7-Don't know
___ Individual e-journals   3-Twice a year
                              4-Once a year
                              5-At some other interval

9. Does your library also collect statistics from its own servers for any of the three categories of e-resources (e.g., hits on an A-Z page)?

Aggregated databases   Yes   No   Don't know
E-journal collections   Yes   No   Don't know
Individual e-journals   Yes   No   Don't know

10. How do you record your library's e-resource usage statistics?

☐ Database   ☐ Spreadsheet   ☐ Word processor
☐ Paper   ☐ Don't record   ☐ Don't know
                     statistics
☐ Other method:

11. How much time is spent recording all types of e-resource usage statistics per collection period?

☐ Less than 2 hours ☐ 4-8 hours ☐ Don't record
☐ 2-4 hours ☐ Over 8 hours ☐ Don't know

12. If your library currently collects e-resource usage statistics, how are they being used? (Please check all that apply.)

☐ Prioritize e-resource purchasing decisions
☐ Decide whether to retain or drop a particular e-resource
☐ Justify the e-resources budget in administrative reports
☐ Choose the type of license or number of licensed users
☐ Analyze faculty requests
☐ Don't collect usage statistics
☐ Don't use statistics effectively (please explain):

13. To the best of your knowledge, how has the e-resource usage at your library changed in the past two years? Please check the box that best describes your usage pattern.

Our e-resource usage has:
☐ Stayed the same ☐ Decreased by 25% or less
☐ Increased by 25% or less ☐ Decreased by more than 25%
☐ Increased by more than 25% ☐ Don't know

14. Does your library use an e-resource management system? (Please check one box.)
☐ Yes
☐ No
☐ No, but we plan to implement an e-resource management system in the near future
☐ Don't know

If you answered Yes to Question 14, please list any e-resource management system(s) that you currently use. If you plan to implement a new system, what system(s) are you considering: _____
_____
_____

Chapter 6

Deriving Usage Statistics from Local Library Management Software

Arun Kumar
Martin P. Brändle

INTRODUCTION

The importance of keeping track of the developments that are taking place in an increasingly competitive scientific research field cannot be overemphasized. However, wading through the maze of information available and knowing which data are the appropriate bunch to pick are often daunting tasks. This chapter will focus on the treatment of the former task, the latter being the domain of research workers (referred to as users or clients in the text to follow). About a decade ago, when some publishers began to electronically capture the entire contents of a physical issue, library users got their first taste of the digital medium. The initial disjunction between print and digital media warranted the establishment of a new mindset, without previous prejudices and inhibitions. Despite the fact that reading an entire article, in Adobe Portable Document Format (PDF) or Hypertext Markup Language (HTML) format, on a computer screen is not a mean achievement, most researchers

[Haworth co-indexing entry note]: "Deriving Usage Statistics from Local Library Management Software." Kumar, Arun, and Martin P. Brändle. Co-published simultaneously in *The Serials Librarian* (The Haworth Information Press, an imprint of The Haworth Press, Inc.) Vol. 53, Supplement No. 9, 2007, pp. 111-128; and: *Usage Statistics of E-Serials* (ed: David C. Fowler) The Haworth Information Press, an imprint of The Haworth Press, Inc., 2007, pp. 111-128. Single or multiple copies of this article are available for a fee from The Haworth Document Delivery Service [1-800-HAWORTH, 9:00 a.m. - 5:00 p.m. (EST). E-mail address: docdelivery@haworthpress.com].

Available online at http://ser.haworthpress.com
doi:10.1300/J123v53S09_07

now prefer e-serials to print serials. In fact, a pilot study undertaken by the Chemistry Biology Pharmacy Information Center (hereafter referred to as Information Center) at Eidgenössische Technische Hochschule (ETH), Zürich (Swiss Federal Institute of Technology), during the years 2003 and 2004, which encompassed ninety-five printed scholarly journals in the fields of chemistry and biology, confirmed the expected *disinterest* of its clients in browsing scientific works in print form. Statistics from this study, while not pertinent to the present chapter, are available upon request from the authors.

In another comprehensive survey on the use of electronic resources (Brändle 2002), 520 members of the Department of Chemistry at ETH, Zürich, were asked to fill out a detailed questionnaire. The return quotient was 34 percent. At that time, the main library of the school had subscriptions to approximately 3,100 electronic titles (developments in the acquisition of e-serials at the school are detailed in the following paragraph). Figure 6.1 displays the reading habits of 178 respondents. It can be seen that reading printed journals does not enjoy the popularity it once did.

Most of the researchers queried, especially doctoral students and postdoctoral research workers, prefer to read printouts of electronic articles. On-screen reading of full-text is preferred the least by the respondents. Diploma students, who have just begun their research career and nonacademic employees, are much less inclined to read electronic journal articles.

The main library of ETH, Zürich, began offering e-serials to its clients in May 1996. An initial collection of fifty e-serials had doubled by the end of the same year (Keller 1997). The number of e-serials climbed to 500 and 1,100 in September 1998 and August 1999, respectively (Keller and Neubauer 1999). Acquisitions received a major boost in 2000, when, according to a decree by the school authorities, 80 percent of the funds allocated for purchasing print journals by the departmental libraries were transferred to the main library for the purpose of acquiring additional e-serials.

Currently, the main library holds subscriptions to more than 7,000 e-serials (http://www.ethbib.ethz.ch/zs_e.html). The majority of the licensing agreements have been signed using the academic-single institution-license model, whereas a few have been negotiated via the academic consortium license model.

FIGURE 6.1. Reading habits of the members of chemistry department of ETH Zurich in 2002 on the basis of feedback by 178 respondents (return rate 34.2%). *Source:* Reproduced with permission of HTW Chur, Switzerland.

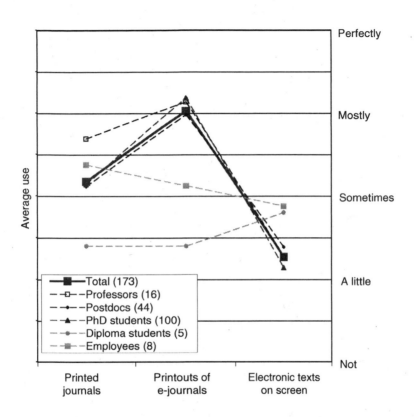

PREREQUISITES FOR A LIBRARY
INFORMATION SYSTEM

In order to gather meaningful usage statistics, a library information system must satisfy the following prerequisites:

1. *Storage:* The fields necessary for online tracking of user activities, such as the searching of titles, user access to certain resources, or changes in user parameters, must be provided. Depending upon the application, this information can be either anonymous or personalized. Storage of time stamps of user

actions should make it possible to obtain perspectives on the evolution of usage over time.

2. *Security:* For personalization services, clients must be able to edit the information contained in databases. However, special security measures must be adopted to prevent possible liability caused by the unauthorized use of information. With the integrated library information system, known as CLICAPS (Chemistry Library Information Control And Presentation System), further described in the section on Cataloging, the Information Center achieves this by splitting the data into separate files with different security levels. The user account file with addresses and lending information is not accessible on the Web. The MyCLICAPS file (mentioned in the following text), which records Web transactions, contains a minimal set of user account information. This user data is a duplicate copy of user account data, but is isolated from the main user account file. The cataloging data, which is open to the public, is a read-only format. Special measures are also taken against URL spoofing by the implementation of a public-private-key encryption. Secure Sockets Layer (SSL) encryption of Web transactions is not presently implemented in CLICAPS.

3. *Easy selection of data:* This is achieved through the powerful search facility offered by the FileMaker database system, in which CLICAPS is programmed.

4. *Easy export of data:* Selected data must be exportable in a format that can be directly read by a statistical or spreadsheet package, or in a format that can easily be transformed. Within the File-Maker, the Information Center commonly uses either WKS (WorKSheet) export or XML (eXtensible Markup Language) export with a subsequent XSLT (eXtensible Stylesheet Language Transformation) into the end format.

5. *Built-in statistical functions:* For on-the-fly statistics within the library system, the underlying database system should offer built-in aggregate functions over a set of records, such as average (), min (), stddev (), etc.

CATALOGING

One major problem with cataloging Web resources is that the medium is dynamic; documents and servers may become outdated as those documents are changed or moved elsewhere (for example, the acquisition of journals by another publisher), and servers change names or port numbers (leading to changes in URLs). Nonetheless, Web resources must be cataloged for accessibility by using appropriate library procedures to create records for retrieval through online catalogs. Before discussing cataloging techniques, it is necessary to further elaborate on the library-management system installed in the Information Center.

CLICAPS: An In-House Library-Management System

In the late 1980s, the Chemistry Library (former name of the Information Center) began to look for a suitable computer-based library- management system. A task group was constituted to evaluate commercially available software, including IBM's DOBIS/LIBIS package. After careful consideration of several factors, such as the advantages and disadvantages of procuring an off-the-shelf product, spare capacity available from already existing systems elsewhere at the school, and also the willingness of school authorities to provide funding, it was decided to develop an in-house system based on the FileMaker Pro database with a user-friendly graphic interface. Apple Macintosh computers were selected in terms of the hardware component, since their operating system was more suitable for running the FileMaker software at that time. The management system was christened the Chemistry Library Information Control And Presentation System (CLICAPS), and this system was implemented in the early 1990s. Over the years, the initially installed modules have been modified and new modules developed to match new developments and ever-changing requirements. In its present form, CLICAPS includes modules for cataloging, serials management, acquisitions, a publishers' database, correspondence, a WebOPAC, a users' database, and circulation and balance sheets. The WebOPAC was introduced in 1998 (http://www. clicaps.ethz.ch). Since then, it has been continuously expanded. In addition to standard searching, it now incorporates navigation along a breadcrumb path, display of acquisitions data, lists of personalized journals, reference linking from chemistry databases to articles and patents, links to the main library catalog and a visual thesaurus.

Serials Cataloging

Currently, the Information Center offers Web access to a collection of more than 2000 active e-serials in a wide range of subject areas. Its policy for cataloging serial resources is as follows:

- Notwithstanding the type of storage media, a single record will ordinarily be used for each serial title. However, within each record is a provision for listing different types of resources with the same or different content. Distinct serial IDs are allocated for each resource.
- A second (or additional) record is used when back-files and the latest issues of e-serials have separate URLs from the main title. For instance, the back-issue archive for the *Biophysical Journal* is provided by PubMed Central, whereas, the Biophysical Society supplies the issues from 1998 onward. The same may also be true in the case of a single provider, for example, the serial *Biopolymers* published by Wiley.

A serial record includes fields for the following query and other relevant parameters, such as: full title, abbreviated title, print ISSN, electronic ISSN, CODEN, URL, coverage, medium, storage location, date of record creation or alteration, and a unique local serial code.

Issues Cataloging

A print-issue module has existed in CLICAPS since 1993. In March 2000, it was expanded to accommodate Web issues as well. The size of the database has grown to more than 330,000 electronic issues as of January 2005. The layout of the records is a suitable modification of the one developed earlier for the printed copies. A record contains the following fields and other related items: resource ID (print and Web resources have individual IDs), the cataloger's name, record index, local serial code, abbreviated serial title, medium, year of publication, volume number, issue number, date of issue registration, frequency of publication, number of issues per volume, nominal date of issue publication, expected date of issue publication on Web, and issue URL.

The following procedures are used to catalog electronic issues on a daily basis:

- A script is invoked to search and collect records for yet to be cataloged issues of active e-serials corresponding to the date in question, that is, the expected date of Web posting. This issue collection is termed as the expected number of Web postings.
- The Web page corresponding to each record, which represents an issue, is browsed to ascertain the posting of that particular issue. When the issue is available, its URL and the date of availability are

entered into the record (automated by means of a script), and a new record–corresponding to next issue to be published–is added to the database. Otherwise, the next inspection is deferred by a predetermined period by activating a script written for this purpose. Generally, the duration of the deferred period is one, two, and three days for weekly, fortnightly, and monthly serials, respectively. Variations in this rule have been incorporated for some journals on the basis of publishers' habits and importance of the journals.

- For statistical purposes, the prediction quotient is recorded from the number of cataloged and expected number of postings.
- A script is run to add the registered issues of the day into the MyCLICAPS accounts (described in the following section) of the library's clients.

At present, the average number of electronic copies cataloged per working day is approximately eighty. The values of the prediction quotient for the years 2003 and 2004 are, respectively, 48.4 percent and 51.2 percent. This infers that almost 160 issues must be tracked down on a daily basis. The time expenditure varies between two and three hours per day for the cataloging procedure described in the preceding text. Attempts to enhance the value of the prediction quotient have yielded little results, mainly because of uncertainty in the issue postings by the publishers.

MyCLICAPS

MyCLICAPS facility is a tool for obtaining current awareness of the scientific literature. Clients can access the latest issues corresponding to all the serials subscribed by them via this service by using the information collected in a single Web page. Login is possible from laboratory, office, home, or Internet café.

Description

The following steps occur when a user logs into the MyCLICAPS from the library catalog (http://www.clicaps.ethz.ch/en/):

- The user clicks on the link to MyCLICAPS.
- A script checks for the presence of a local cookie (which will not be present when a user logs in for the very first time or if s/he has ended his or her earlier MyCLICAPS session by logging out). If it is

not found, the user is directed to a login screen (Figure 6.2) that requests a username and password. Authentication is checked via connection to the Information Center user database. If the login is successful, a cookie is stored in user's browser.

- There are then two possible scenarios. A new client, with no journal credited to his or her MyCLICAPS account, is redirected to an "Add journal" screen (Figure 6.3). Herein, he or she is requested to type the title (in full or abbreviated form) of the e-serial of his or her preference. Results obtained by clicking on the Search button for the search string that is typed are obtained on a new screen (Figure 6.4). The client now adds his or her favorite serial to his or her account by selecting the appropriate title from the shown list and clicking on the corresponding down-arrow button. When this is accomplished, the client is directed to his or her MyCLICAPS page (Figure 6.5). Since the "Add journal" step is redundant in the case of an old client, he or she accesses his or her MyCLICAPS page directly, with or without login as previously explained.
- Various tasks may then be accomplished.

1. In Figure 6.5, the number of latest issues displayed corresponding to both the journals is five. This default value can be changed at will by clicking on the link to "Settings." Values between one and ten are permissible. Further, clicking on the "+" or "−" buttons allows a local increase or decrease in the number of displayed issues for the selected serial.

2. A client may access the Web page with the contents of a particular issue by clicking on the corresponding issue link. In order to display the contents in a new browser window, the option to block popup windows must be disabled. If the Web page for an issue is accessed, a script writes a check mark in the box right adjacent to the issue number (Figure 6.5). This feature spares the clients the inconvenience of having to write notes.

3. A client can also access the Home page of a journal by clicking on the link to the title.

4. The "Add journal" feature, explained previously, may be used to include additional journals. It may be noted that, no matter when journals are added, a built-in routine automatically sorts all serial titles alphabetically.

5. The deletion of one or more serials already placed in an account is also possible. This facility is needed if a client happens to include an incorrect serial title or if he or she finds a journal to no

longer be useful for his or her research work. Clicking on the up-arrow button in Figure 6.5 accomplishes this task.

- A client may end his or her MyCLICAPS session by clicking on the Logout button.

OTHER AVAILABLE SERVICES

Getting information via e-mail alerting services offered by many publishers is fairly popular among many research workers. To avail such a service, a user must sign up to receive regular e-mail notifications of recently posted issues of serials. Each e-mail contains a direct link to an issue's table of contents. The main disadvantage of this approach is that a user must go through a number of alerts, many of which may not be useful, and follow them up. This is an inefficient use of time and may further require note taking. Two such services are described in the following text.

FIGURE 6.2. Login screen for MyCLICAPS tool.

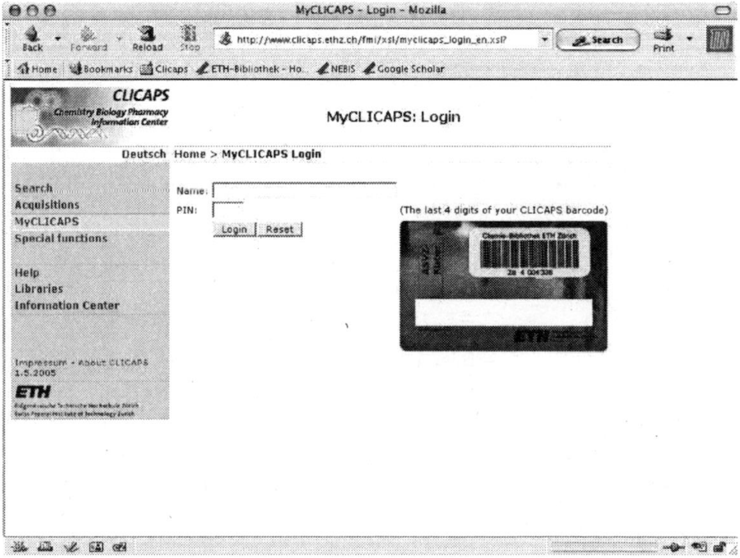

FIGURE 6.3. Search for an e-serial to be added.

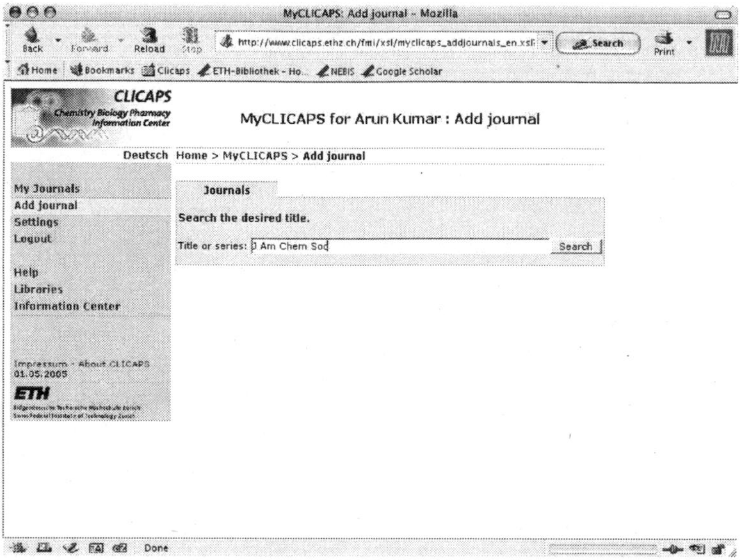

FIGURE 6.4. Selection screen for adding an e-serial to a client's account.

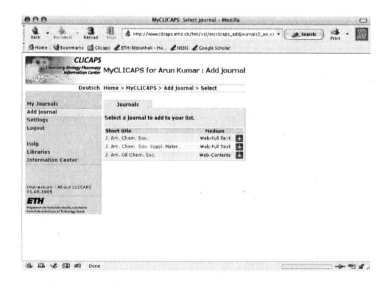

FIGURE 6.5. MyCLICAPS screen.

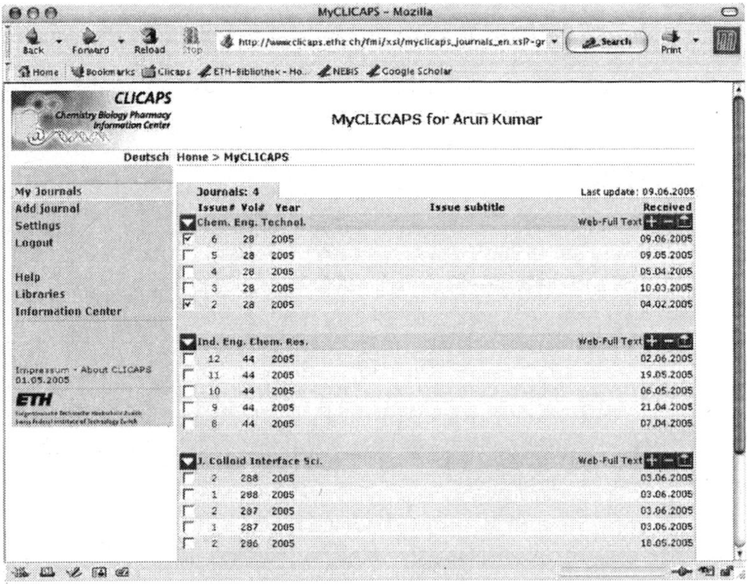

Scopus™ (a registered trademark of Elsevier B. V.), the largest abstract database of scientific literature, encompassing over 14,000 serials, was offered to the public toward the end of 2004. Search alerts are just one among the various available features. For example, results from keyword searches can be used to setup alerts, enabling the user to receive new results by e-mail. Furthermore, it is possible to run search alerts daily, weekly, or monthly. Scopus thus offers an attractive method to keep a researcher abreast of the latest developments in his or her research field. An institution can buy Scopus at an annual subscription fee, with the price dependent upon the size of the institution. Elsevier offered the chemistry department at ETH, Zürich free access to their database during summer of 2004, however, usage statistics are not available for this trial period.

Current Contents Connect® from the Institute for Scientific Information (ISI) provides access to bibliographic information from over 8000 scholarly journals. Various search features similar to those in Scopus are available. The use of an alerting option enables weekly updated search results to be automatically e-mailed to users. A recently introduced open URL linking process connects users directly to 1Cate, SFX, and other open URL systems. Web of Science, as part of the Web of Knowledge package, offers the same functionality.

PROMOTION

The marketing and promotion of the MyCLICAPS facility are undertaken by the following activities:

- Distributing promotional materials of Information Center, such as brochures and information packets
- Providing verbal and written information to new clients, when they register themselves as Information Center members
- Informing and/or reminding the clients about the MyCLICAPS tool, while conducting introductory courses in using resources provided by the Information Center
- Providing personal assistance to potential clients in opening and operating MyCLICAPS account, while educating them on locating information and interpreting catalogs available on the Web pages of the Information Center.

USAGE STATISTICS

Vendors of electronic serials are usually able to supply reliable statistics on e-serials usage, and the evaluation of these statistics can be helpful in guiding librarians in deciding which subscriptions should be retained, and which should be cancelled. Unfortunately, such statistics do not differentiate between channels, such as browser bookmarks, WebOPACs, library Web sites, reference-linking software, database links, reference management software, etc. Furthermore, they are much less revealing of overall usage habits; it is not possible to distinguish whether a user accessed an article by using a reference database or simply while browsing an issue, since the "hit" on the article in both the cases is via the issue's table of contents. Statistical data obtained from library Web sites, WebOPACs, and reference-linking schemes may provide a complement to the overall picture. Only a rough insight can be provided by the evaluation of access logs of the e-serials library Web pages. They may yield information on the relative popularity of browsing journal titles alphabetically, browsing by category, or by searching (Figure 6.6).

FIGURE 6.6. Information Center's e-journals Web page.

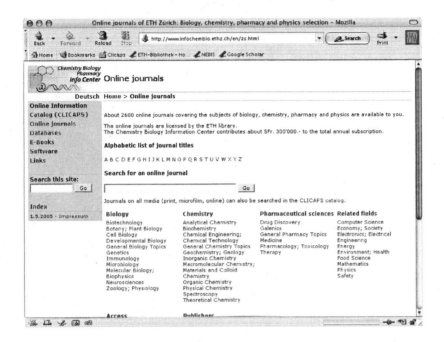

Although it is not ordinarily possible to know of the specific journal link that was clicked on, these can be tracked down by implementing, for example, the JavaScript onClick function, which would populate a link-click database. This remark also applies to the results obtained from searches in library WebOPACs. Statistics from reference-linking products such as SFX, LitLinkFinderPlus, or home-grown implementations (mentioned previously) can give trends in relative database usage. However, article usage results derived from log files will depend on the extensiveness of journal coverage of the concerned databases.

Web services that allow for the personalization of information sources can be used to gather precise statistics on the usage of these sources because every user action is fed back to the service database. The following paragraphs present the results extracted from MyCLI-CAPS.

As of January 14, 2005, 448 subscribers (of which 33 percent operate their accounts in English) of the MyCLICAPS service have added 4,192 titles to their accounts. Active journal entries total 3,602, with the corresponding issues being updated by library staff on a regular basis. About 271,000 issues have been added to the MyCLICAPS database since the service began in September 2000. On an average, a user subscribes to eight journals, which appears to be a reasonable number. Figure 6.7 displays the distribution of users in terms of the number of subscribed journals. It can be seen that the breadth of the journals is quite extensive. At the lower end, 183 users (40.8 percent) subscribe to one or two titles only.

These accounts may sometimes be considered as inactive, since most of them were created while demonstrating the MyCLICAPS facility to potential users. At the upper end, one account contains seventy-five titles, and another has sixty-nine titles. As far as the library knows, these accounts belong to two staff scientists, who maintain the lists for their research groups. Generally, the number of e-serials subscribed to by most of the users varies between three and twenty.

By counting the number of users per title, one can pinpoint favorite journals and subject areas. Up until January 14, 2005, 618 different journals, or 30 percent of the active electronic titles available in our CLICAPS WebOPAC were covered by MyCLICAPS accounts. This indicates a rather broad subject area covered by research groups at the university. Figure 6.8 shows the distribution of titles that

FIGURE 6.7. Distribution of users in terms of subscribed journals in the MyCLICAPS Web service.

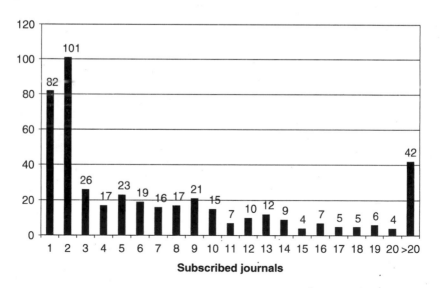

FIGURE 6.8. Variation in the number of different titles (ordinate) with the given number of usrs per title (abscissa).

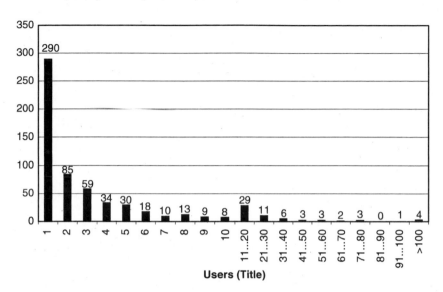

MyCLICAPS users have in common. For 290 titles, there is only one user for each title.

Table 6.1 shows details on the coverage of subjects. Except for geochemistry, for which no research group exists at the Department of Chemistry and Applied Biosciences, the other chemistry disciplines are adequately represented in terms of the number of subscribed journals. Compared to chemistry and its related disciplines, biology subjects are less prominent. This is probably because of the fact that most of the biology institutes are located outside the Department of Chemistry building, which houses the Information Center, so a strong relationship does not exist between the Information Center and its clients from biology. Physics journals occupy a prominent position because of the overlapping of subjects in the fields of physics, physical chemistry, and crystallography.

Table 6.2 ranks twenty most popular journals in terms of the number of subscribed users. The results reveal that researchers give preference to general science, general chemistry, and organic chemistry journals. Seven titles published by the American Chemical Society are among the twenty top journals. The *Journal of the American Chemical Society* is the top choice, followed by the *Journal of Organic Chemistry*.

TABLE 6.1. Number of journals for subjects covered by journals in MyCLICAPS facility.

Chemistry	Number (%)	Biology	Number (%)	Related subjects	Number (%)	Miscel-laneous
General Chemistry	47 (7.6)	Molecular Biology	35 (5.7)	Physics	106 (17.2)	
Chemical Engineering	46 (7.4)	Cell Biology	19 (3.1)	Environmental Science	46 (7.4)	
Analytical Chemistry	41 (6.6)	General Biology	17 (2.8)	Medicine	20 (3.2)	
Macromolecular Chemistry	39 (6.3)	Genetics	14 (2.3)	Pharmaceutical Sciences	17 (2.8)	
Organic Chemistry	34 (5.5)	Neurosciences	10 (1.6)	Energy	7 (1.1)	
Physical Chemistry	23 (3.7)	Biotechnology	8 (1.3)	Safety	6 (1.0)	
Inorganic Chemistry	15 (2.4)	Microbiology	8 (1.3)	Food/Agro Sciences	4 (0.6)	
Biochemistry	14 (2.3)	Immunology	5 (0.8)	Economy	2 (0.3)	
Theoretical Chemistry	11 (1.8)	Zoology	5 (0.8)	Electronics	1 (0.2)	
Geochemistry	1 (0.2)	Botanic	4 (0.6)			
Totals	271 (43.9)		125 (20.2)		209 (33.8)	13 (2)

Angewandte Chemie is split up into international (rank four) and German (rank nine) versions. If the user counts corresponding to the two versions were added, it would be placed in rank two. Barring *Helvetica Chimica Acta,* the values of the impact factor for all other journals exceed two.

Although the titles listed in Table 6.2 seem to be highly popular, their elevated rankings do not necessarily indicate that they are consulted on a regular basis. To evaluate the effective usage, the ratios of clients who have browsed through the latest issues to all clients were calculated for each of the serials listed in Table 6.2. Normally, the number of latest issues displayed for each journal is set between three and five by the users. Periods covered thus vary between three and five weeks for weekly journals, and three and five months for monthly journals. The values of the effective usage, listed in the last column of Table 6.2, lie between 5 and 29 percent. These values, which appear to be low, are affected by two factors. First, user visits to the Web service may not be within the time frame covered by the display window. For journals with a high

TABLE 6.2. Data for 20 top favorite journals in MyCLICAPS Web service as of January 14, 2005.

Rank	Short title	Publisher	Users	IF[1]	Eff. usage (%)
1	*J. Am. Chem. Soc.*	ACS	203	6.516	9.9
2	*J. Org. Chem.*	ACS	118	3.297	11.0
3	*Nature (London)*	Nature Publishing Group	112	30.979	10.7
4	*Angew. Chem., Int. Ed.*	Wiley-VCH	106	8.427	13.2
5	*Science (Washington D.C.)*	Am. Assoc. Adv. Sci.	91	29.781	16.5
6	*Chem. Rev.*	ACS	76	21.036	28.9
7	*Org. Lett.*	ACS	73	4.092	16.4
8	*Tetrahedron Lett.*	Pergamon	72	2.326	6.9
9	*Angew. Chem.*	Wiley-VCH	70	–	20.0
10	*Helv. Chim. Acta*	Schweiz. Chem. Gesellschaft	68	1.861	13.2
11	*Chem. Commun.*	RSC	60	4.031	21.7
12	*Chem. - Eur. J.*	Wiley-VCH	57	4.353	24.6
13	*Tetrahedron*	Pergamon	56	2.641	12.5
14	*Eur. J. Org. Chem.*	Wiley-VCH	46	2.227	17.4
15	*Acc. Chem. Res.*	ACS	42	2.168	21.4
16	*Inorg. Chem.*	ACS	41	3.389	24.4
17	*Tetrahedron Asymmetry*	Pergamon	39	2.178	5.1
18	*Proc. Natl. Acad. Sci. USA*	National Acad. Sci.	38	10.272	21.1
19	*Organometallics*	ACS	33	3.375	24.2
20	*J. Chem. Phys.*	AIP	33	2.950	21.2

[1]Impact Factors 2003, courtesy of Institute for Scientific Information.

publication frequency (for example, the weekly *Tetrahedron Letters*), the value of the effective usage, therefore, is low. Second, the values are reduced by the presence of dead accounts. For the most favorite serial, the *Journal of the American Chemical Society,* the effective usage is only 9.9 percent. This low value can be attributed to the fact that this title often occurs in dead accounts where it was added as an example during the demonstration of the MyCLICAPS Web service. On the other hand, less popular titles are often consulted on a regular basis because of special research interests of researchers in such titles. For all subscribed titles, the average effective usage is 24 percent (65,928 hits per 270,779 issues).

CONCLUSIONS

In-house library-management software developed by the Chemistry Biology Pharmacy Information Center at ETH, Zürich has been described in this chapter. In its present form, it includes modules for performing various contemporary library tasks. By using the MyCLICAPS module, registered clients can access recently posted Web issues corresponding to all the e-serials subscribed by them. All information that is part of a user account is collected on a single Web page. New e-serials may be added at will to an already existing account by authorized users. Similarly, previously added titles may be deleted. On the basis of 448 MyCLICAPS accounts examined, usage statistics of e-serials are presented. The average value of the number of serials subscribed by the clients is eight. There is some indication that the more popular e-serials with high publication frequencies have lower effective usage. On the other hand, users show more dedication to the use of less popular serials, which are specific to their narrower research interests.

NOTE

Figures 6.2-6.8 are reprinted with permission from the Chemistry Biology Information Center, ETH Zürich.

REFERENCES

Brändle, Martin. "Nutzung elektronischer wissenschaftlicher Information durch Hochschulabsolventen in der Chemie an der ETH Zürich. Untersuchungen und Vorschläge zur Vermittlung von Informationskompetenzen." Diploma thesis NDS I+D, HTW Chur, Switzerland, 2002.
Keller, Alice, 1997. Elektronische Zeitschriften in Bibliotheken–Ein Erfahrungsbericht aus der ETH-Bibliothek. *Nachrichten für Dokumentation* 48:131-136.
Keller, Alice, and Wolfram Neubauer, 1999. Dienstleistungsangebote von Bibliotheken in elektronischer Form–Eine Benutzungsstudie der ETH-Bibliothek. *Nachrichten für Dokumentation* 50:407-412.

doi:10.1300/J123v53S09_07

Chapter 7

Serials Solutions
and the Art of Statistics Gathering

David C. Fowler

INTRODUCTION

In 2000, a company named Serials Solutions was founded by a group
of library entrepreneurs led by Peter McCracken, a librarian who had
formerly worked at East Carolina State University and the University of
Washington. McCracken and his team made one of the first significant
attempts at corralling the increasingly vast array of paid, complimentary
with print, and open-access electronic serials into a customizable database that could be manipulated and personalized by every subscribing
library. This database initially presented libraries with a fairly limited
ability to select groups of subscribed journal collections with default
holdings dates, and these were, in turn, presented to library patrons in the
form of static title lists of e-journals at their libraries. In these early days,
there was little ability to customize features, and no capability at all to
generate any kind of usage statistics.

Now, several years later, Serials Solutions has evolved in many positive ways to become a much more flexible and nimble tool for librarians

The author would like to thank Mike Showalter at Serials Solutions for providing
some information and answering several questions that he had in the course of writing
this chapter. Screen captures of the Serials Solutions usage statistics module are reprinted with permission.

[Haworth co-indexing entry note]: "Serials Solutions and the Art of Statistics Gathering." Fowler, David C.
Co-published simultaneously in *The Serials Librarian* (The Haworth Information Press, an imprint of The
Haworth Press, Inc.) Vol. 53, Supplement No. 9, 2007, pp. 129-149; and: *Usage Statistics of E-Serials* (ed: David C. Fowler) The Haworth Information Press, an imprint of The Haworth Press, Inc., 2007, pp. 129-149. Single or multiple copies of this article are available for a fee from The Haworth Document Delivery Service [1-
800-HAWORTH, 9:00 a.m. - 5:00 p.m. (EST). E-mail address: docdelivery@haworthpress.com].

doi:10.1300/J123v53S09_08

to list, count, sort, and present their serial electronic resources to the public. Other chapters in this book have discussed elements of TDNet, SFX, and EBSCO A-Z. This chapter will examine the development of Serials Solutions and the statistics management options that it can and cannot provide.

SALE TO PROQUEST

In July 2004, Serials Solutions was acquired by ProQuest Information and Learning, which provided it with crucial financial, personnel, and other backing. This backing gave it a more stable base from which to compete with larger peers, such as EBSCO, and to continue to develop and evolve innovations, such as its Electronic Resource Management Service (ERMS) and a new federated search engine.

SERIALS SOLUTIONS AND THE COMPETITION

Although Serials Solutions is not a subscription vendor, like EBSCO or Swets, it has managed to maintain a competitive product on the market, a product generally innovative enough to compete with the larger players in the market. Other similar products on the market include EBSCO A-Z, provided of course, by EBSCO in Birmingham, Alabama; TDNet, based in Tel Aviv, Israel; and SFX, provided by Ex Libris in Chicago, Illinois. Each product has different cost factors, and offers somewhat different ranges of services, so every library that utilizes them has had to do an analysis of their requirements and cost limitations versus the services provided and make a decision on which to purchase based on their own local circumstances. There is not necessarily one right or wrong answer to which service is best for a particular site–every organization must make its own decision. Circumstantial evidence seems to suggest that relatively few institutions switch vendors once they have selected one.

SITE STATISTICS FROM SERIALS SOLUTIONS

Statistics and the Electronic Resources Management System

Serials Solutions began compiling and providing usage statistics for its clients in mid-2004. What statistics then can currently be derived from

Serials Solutions, using their Electronic Resources Management System? The ERMS statistics module is located in the Data Management header under the subheading, "Data Summary and Analysis Tools." Within that subheading is the "Usage Statistics" module, which will be the focus of this section.

Basic Numbers

ERMS provides three basic numbers at the top of the page (Figure 7.1):

1. *Total Holdings:* It is the total number of titles tracked by Serials Solutions, regardless of the number of different databases they are counted in. In this case, 62,301 titles are being tracked. Contrast this count with the second number.

2. *Total Unique Titles:* It is the total number of discrete titles tracked by Serials Solutions, in this case, 29,438 titles. This statistic disregards the number of multiple times a single title might be accounted for. For example, consider the *Journal of Academic Librarianship.* This single journal is made available from five distinct resources. Four of the five are listed in various EBSCOHost EJS databases, and one is listed in ScienceDirect. Thus, for the purposes of the first number, Total Holdings, the *Journal of Academic Librarianship* is counted five times. However, for the purposes of the second number, Total Unique Titles, it counts only once, as all unique titles would.

3. *Total Databases:* In this case, 235 databases, which simply reflects the total number of unique databases that the institution subscribes to, and that the journals in total holdings and total unique titles are part and parcel of the total databases.

Search Statistics

The types of statistics that help an institution determine which electronic resources are being used, or not being used, are search statistics. While the statistics found in Serials Solutions may not be as comprehensive as those obtained from many journal vendors, they can provide some insights into which resources are and are not being searched at an institution. These statistics are found in the first tab of Figure 7.2. In the first dropdown menu, two options can be selected, Search Types and Subjects.

FIGURE 7.1.

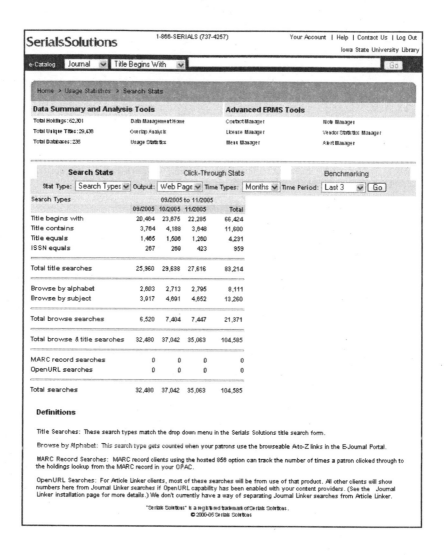

Data output can be manipulated and customized by the user in several different areas. The first option is Output. The user can choose either a Web page option (the default option), or a CSV (comma separated value) file option. In all cases, the most recent three months of statistics will be the default output, but this can be manipulated extensively by the

FIGURE 7.2.

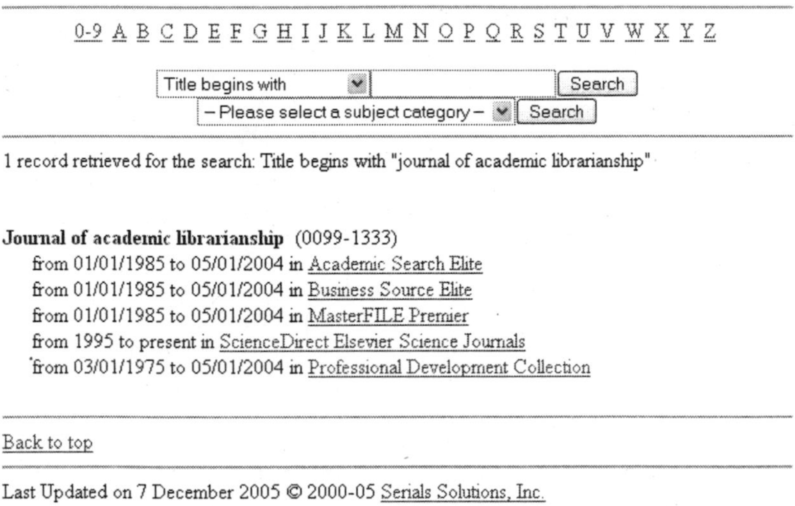

0-9 A B C D E F G H I J K L M N O P Q R S T U V W X Y Z

| Title begins with | ▾ | | Search |

| – Please select a subject category – ▾ | Search |

1 record retrieved for the search: Title begins with "journal of academic librarianship"

Journal of academic librarianship (0099-1333)
    from 01/01/1985 to 05/01/2004 in Academic Search Elite
    from 01/01/1985 to 05/01/2004 in Business Source Elite
    from 01/01/1985 to 05/01/2004 in MasterFILE Premier
    from 1995 to present in ScienceDirect Elsevier Science Journals
    from 03/01/1975 to 05/01/2004 in Professional Development Collection

Back to top

Last Updated on 7 December 2005 © 2000-05 Serials Solutions, Inc.

account administrator. Search Types is arguably the most useful option of the two.

In the previous example (Figure 7.1), we can see various statistics that have been extracted from this institution's profile:

1. *Title Begins With:* This statistic indicates 66,424 searches in the default timeframe using this field. If a user was searching the *Journal of Economic Literature,* a search of this type could be conducted for *"Journal of Economic Literature," "Journal of Economic,"* or even *"Journal of,"* regardless of the relative futility of the construction of the latter search. This is also the default search, when using the Serials Solutions end user interface. The high numbers in this field would partially be explained by this particular circumstance, but those numbers could also be supplemented by the fact that this is seemingly the most commonsense approach for experienced and novice users alike, and thus, it can be presumed that it would be the tactic utilized by the average library user.

2. *Title Contains:* This statistic indicates 11,600 searches in this field. Using the aforementioned title again, examples that could be used to search in this manner would be *"Economic Literature,"* or, far

more broadly, *"Economic,"* or *"Literature."* Even in theory, the overly broad phrase *"Journal of"* could again be used in this field.

3. *Title Equals:* In order to obtain a search result other than "zero," an exact title must be entered, using this criteria. This example shows 4,231 searches accomplished in this field. Using the previous example, the only possible successful search would have to be *"Journal of Economic Literature,"* hence the much smaller number of searches found. Any other examples in the previous two search types would result in zero records being returned.

4. *ISSN Equals:* This is unsurprisingly the least popular search, with only 959 examples, undoubtedly because only library professionals or fairly sophisticated library users would know what an ISSN (International Standard Serial Number) is, where to find it, and where and why to search it.

5. *Total Title Searches:* It is simply the subtotal of the first four fields, or 83,214.

6. *Browse by Alphabet:* 8,111 browses in this mode are recorded. For *Journal of Economic Literature,* this means, a library patron using the main library interface selected *"J,"* then *"Jou,"* and then scrolled down the list, until the desired title was found. (For any title beginning with *"Journal of,"* this would be a very torturous route to take.)

7. *Browse by Subject:* This presupposes a more general and less title-focused browse by the patron. Again, using the main library interface, the user this time chose the Subject Browse utility, selected the "Business and Economics" subject heading, and then scrolled down to find the title, *Journal of Economic Literature.* 13,260 browses were recorded here, making it a somewhat more popular option than Browse by Alphabet.

8. *Total Browse Searches:* It is the subtotal of the above two fields, or 21,371.

9. *Total Browse and Title Searches:* It is the sum of Total Title Searches and Total Browse Searches, or 104,585.

10. *MARC Record Searches:* This institution does not possess this particular utility so the total is zero.

11. *OpenURL Searches:* This institution also does not possess this utility so the total is again zero.

12. *Total Searches:* The grand total of Total Browse and Title Searches, MARC Record Searches, and OpenURL Searches, or 104,585 searches.

Subject Statistics

Serials Solutions does not currently use either Library of Congress (LC) subject headings, or *Ulrich*'s subject classifications. Instead, it uses its own in-house subject classification system. While the Serials Solutions headings are reasonably clear in their organization and composition, they are likely to be of limited utility to libraries that are organized to use either LC or *Ulrich*'s headings. Thus, for these libraries, the Serials Solutions headings are likely to be useful only for a more general snapshot of subjects being searched and browsed at a library, rather than a detailed breakdown by a library's fund codes that are more likely to be tied to either LC or *Ulrich*'s headings.

The fourteen major Serials Solutions subject headings (see Figure 7.3) and the number of searches depicted in our example in each area are:

1. Business and Economics 431
2. Earth and Environmental Sciences 492
3. Fine Arts and Music 213
4. Gender and Ethnic Studies 398
5. General Interest Periodicals 67
6. Government, Law and Public Policy 317
7. Health Sciences 1238
8. Humanities and Reference 368
9. Life Sciences and Agriculture 1061
10. Physical Sciences and Mathematics 268
11. Religion and Philosophy 166
12. Social and Behavioral Sciences 1255
13. Sports, Leisure and Hobbies 254
14. Technology and Applied Sciences 435

Within these fourteen headings, there are numerous subheadings (that will not be broken down here), and in some cases, even sub-sub-headings which also have their search numbers broken out as well. At present, there are 135 subheadings and 206 sub-subheadings used.

Again, while not adhering strictly to LC or *Ulrich*'s headings, library bibliographic specialists can at least glean a basic understanding of which journals, in which subject areas and subject area specializations, are being utilized by patrons. Although ERMS obviously cannot track journal searches or browses initiated from the library OPAC or by on-campus patrons who access directly from vendor Web sites, it can provide li-

FIGURE 7.3.

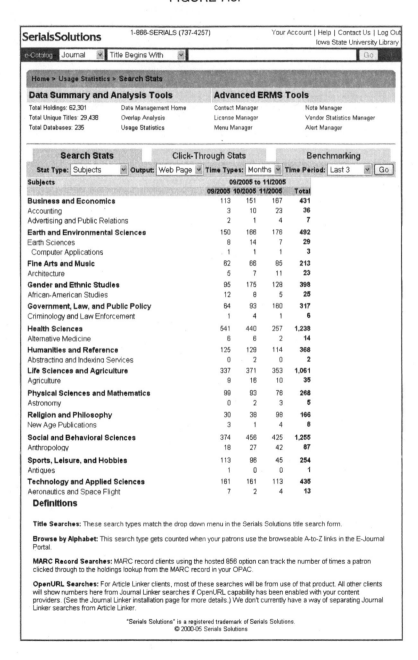

SerialsSolutions	1-888-SERIALS (737-4257)	Your Account	Help	Contact Us	Log Out
		Iowa State University Library

e-Catalog | Journal | Title Begins With | | Go

Home > Usage Statistics > Search Stats

Data Summary and Analysis Tools   Advanced ERMS Tools

Total Holdings: 62,301	Data Management Home	Contact Manager	Note Manager
Total Unique Titles: 29,438	Overlap Analysis	License Manager	Vendor Statistics Manager
Total Databases: 235	Usage Statistics	Menu Manager	Alert Manager

Search Stats	Click-Through Stats	Benchmarking

Stat Type: Subjects | **Output:** Web Page | **Time Types:** Months | **Time Period:** Last 3 | Go

Subjects	09/2005 to 11/2005			
	09/2005	10/2005	11/2005	Total
Business and Economics	113	151	167	**431**
Accounting	3	10	23	**36**
Advertising and Public Relations	2	1	4	**7**
Earth and Environmental Sciences	150	166	176	**492**
Earth Sciences	8	14	7	**29**
Computer Applications	1	1	1	**3**
Fine Arts and Music	62	66	85	**213**
Architecture	5	7	11	**23**
Gender and Ethnic Studies	95	175	128	**398**
African-American Studies	12	8	5	**25**
Government, Law, and Public Policy	64	93	160	**317**
Criminology and Law Enforcement	1	4	1	**6**
Health Sciences	541	440	257	**1,238**
Alternative Medicine	6	6	2	**14**
Humanities and Reference	125	129	114	**368**
Abstracting and Indexing Services	0	2	0	**2**
Life Sciences and Agriculture	337	371	353	**1,061**
Agriculture	9	16	10	**35**
Physical Sciences and Mathematics	99	93	76	**268**
Astronomy	0	2	3	**5**
Religion and Philosophy	30	38	98	**166**
New Age Publications	3	1	4	**8**
Social and Behavioral Sciences	374	456	425	**1,255**
Anthropology	18	27	42	**87**
Sports, Leisure, and Hobbies	113	96	45	**254**
Antiques	1	0	0	**1**
Technology and Applied Sciences	161	161	113	**435**
Aeronautics and Space Flight	7	2	4	**13**

Definitions

Title Searches: These search types match the drop down menu in the Serials Solutions title search form.

Browse by Alphabet: This search type gets counted when your patrons use the browseable A-to-Z links in the E-Journal Portal.

MARC Record Searches: MARC record clients using the hosted 856 option can track the number of times a patron clicked through to the holdings lookup from the MARC record in your OPAC.

OpenURL Searches: For Article Linker clients, most of these searches will be from use of that product. All other clients will show numbers here from Journal Linker searches if OpenURL capability has been enabled with your content providers. (See the Journal Linker installation page for more details.) We don't currently have a way of separating Journal Linker searches from Article Linker.

"Serials Solutions" is a registered trademark of Serials Solutions.
© 2000-05 Serials Solutions

brarians with at least a snapshot of the areas that are receiving the most usage, and can also provide library administrators with some general guidance in allocating acquisitions budget money to assigned subject areas, even if the titles used here do not directly dovetail with those used at a given institution.

Manipulating Date Ranges

Date ranges can be arranged in a variety of configurations, depending on what the user needs. For instance, the default range set by Serials Solutions is for the previous three months' worth of usage statistics. The user can just as easily select only the previous month, three months, the previous year, or any date range within the library of statistics that is being kept, and run their own customized report, utilizing this feature in ERMS.

Click-Through Statistics

A click-through statistic represents any instance where a user clicks on a journal link within Serials Solutions. Thus, an institution can get a decent idea of how many times each database, each journal title within that database, or each journal title individually, has been accessed using the Serials Solutions interface. Reports can again be generated by Web page (the default option) or CSV file, and date range can be customized to current year, previous year, and the last twelve months.

Serials Solutions provides click-through statistics in a variety of configurations. The statistics module defaults to presenting hits by Database.

Citing this institution's example, the first column lists all subscribed databases. Each database name is clickable, which will take the administrator into a new report, just for that database, which lists each journal title, and the hits on those individual titles (Figure 7.4). The second column lists each database's provider (e.g., ACM Digital Library, Metapress, etc.). The following columns then list the number of hits for the twelve months of 2005 to date of writing this chapter, for each database, followed by a total column. So, looking at the figures for ABI/Inform Complete, the monthly figures are 532 for January 2005, 638 for February 2005, etc., with a total of 5,593 for 2005 to date of this writing.

Also, at the top of this screen there are total hits for each month for all databases. In this example, January 2005 has 11,009 hits, February

FIGURE 7.4.

SerialsSolutions — 1-866-SERIALS (737-4257) — Your Account | Help | Contact Us | Log Out — Iowa State University Library

e-Catalog | Journal | Title Begins With | | Go

Home > Usage Statistics > Click-Through Stats

Data Summary and Analysis Tools | **Advanced ERMS Tools**

Data Summary and Analysis Tools		Advanced ERMS Tools	
Total Holdings: 62,501	Data Management Home	Contact Manager	Note Manager
Total Unique Titles: 29,468	Overlap Analysis	License Manager	Vendor Statistics Manager
Total Databases: 236	Usage Statistics	Menu Manager	Alert Manager

Search Stats | **Click-Through Stats** | Benchmarking

Stat Type: Databases | Output: Web Page | Time Types: Months | Time Period: This Year | Go

Databases
Total for all Databases: 11009 13741 15641 15585 9610 10634 7873 10550 17479 20459 18803 5400 156784

01/2005 to 12/2005

Database Name	Provider	01/2005	02/2005	03/2005	04/2005	05/2005	06/2005	07/2005	08/2005	09/2005	10/2005	11/2005	12/2005	Total
informel	Thomson Gale	0	0	0	0	0	0	0	0	14	4	7	1	26
ABI/INFORM Complete	ProQuest	532	638	531	572	257	339	236	355	601	609	753	170	5593
Academic Search Elite	EBSCOhost	0	0	0	0	0	332	393	483	1193	1380	1248	359	5368
Academy of Management	MetaPress	0	0	0	0	0	0	0	0	0	12	6	0	18
Access World News	Newsbank	0	0	0	0	0	0	4	32	30	24	31	18	139
ACM Digital Library	ACM Digital Library	87	68	32	35	32	31	32	24	60	60	30	18	479
AERA SIG Communication of Research	AERA SIG	16	21	20	33	15	17	9	15	16	21	18	6	207
African American Newspapers: The 19...	Accessible Archives	0	0	0	2	0	3	0	2	0	12	3	0	22
Emerald Journals	Emerald	27	43	58	61	50	62	24	55	77	93	55	19	624
AlphaMed Press	AlphaMed Press	0	0	0	0	0	0	0	0	0	0	2	0	2
University of California Press Jour...	University of California Press	19	54	44	61	12	10	11	9	10	14	25	5	274
University of Chicago Press	University of Chicago Press	29	50	46	36	14	26	14	20	50	53	61	13	412
Urban & Vogel GmbH	MetaPress	0	0	0	0	0	0	0	1	0	0	0	6	7
Veterinary Science and Veterinary M...	Elsevier Science	0	0	0	0	12	12	10	16	21	30	25	8	134
Walter de Gruyter Journals	Walter de Gruyter	14	15	10	17	2	16	4	6	7	7	16	6	120
Wiley InterScience Journal of Patho...	Wiley Interscience	0	0	0	0	0	0	0	1	0	0	2	0	3
Wiley Interscience Journals	Wiley Interscience	377	431	550	469	458	478	342	434	489	538	607	196	5369
World Scientific Journals	World Scientific Publishing	3	5	2	9	19	7	7	4	5	5	3	1	70

2005 has 13,742 hits, etc. The total number of hits for the year 2005 to date of writing this chapter is 156,784.

Looking at Figure 7.5, which is reached by clicking on "ABI Inform Complete" on the Figure 7.4 screen, we can see the breakdown of each individual title within this database. This screen lists each journal title, its ISSN, and then the monthly hits for each title, as well as the total for year-to-date. In this example, hits are fairly sparse for each individual ti-

FIGURE 7.5.

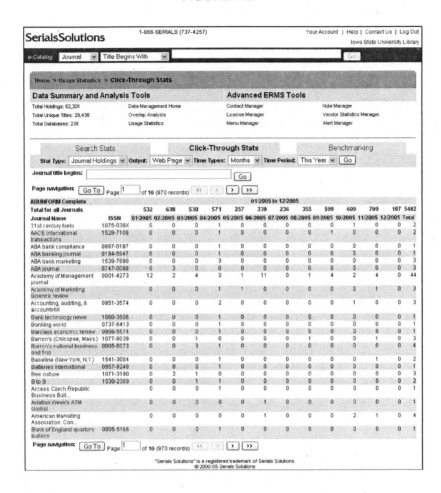

tle (only two hits all year for *21st Century Fuels*), but as ABI Inform contains 970 titles, the total for all titles is significant (5,482). Again, monthly and annual totals for all included titles are listed at the top of the page (Figure 7.4).

Yet another granular level of data can be viewed by jumping from the titles in Figure 7.5 by clicking on the individual titles listed. This provides listings for titles that exist on multiple platforms. Looking at *21st Century Fuels* in Figure 7.6, we can see that it is also available on another platform, Lexis-Nexis Academic.

FIGURE 7.6.

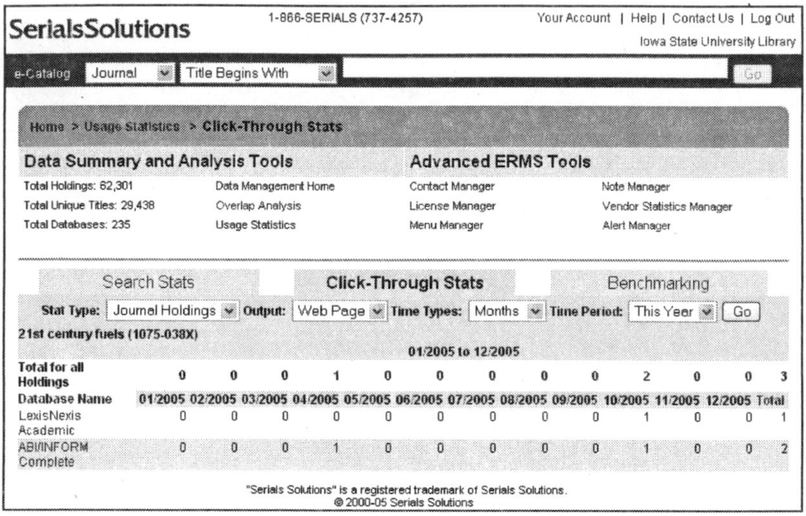
SerialsSolutions 1-866-SERIALS (737-4257) Your Account | Help | Contact Us | Log Out
Iowa State University Library

e-Catalog Journal Title Begins With Go

Home > Usage Statistics > Click-Through Stats

Data Summary and Analysis Tools | Advanced ERMS Tools

Total Holdings: 62,301 | Data Management Home | Contact Manager | Note Manager
Total Unique Titles: 29,438 | Overlap Analysis | License Manager | Vendor Statistics Manager
Total Databases: 235 | Usage Statistics | Menu Manager | Alert Manager

Search Stats | Click-Through Stats | Benchmarking

Stat Type: Journal Holdings Output: Web Page Time Types: Months Time Period: This Year Go

21st century fuels (1075-038X)

01/2005 to 12/2005

Total for all Holdings	0	0	0	1	0	0	0	0	0	2	0	0	3
Database Name	01/2005	02/2005	03/2005	04/2005	05/2005	06/2005	07/2005	08/2005	09/2005	10/2005	11/2005	12/2005	Total
LexisNexis Academic	0	0	0	0	0	0	0	0	0	1	0	0	1
ABI/INFORM Complete	0	0	0	1	0	0	0	0	0	1	0	0	2

"Serials Solutions" is a registered trademark of Serials Solutions.
© 2000-05 Serials Solutions

The same basic information is provided, as in previous screens. In this example, *21st Century Fuels* has two hits noted in ABI/Inform, plus one additional hit in Lexis-Nexis, for a total of three for the year 2005.

Once again, the title of the database provider can be clicked on, and this takes the administrator back to the page (Figure 7.5).

Several other display options are available to view click-through statistics. Figure 7.7 depicts these statistics by "Journal holdings." This page is the first of 189 pages that depicts the click-through statistics for this institution.

Each journal title held by this institution is listed alphabetically, along with its ISSN (where available) and the database platform (or platforms) on which it is presented. For titles that are available on multiple platforms, each title is listed on a separate line for each database in which it is represented. Thus, in this example, *123Jump* and *2.5G-3G,* for example, are on two lines each, and *33 Metal Producing,* is listed on three lines.

The next option is click-through statistics by "Journal titles" (Figure 7.8). This is somewhat similar to the information displayed in Figure 7.7, but takes out the information relating to database platforms and treats each journal title as a unique entity, rather than as a subcomponent

FIGURE 7.7.

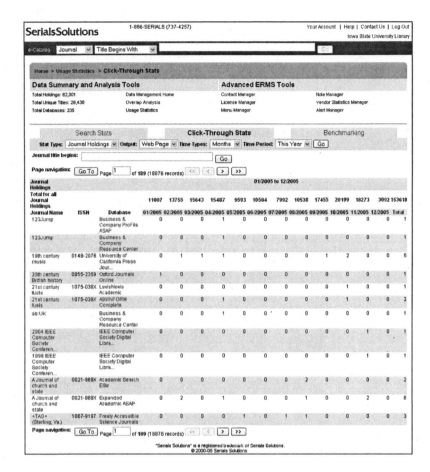

of the larger database platform; thus, the aforementioned titles appear only once on this listing rather than several times.

The fourth display option is for "Providers Databases (DBs)" (Figure 7.9), which uses the database provider as the primary key for which information is displayed.

The first column depicted is for the provider itself, such as Accessible Archives, or the American Chemical Society, etc. The second column lists each database within each provider. In most cases, there will be only one database per provider, but in several cases there are two or more. For in-

FIGURE 7.8.

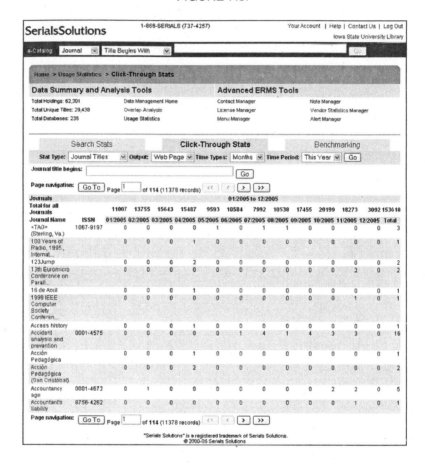

stance, in this example, Accessible Archives provides both "African-American Newspapers" and *"Godey's Lady's Book."* This screen provides a total figure for all providers running across the top, and also subtotals for all databases within each provider. The database totals add up to the provider subtotals, which then add up to total figure for all providers.

The fifth and final display option is for "Providers," similar to Figure 7.9, but which eliminates the individual databases from the equation (Figure 7.10).

This option lists each provider only, and then the monthly and year-to-date totals for each provider, along with the usual "Total for All Providers" across the top.

FIGURE 7.9.

SerialsSolutions	1-866-SERIALS (737-4257)	Your Account	Help	Contact Us	Log Out

Iowa State University Library

e-Catalog | Journal ∨ | Title Begins With ∨ | | Go

Home > Usage Statistics > **Click-Through Stats**

Data Summary and Analysis Tools			Advanced ERMS Tools	
Total Holdings: 62,301	Data Management Home		Contact Manager	Note Manager
Total Unique Titles: 29,438	Overlap Analysis		License Manager	Vendor Statistics Manager
Total Databases: 235	Usage Statistics		Menu Manager	Alert Manager

Search Stats	**Click-Through Stats**	Benchmarking

Stat Type: Providers (DBs) ∨   Output: Web Page ∨   Time Types: Months ∨   Time Period: This Year ∨   Go

Providers (by DB)   01/2005 to 12/2005

Provider	Database	01/2005	02/2005	03/2005	04/2005	05/2005	06/2005	07/2005	08/2005	09/2005	10/2005	11/2005	12/2005	Total
Total for all Providers		11009	13741	15641	15585	9610	10634	7873	10550	17479	20459	18903	3107	154491
Accessible Archives	Totals for all databases	0	0	0	3	0	3	0	2	4	12	3	0	27
	African American Newspapers: The 19...	0	0	0	2	0	3	0	2	0	12	3	0	22
	Godey's Lady's Book	0	0	0	1	0	0	0	0	4	0	0	0	5
ACM Digital Library	Totals for all databases	67	58	32	35	32	31	32	24	60	60	30	7	468
	ACM Digital Library	67	58	32	35	32	31	32	24	60	60	30	7	468
AERA SIG	Totals for all databases	16	21	20	33	15	17	9	15	16	21	18	4	205
	AERA SIG Communication of Research	16	21	20	33	15	17	9	15	18	21	18	4	205
AlphaMed Press	Totals for all databases	0	0	0	0	0	0	0	0	0	0	2	0	2
	AlphaMed Press	0	0	0	0	0	0	0	0	0	0	2	0	2
University of New Mexico	Totals for all databases	0	0	0	0	0	7	2	9	23	16	24	0	81
	SORA - Searchable Ornithological Re...	0	0	0	0	0	7	2	9	23	16	24	0	81
Wiley Interscience	Totals for all databases	377	431	550	469	458	478	342	435	489	538	609	129	5305
	Wiley InterScience Journal of Patho...	0	0	0	0	0	0	0	1	0	0	2	0	3
	Wiley Interscience Journals	377	431	550	469	458	478	342	434	489	538	607	128	5302
World Scientific Publishing	Totals for all databases	3	5	2	9	19	7	7	4	5	5	3	0	69
	World Scientific Journals	3	5	2	9	19	7	7	4	5	5	3	0	69

"Serials Solutions" is a registered trademark of Serials Solutions.
© 2000-05 Serials Solutions

Benchmarking

Clicking on the "Benchmarking" tab takes you to a screen that compares and contrasts the median statistics at your institution versus those at Serials Solutions-subscribing peer institutions, and also versus all Serials Solutions-subscribing institutions (Figure 7.11). Serials Solutions assigns all of its participating clients to one of three peer-groups: academic libraries, special libraries, and public libraries. Academic libraries are then assigned into subgroups, based upon their Carnegie classification. Special libraries are assigned to subgroups based upon "generally recognized" special library groups, such as law, medical, or

FIGURE 7.10.

SerialsSolutions   1-866-SERIALS (737-4257)   Your Account | Help | Contact Us | Log Out   Iowa State University Library

e-Catalog | Journal ▾ | Title Begins With ▾ | | Go

Home > Usage Statistics > Click-Through Stats

Data Summary and Analysis Tools   **Advanced ERMS Tools**

Total Holdings: 62,301	Data Management Home	Contact Manager	Note Manager
Total Unique Titles: 29,438	Overlap Analysis	License Manager	Vendor Statistics Manager
Total Databases: 235	Usage Statistics	Menu Manager	Alert Manager

Search Stats   **Click-Through Stats**   Benchmarking

Stat Type: Providers ▾   Output: Web Page ▾   Time Types: Months ▾   Time Period: This Year ▾   Go

01/2005 to 12/2005

Providers	01/2005	02/2005	03/2005	04/2005	05/2005	06/2005	07/2005	08/2005	09/2005	10/2005	11/2005	12/2005	Total
Total for all Providers	11009	13741	15641	15585	9610	10634	7873	10550	17479	20459	18803	3107	154491
Provider	01/2005	02/2005	03/2005	04/2005	05/2005	06/2005	07/2005	08/2005	09/2005	10/2005	11/2005	12/2005	Total
Accessible Archives	0	0	0	3	0	3	0	2	4	12	3	0	27
ACM Digital Library	67	58	32	35	32	31	32	24	60	60	30	7	468
AERA SIG	16	21	20	33	15	17	9	15	16	21	18	4	205
AlphaMed Press	0	0	0	0	0	0	0	0	0	0	2	0	2
American Association for Cancer Res...	2	2	3	3	0	2	0	2	0	0	3	0	17
American Ceramic Society	0	0	0	4	7	4	4	13	1	7	5	2	47
American Chemical Society	383	445	564	470	463	727	487	437	526	613	619	122	5856
American Heart Association	0	0	0	0	0	0	0	0	0	3	7	2	12
American Institute of Aeronautics a...	21	13	5	10	9	9	5	12	20	8	8	1	119
American Institute of Physics	117	129	172	171	201	154	83	106	171	147	167	39	1657
American Library Association	0	0	0	0	0	0	0	0	0	0	8	0	8
Walter de Gruyter	14	15	10	17	2	16	4	6	7	7	16	3	117
Wiley Interscience	377	431	550	469	458	478	342	435	489	538	609	129	5305
World Scientific Publishing	3	5	2	9	19	7	7	4	5	6	3	0	69

Page navigation: Go To | Page 1 of 2 (136 records) | << < > >>

"Serials Solutions" is a registered trademark of Serials Solutions.
© 2000-05 Serials Solutions

corporate libraries. Public libraries are similarly assigned to subgroups based upon the number of residents they serve. Foreign libraries that use Serials Solutions but do not possess a Carnegie classification or IPEDS (Integrated Postsecondary Education Data System) enrollment figure are classified according to an estimate of where they would fall within the Carnegie system, based upon a consultation between Serials Solutions and the participating foreign library. Not all client libraries have their statistics entered in the Benchmarking tab, but approximately 1,300 libraries do.

FIGURE 7.11.

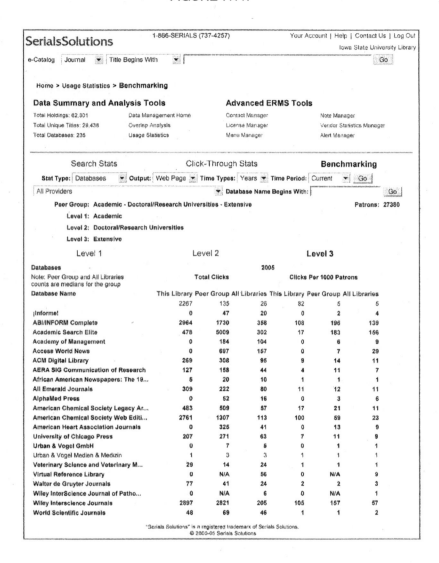

Serials Solutions uses medians rather than averages, as click-through statistics will show dramatic differences between institutions on either pole of a given category. Median figures are used simply to "smooth out" the statistical effects of such institutions versus the more average institutions in the middle. The benchmarking statistics provided look at two metrics: total clicks, which are the total clicks for search types, databases, and subjects for your library, versus the median of peer institutions and all institutions; and also clicks per 1,000 patrons, which controls for the different populations served by dividing the total clicks by the number of patrons in thousands.

In the default page (Figure 7.12), this institution is shown to be in the Academic peer group, and its subgroup is for Extensive institutions (Level 3). Its benchmarked statistics are shown for database use, and its Level 3 peer institutions are also depicted.

Total clicks for the institution, for its peer group, and for all libraries, are shown across the top of the graph and are depicted both in terms of Total Clicks and Clicks per 1,000 patrons. Beneath that, each database is listed and their total clicks are similarly listed out.

For example, the ACM Digital Library had 269 total clicks at this institution, versus a median of 222 clicks at its peer institutions, and a median of sixty clicks at all libraries. It also shows that the ACM Digital Library had nine clicks per 1,000 patrons at this institution, versus a median of ten clicks per 1,000 patrons at its peer institutions, and a median of seven clicks per 1,000 patrons at all institutions.

Although not shown in this chapter, an institution can compile similar statistical comparisons in this utility for Search Types and Subjects. An institution in one Carnegie category (such as Level 3/Extensive), can also select the Level 1 or Level 2 tabs to compare itself versus other Carnegie categories.

In spite of the dropdown menus, at this time these reports can only be generated in Web page format and can be expressed chronologically only in terms of years. An institution can generate figures for the current year, the previous year, or both.

Overlap Analysis Collection

Serials Solutions also provides a helpful tool to determinate the amount of title analyzing, taking the count of titles of each collection possessed by an institution. The default mode has all collections that are held preselected, but the institution doing the analysis can deselect any collections it wishes to be excluded if it wishes to focus the analysis on a particular subset of providers. An administrator can also select one or more collections for a specific analysis.

The databases subscribed are listed in the first column (Figure 7.12); the statistical information is listed in each of the following columns:

FIGURE 7.12.

SerialsSolutions   1-866-SERIALS (737-4257)   Your Account | Help | Contact Us | Log Out

Iowa State University Library

e-Catalog | Journal ▼ | Title Begins With ▼ | | Go |

Home > Overlap Analysis > **Databases**

Data Summary and Analysis Tools

Total Holdings: 62,301	Data Management Home	
Total Unique Titles: 29,438	Overlap Analysis	
Total Databases: 235	Usage Statistics	

Advanced ERMS Tools

Contact Manager	Note Manager
License Manager	Vendor Statistics Manager
Menu Manager	Alert Manager

Serials Solutions Overlap Analysis

View the amount of overlap in your collection

- The results below indicate the unique and common holdings in each of the selected databases and the totals for the entire collection.
- Press Start Over button to create a new database list.
- Press Edit Collection button to modify your database list.
- Click on the numbers in the holdings columns to view a list of the journal holdings
- Please read the Overview of Overlap Analysis.

Overlap Analysis Results

              | << Edit Collection | Start Over >> |

Holdings Summary	Title Unique	Holding Unique	Total Unique	Full Holding Overlap	Partial Holding Overlap	Total Holding Overlap	Title Overlap	Total	Percent Full Overlap	Percent Unique
¡Informe!	111	0	111	18	16	34	0	145	12.4	76.6
ABI/INFORM Complete	807	175	982	1274	791	2065	3	3051	41.8	32.2
Academic Search Elite	206	4	210	1634	176	1810	0	2020	80.9	10.4
Academy of Management	0	0	0	2	1	3	0	3	66.7	0.0
Access World News	701	4	705	856	36	892	0	1597	53.6	44.1
ACM Digital Library	249	86	335	12	46	58	0	393	3.1	85.2
AERA SIG Communication of Research	59	1	60	102	18	120	0	180	56.7	33.3
African American Newspapers: The 19th Century	7	0	7	0	0	0	0	7	0.0	100.0
AlphaMed Press	0	0	0	2	0	2	0	2	100.0	0.0
American Association for Cancer Research	1	0	1	4	2	6	0	7	57.1	14.3

Journal Holdings Totals

Total holdings in collection*	14503	1406	15909	40259	5835	46094	298	62301	64.6	25.5

*Total holdings is the sum of all of the holdings in the databases listed in the table above. However, the total holdings number on this page will change based on the list of databases used in your overlap analysis query.

Holding Type	Description
Total Unique	The sum of title unique and holding unique holdings.
Full Overlap	Journal holdings available in more than one database. The coverage dates of the reference holding are completely overlapped by at least one of the comparison holdings.
Partial Overlap	Journal holdings available in more than one database. The coverage dates of the reference holdings are only partly overlapped by at least one comparison holding
Title Overlap	Journal titles available in other databases, but the date ranges are incalculable due to missing dates.
Total Overlap	The sum of full and partial overlap holdings
Total Holdings	The sum of the total unique holdings, total overlap holdings and non-distinct total overlap titles.
Percent Full Overlap	Percentage of all holdings in a database that are completely overlapped by at least one other holding from another database.
Percent Unique	Percentage of all holdings in a database that are either title unique or holding unique.

Unique Journals Summary

Unique journal titles that appear in only one database	14503
Unique Journal titles that appear in more than one database (counted only once)	14935
Total Unique Journal titles in your collection	**29438**
Percent of your Unique Journal titles that appear in only one database	49.3

"Serials Solutions" is a registered trademark of Serials Solutions.
© 2000-05 Serials Solutions

1. *Title unique:* Journal holdings available in only that particular database
2. *Holding unique:* Journal holdings available in more than that one particular database, but which do not overlap in coverage dates
3. *Total unique:* The total of title unique and holding unique
4. *Full holding overlap:* Journal holdings available in more than this particular database. The coverage dates of the reference holding are completely overlapped by at least one of the comparison holdings.
5. *Partial holding overlap:* Journal holdings available in more than this particular database. The coverage dates of the reference holdings are only partly overlapped by at least one comparison holding.
6. *Total holding overlap:* It is the total of full and partial holdings
7. *Title overlap:* Journal titles that are available in other databases, but the date ranges are incalculable due to missing dates
8. *Total holdings:* The sum of the total unique holdings, the total overlap holdings, and the nondistinct total overlap titles
9. *Percent full overlap:* The percentage of all holdings in a database that are completely overlapped by at least one other holding from another database
10. *Percent unique:* The percentage of all holdings in a database that are either title unique or holding unique

Finally, Serials Solutions provide a summary of unique journals in an institution's collection. For this institution, the totals are as follows:

Unique journal titles that appear in only one database:	14,503
Unique journal titles that appear in more that one database (counted only once):	14,935
Total unique journals in the collection:	29,438
Percent of unique journal titles that appear in only one database:	49.3

Future Statistics

A number of future enhancements are currently planned by Serials Solutions and will be introduced in the near future, including adding the ability to track user sessions; the ability to provide more granular statistics for each product (such as Article Linker and Central Search), so that libraries will not only be able to ascertain when a user has begun a search, but also what they are finding on those searches, and what they are clicking on; providing Project COUNTER-compliant statistics aggregations and reports; and, finally, creating a method to determine what resources library patrons are looking for but not finding in their search of a particular library's collection.

CONCLUSIONS

Serials Solutions is not the only provider of electronic journal listings on the market, and is eclipsed in size by larger services, such as EBSCO A-Z. However, the company has remained in the forefront of its niche in the market, consistently providing new and expanded services and features to its product, including its Data Management module for site administrators. While the breadth and depth of the statistics it provides are impressive, they do not, as yet, serve as an alternative or replacement for the site statistics provided directly by journal providers, or journal platforms, such as Ingenta or Metapress. They can, however, provide valuable adjunct statistics to complement and fill out these other statistics. In the cases where a particular journal title has no statistics provided by its platform or producer, Serials Solutions may, in fact, be the only resource available for providing any usage statistics at all. Further, Serials Solutions can provide useful tools for determining the amount of unique or duplicated titles in a library's collection, which possibly may not be determined by any other method. It is hopeful that statistical packages and tools in Serials Solutions, and in its competitors, will continue to advance and evolve in future years, so that the library profession can continue to refine and develop its methods for gathering and analyzing usage statistics.

REFERENCES

Serials Solutions ERMS (Electronic Resource Management System) User Guide, Version 1.0. Seattle, WA: 2005.
Serials Solutions Web site. http://www.serialssolutions.com/home.asp

doi:10.1300/J123v53S09_08

Chapter 8

Application of Electronic Serial Usage Statistics in a National Laboratory

Christine F. Noonan
Melissa K. McBurney

INTRODUCTION

With the growth of online products being delivered to library customers, the traditional measures of library performance–counts of walk-in visitors, the number of users attending presentations, the number of classes, and the number of individual subscriptions processed, etc.–no longer, accurately reflect the increased activity and use of library products and services. E-serials usage statistics give us a myriad of information on user behavior, research trends, and collection development, and can act as important analytical tools that can in turn support resource allocation analysis, reporting, and managerial decision making. Although librarians very much need these statistics in order to assist their decision making, the usage data provided is not always suitable for local needs analysis, and librarians, including the authors, are looking for new ways to provide the information that is needed, both locally and for the profession as a whole.

[Haworth co-indexing entry note]: "Application of Electronic Serial Usage Statistics in a National Laboratory." Noonan, Christine F., and Melissa K. McBurney. Co-published simultaneously in *The Serials Librarian* (The Haworth Information Press, an imprint of The Haworth Press, Inc.) Vol. 53, Supplement No. 9, 2007, pp. 151-160; and: *Usage Statistics of E-Serials* (ed: David C. Fowler) The Haworth Information Press, an imprint of The Haworth Press, Inc., 2007, pp. 151-160. Single or multiple copies of this article are available for a fee from The Haworth Document Delivery Service [1-800-HAWORTH, 9:00 a.m. - 5:00 p.m. (EST). E-mail address: docdelivery@haworthpress.com].

The Hanford Technical Library (HTL) is a research and technical library located in Richland, Washington, and is operated by the Pacific Northwest National Laboratory (PNNL) for the United States Department of Energy. Approximately 4,000 PNNL staff members in multiple geographic locations are served by the HTL, in addition to another estimated 7,000 employees from the Department of Energy (DOE), as well as DOE contractors on the Hanford Site. The library is collocated with the Washington State University (WSU) Tri- Cities Max Benitz Memorial Library and the DOE Public Reading Room in the Consolidated Information Center on the WSU Tri-Cities campus.

The HTL is physically removed from the main campus of PNNL, necessitating a robust online presence in order to effectively reach and provide services to library users and save them the time of driving to the library. In today's networked environment, the library is an information access point for local patrons and for remote users at satellite offices across the United States. The ability of the HTL to provide users access to online content is a necessity to both support research initiatives and to provide up-to-date scientific and technical information.

The HTL currently provides access to over 8,000 online journals, and usage data provided by publishers and vendors is needed in order to assist in convincing the Laboratory management to continue to invest in funding the library at increasing levels of demand for library services.

USAGE STATISTICS DEFINED

According to Rous, at the most fundamental level, e-serial usage statistics "are nothing more than the artifacts of online transactions, stored in Web server logs; but at the most abstract level, they represent nothing less than an effort to understand changing patterns of scholarly behavior by tracing and analyzing scholars' interactions with online resources through time."[1] Looking at the first part of Rous's definition, we can identify transactions as access to the abstract, table of contents, or as downloading of HTML or PDF electronic journal content. In some cases, publishers and vendors may also record usage transactions as queries, sessions, or views. These statistics are often difficult to compare because of the terminology used by the vendor. In many cases, they do not tell us which individual articles are being downloaded, why a particular article has been downloaded, or from what location it is being downloaded. The lack of standardization across vendors and publishers, coupled with the lack of end user information supplied, can be very problematic to collection development, as alluded to by the second portion of Rous's definition of usage statistics. This is especially true when there is a need to analyze the use of titles in a particular subject area, to conduct a systematic review of the library's holdings, or to initiate a review of consortia arrangements and packages.

One attempt aimed at standardizing vendor-supplied usage statistics is the Counting Online Usage of NeTworked Electronic Resources (COUNTER) Project. COUNTER is "an international initiative designed to serve librarians, publishers, and intermediaries by facilitating the recording and exchange of online usage statistics."[2] The COUNTER Code of Practice, released in December 2002, provides guidance on data elements and definitions of usage data for online journals and databases. This guidance provides consistent terminology and a framework for generating usage data. COUNTER currently lists forty registered vendors that are providing COUNTER-compliant usage statistics to libraries, publishers, and intermediaries. Libraries are thus able to compare usage data from different vendors in an unvarying fashion. In addition, publishers can provide data in an easily accessible way, requiring less time-intensive interpretation and data manipulation. Ideally, usage statistics are available on a monthly basis; however, many vendors only provide usage data quarterly, biannually, or upon request, or are not currently COUNTER-compliant.

WHY DO WE NEED USAGE STATISTICS?

Librarians have difficulty determining who is using which e-resource and the degree to which a given resource is meeting user needs.[3] Usage statistics are necessary for collection development, to indicate research trends (as is done at the Laboratory), to aid in marketing and managerial decision making, and to assist in Web site usability and redesign projects. Furthermore, libraries must be accountable and must show effective use of financial resources. For the HTL, approximately 70 percent of the library's collection budget is spent on electronic journals and 26 percent of the collection budget is spent on other electronic resources, including e-books and databases. In addition, at the Lab, Federal regulations require that any purchase over $10,000 need to have a sole source justification written to show that no other vendor can supply the information provided in the resource. It then becomes important to have the usage statistics available, which demonstrate that there will be a negative impact if a title is not retained, and to support library budget requests and purchasing decisions.

The analysis of statistics plays a large role and is a valuable tool in collection development. Statistical information helps the library to identify journals for cancellation and to justify subsequent cancellation decisions. When making cancellation decisions, HTL staff uses the following pieces of data in the analysis: electronic usage, print usage (if the print is still carried), cost-per-use, customer feedback, the impact factor of the title as determined by ISI's Journal Citation Reports, the number of articles published in that journal by PNNL staff, and current and evolving PNNL research focuses. The HTL does not solely rely upon any one piece of data to create the entire picture. When deciding whether to cancel a journal, the following questions need to be answered: Are patrons actually downloading articles from the title? If so, what is the cost-per-use (journal cost divided by the number of downloads)? If it has a high cost-per-use, would it be more effective to cancel the title and provide it when needed through document delivery? Cancellation, in this example, places the cost back upon the user since the HTL charges for document delivery services. However, the library cannot afford to subscribe to a title for only one or two people. That said, in some cases, even if the usage for a title is low, the library may not cancel it. For example, the usage statistics provided by a vendor may show that a journal has only had three articles downloaded over the course of a year, but when the HTL solicits user feedback, it may discover that a program in that subject area is emerging as a new focus of research. The decision may then be made to keep the journal on a watch list and to revisit the usage in the following year in order to see if the usage did indeed improve enough so as to justify retaining the title.

Electronic usage statistics are analyzed in combination with print usage statistics to decide if the print version should be cancelled. If the electronic version is getting the majority of use, then the HTL solicits user feedback to determine justifications for retaining the print. In most cases, there has been no need to do so. However, for those titles which have better print graphics than the online version, the HTL has retained the bound volumes. Print is cancelled or suppressed to save on shelf space, reduce bindery costs, and decrease staff time previously spent on receiving and binding serials.

The HTL currently carries only thirty journals with no online access. Based on analysis of print and online usage statistics, the HTL has decided not to receive and claim print issues that are available electronically, and not to bind print titles that are available online. Because of these decisions and the amount of print that has been cancelled altogether, one staff member who works in serials is now available to work on new projects.

Research trends change periodically at PNNL because of new scientific fields emerging, funding from the Department of Energy fluctuating, the ebb and flow of grant and proposal cycles, etc. Usage statistics often mirror the research landscape–its natural ups and downs and the changing of directions into new emergent areas. The information of what were once core research journal collections for library users evolve, and the HTL librarians must respond accordingly by providing users with new resources and subscriptions. Usage statistics can play a role in helping the library determine the requirement of new resources. Based upon usage data provided by several vendors, the HTL has been able to identify use of titles for which it does not subscribe, and it has made the decision to add the titles to its collections. Thus, usage statistics are incorporated into renewal and cancellation decisions and, when necessary, the decision making process for acquiring new products.

GATHERING THE DATA

Currently at the HTL, usage statistics are downloaded, interpreted, and tracked in an Excel spreadsheet. The data for each vendor or publisher is kept in a separate worksheet within the spreadsheet and is updated at appropriate intervals. The HTL currently has two staff members assigned to this task. The electronic library specialist is responsible for setting up, troubleshooting, and maintaining access to online products, and as well as monitoring and recording the usage data that requires some form of manipulation or interpretation. A paraprofessional staff member inputs the usage data into Excel for those vendors and publishers who do not require as much examination. The HTL currently tracks e-serial usage statistics from twenty-nine publishers and/or vendors. These include journals that are included as part of a large fulltext database, large journal packages from a single publisher or provider, and journals purchased as individual titles from small societies or publishers. The most common data point recorded is the sum total of HTML and PDF downloads, since this indicates financial impact if a title is cancelled. The HTL does not track how many users access the abstract or table of contents level of a journal, although the data point may indicate usage. Many vendors do not include titles with zero hits in their statistics, and others such as the Institute of Electrical and Electronics

Engineers' *IEEE Xplore* do not provide individual title usage. Every vendor provides data in slightly different formats, which makes comparisons difficult. Due to the myriad types of reporting available, dedicated staff-time to interpret the data is essential. Currently, the two staff members involved expend approximately ten hours per month gathering the usage data and entering it into the Excel spreadsheet.

Although the HTL tracks usage data from over two dozen vendors, who provide usage data in several formats (not just COUNTER), there are a handful of small publications purchased individually that provide no statistics whatsoever. This lack of information makes it very difficult for the library to make informed collection development decisions. In addition, relatively few of the e-serials usage statistics collected provide statistics by IP (Internet Protocol) address. Every computer or proxy server communicating over the Internet has a unique IP address. Because of the multiple companies this library serves, it would be beneficial to have such IP statistics to ascertain which companies are using which of the resources supplied by the library. In addition, this data would allow the HTL to tailor its marketing efforts and library education classes more appropriately.

PUTTING THE DATA IN CONTEXT

Of course, usage statistics availablility does not mean the library can always utilize them if it has purchased bundled packages, or if the library is locked into a multiyear deal. In general, libraries want to provide greater access to more information at less cost. Consortial buying is a growing trend, as Hanson indicates.[4] It is an attempt to bring down the prices of electronic products, while simultaneously increasing access. The HTL engages in consortial licensing on numerous products with other Department of Energy Laboratories and research institutes. Analyzing the usage on these types of subscriptions may indeed show several titles that are not being used at all. However, when the library compares the cost-per-use of the entire package, the monetary investment proves justifiable; the HTL is certainly providing access to more than it would be able to if it had been required to purchase each title separately. If an analysis identifies a subscription that is not cost-effective, the library would now be able to use that information as a negotiation point for renewal. Anticipating end user questions about subscribing to journal titles outside of a Lab research area, the HTL has added a section in its collection development policy about bundled packages.

Lack of usage of a particular title can also illuminate opportunities for marketing on the Library's end. Can it trust that the researchers know how to access online resources, or should it interpret and attribute little or no use on the changing research landscape? By collecting user feedback and analyzing it for Web site usability issues, the HTL can fold the data into a more robust Web site usability analysis, in order to effectively market its online resources to staff in Richland, Washington, as well as at remote satellite offices. In addition, when the HTL purchases an individual title or package of titles based upon specific request from a research group, it can monitor the usage closely. If there are minimal downloads, librarians can request promotional materials from vendors and can modify their bibliographic instruction classes to cover these resources. The HTL also has librarians assigned to subject areas, and they assist in promoting the journals to the groups for which they are a liaison.

PROBLEMS WITH THE DATA

The HTL currently relies solely on the vendor to provide data on how and if the products are being used, but usage statistics are often unavailable, unreliable, and not comparable across vendors.[5] Duy suggests that libraries consider developing an in-house system to collect basic usage data on all electronic resources to: (1) provide minimal usage data on those products for which vendors do not provide usage statistics, (2) supplement the data that is provided, and (3) serve as a complementary metric for vendor-supplied incorrect or faulty usage data due to system malfunctions.[6]

For those titles with which the library receives no vendor-supplied usage statistics, it is currently investigating its own form of tracking the usage data by using redirect URLs from the e-journals list on its Web site and monitoring the number of click-through from the Web site to the publisher site. E-serials are made available to the research community on the HTL Web site in an A-Z list, and via forty-five subject headings and the library OPAC, *Leona*.[7] Usage statistics provided by the publisher or vendor do not differentiate between the two patron-access points, and the proposed method would only capture user access of online titles that originate from the library Web site. Although this method will not provide the library with the number of HTML or PDF downloads at the article level, it will give librarians a better indication of usage than no indication at all. In addition, and when appropriate, the HTL is using SFX-generated statistics to augment vendor-supplied data. Ideally, the library would like to develop an in-house electronic resource management system that would enable analysis of statistics from different vendors much faster and easier. This would assist librarians in looking at the collection in its entirety.

Gathering usage data from vendors or from the library's Web logs will provide the staff only with quantitative data, which lends nothing to the assessment of a publication's quality or its intended use by the patron. Indeed, as users are accessing journal articles in full-text format, it needs to be examined–do the resources satisfy a research need or question? The reverse may also be true–if a vendor reports little or no usage for a product, it does not necessarily mean the resource should be on the next cancellation list, as many vendors are concerned that low usage data may mean cancellation of their product.[8] It may be an indication that the resource is not visible enough on the library Web site and users either cannot find it or may not know of its acquisition. Indeed, as a study in an academic library setting discovered, a resource must be available to users for a minimum of twelve to eighteen months before heavy use is observed.[9]

NEXT STEPS:
GENERATING ACCOUNTABILITY
AND PROVIDING SOLUTIONS

As discussed, usage statistics are absolutely necessary for collection development, and they can and do indicate research trends at the Laboratory, aid in targeted marketing to groups and/or companies, lend a hand in managerial decision making (funding, budget allocation, and staffing), and can assist in Web site usability and redesign projects.

It is nearly impossible for librarians to compare data among vendors. And, in a sense, libraries have come to expect these "apples to oranges" comparisons. Standardization efforts, such as the COUNTER Code of Practice, will allow library staff to make comparisons that are more meaningful across multiple sets of usage data. Unfortunately, this is the best tool that librarians have at the moment, so they need to make the most of all available resources for capturing and interpreting usage data as best as they can, whether it is Web site log files, SFX statistics, or vendor-supplied data. Shim, Murphy, and Brunning identify three main methods of analysis for assessing usage statistics and their potential to provide insight on library systems, resources, and services.[10] These methods are: (1) user behavior and demand, which provides insight into the information-seeking behavior of patrons and demand for information; (2) electronic resource efficiency and limitations, which helps identify the strengths and weaknesses of different e-resources; and (3) system design and configuration, which provides system assessments by identifying over- or under-utilization and by designing efficient systems capabilities. In addition to these forms of analysis, the HTL has identified three additional areas of library assessment that can be supported with e-serial usage statistics, including the evaluation of consortia arrangements or package deals, collection development–confirmation of subject strengths and weaknesses and acquisitions emphases, and staffing resources and needs.

CONCLUSIONS

The main solutions that libraries today are trying to find reside within the libraries themselves. The library community must encourage publishers and vendors to provide it with standardized usage statistics and to become COUNTER-compliant. Libraries need to develop or acquire systems that can link acquisitions, budget, and usage statistics data, and therefore reduce staff time currently spent on manually inputting usage statistics. Finally, libraries need to fully exploit all the data points that are available to them, quantitatively as well as qualitatively, in order to gain a more holistic understanding of e-resources usage in general, and of e-serials usage in particular. These solutions would provide a better understanding of user behavior, could highlight resources with poor design, could illuminate areas where the collection is strong or weak, and could streamline the workflow process, and free up staff time to devote to enhancing programs and services to patrons.

NOTES

1. Bernard, Rous. 2004. "Introduction: Use and Abuse of Online Statistics: Overview," In *Online Usage: A Publisher's Guide*. Ed. Bernard Rous, pp. 1-16.

2. Project COUNTER, "About COUNTER," Introduction, http://www.project counter.org/about.html (accessed on March 27, 2005).

3. Peggy, Johnson. 2004. Fundamentals of Collection Development and Management. American Library Association: Chicago.

4. Kathleen, Hanson. 2003. "Electronic Serials Costs: Sales and Acquisitions Practices in Transition," In *E-Serials–Publishers, Libraries, Users, and Standards*. Ed. Wayne Jones, pp. 29-40.

5. Joanna, Duy and Liwen Vaughan. 2003. "Usage Data for Electronic Resources: A Comparison between Locally Collected and Vendor-Provided Statistics." *The Journal of Academic Librarianship* 29(1): 16-22; Luther, Judy. 2000. White Paper on Electronic Journal Usage Statistics. Council on Library and Information Resources, Washington, D.C.; Stemper, James A. and Janice M. Jaguszewski. 2003. "Usage Statistics for Electronic Journals: An Analysis of Local and Vendor Counts." *Collection Management* 28(4): 3-22.

6. Joanna, Duy. 2004. "Usage Data: Issues and Challenges for Electronic Resource Collection Management," In *E-Serials Collection Management–Transitions, Trends, and Technicalities.* Ed. David C. Fowler, pp. 111-139.

7. The Hanford technical Library Web site is publicly accessible at http://libraryweb.pnl.gov. The HTL OPAC is available at http://libcat.pnl.gov.

8. Duy and Vaughan, "Usage Data," 17.

9. Townley, Charles T., and Leigh Murray. 1999. "Use-Based Criteria for Selecting and Retaining Electronic Information: A Case Study." *Information Technology and Libraries* 18(1): 32-39.

10. Wonsik, Shim, Kurt Murphy, and Dennis Brunning. 2004 "Usage Statistics for Electronic Services and Resources: A Library Perspective," In *Online Usage: A Publisher's Guide.* Ed. Bernard Rous, pp. 34-46.

doi:10.1300/J123v53S09_09

Chapter 9

Usage Statistics of Electronic Government Resources

Susan L. Kendall
Celia Bakke

INTRODUCTION

The San Jose State University (SJSU) Library, a participant in the United States Government Printing Office Federal Depository Library Program (FDLP), has maintained and provided access to Federal government publications for the campus and local community since the early 1960s. The FDLP began the transition from tangible (print) publications to electronic format in 1994, and now, ten years later, 66 percent of new titles added to the FDLP were electronic online titles.[1] The SJSU Library online catalog, as the primary access point to the Library's resources, reflects traditional cataloging practice in which full bibliographic records are included for all items. With the emergence of electronic resources, the SJSU Library recognized the continuing importance of having all publications and formats represented in the catalog. Therefore, the Library provides bibliographic records for all formats of government publications, rather than relying solely on links for electronic government resources from local Web pages.

Usage statistics help to make informed decisions concerning collection development and management, library instruction, and public ser-

[Haworth co-indexing entry note]: "Usage Statistics of Electronic Government Resources." Kendall, Susan L., and Celia Bakke. Co-published simultaneously in *The Serials Librarian* (The Haworth Information Press, an imprint of The Haworth Press, Inc.) Vol. 53, Supplement No. 9, 2007, pp. 161-172; and: *Usage Statistics of E-Serials* (ed: David C. Fowler) The Haworth Information Press, an imprint of The Haworth Press, Inc., 2007, pp. 161-172. Single or multiple copies of this article are available for a fee from The Haworth Document Delivery Service [1-800-HAWORTH, 9:00 a.m. - 5:00 p.m. (EST). E-mail address: docdelivery@haworthpress.com].

Available online at http://ser.haworthpress.com
© 2007 by The Haworth Press, Inc. All rights reserved.
doi:10.1300/J123v53S09_10

vice. But the catalog does not reflect the level of use of electronic resources. The SJSU Library developed a software program to capture these usage statistics for electronic government resources. The following section examines several articles that address either providing access to electronic resources in the online catalog or usage studies of government publications.

LITERATURE REVIEW

Studies concerning the use of government publications and category of users, prior to the availability of electronic publications, have been covered in depth by Margaret A. Renton in *Government Publications: A Comparative Use Study* (1991). Renton identifies several reasons for collecting usage statistics. "Such data can be useful for collection development and storage decisions" She also notes, "Data by [Superintendent of Documents] SuDoc class and borrower are also useful for planning bibliographic instruction services." Renton suggests that inclusion of government publications in the catalog would increase their usage, regardless of their publication date.

Although an essay by Eric Lease Morgan, "Adding Internet Resources to our Opacs" (1995) does not discuss government publications, he advocates adding bibliographic records for Internet-based electronic serials to online library catalogs, to emphasize not just ownership but access (Morgan, 1995). The concept of providing free access to Federal government publications is the core of the Federal Library Depository Program. Besides access, Morgan identifies several issues concerning Internet resources in the catalog. Some of these issues, such as inaccessible URLs, are still of importance even today. In 1995, the concept of a persistent URL was just being developed. Also, at that time, most libraries had public terminals, which were limited in their ability to access the Internet. Today, computers serve as public access terminals that allow for much more diversified use. The Internet itself has also evolved with the addition of graphical user interfaces.

An article by Burke, Gerald, Germain, and Van Ullen discussed incorporating free Internet-based resources into the online catalog. The authors questioned whether addition of this type of resource might diminish the accuracy and reliability of the catalog. Their study identified an error rate of 14.58 percent for free URL resources and 7.57 percent for inaccessible Federal government PURL (Persistent Uniform Resource Locator) sites (Burke et al., 2003). Although the error rate for the

PURLs is of concern for the profession, generally, the inclusion of electronic government resources in the catalog is critical for access, which is based on the transition by the United States Government Printing Office from the tangible formats to the electronic environment.

Despite inaccessible PURLs, the addition of these electronic government resources to the online catalog enhances access, consistent with the principle of collocation. Brown's article, "Knowing Where They're Going" (2004), focuses on issues related to measuring online document use. The reasons he related for capturing usage statistics included URL maintenance, collection management, and outreach strategies (Brown, 2004). The need for these statistics led Brown to develop a software program that identifies use of resources by agency, title, and Superintendent of Documents (SuDocs) classification number.

SAN JOSE STATE UNIVERSITY LIBRARY

In August 2003, the SJSU Library, in collaboration with the San Jose Public Library (SJPL), opened the doors to a new eight-story building, the Dr. Martin Luther King Jr. Library. The five-year planning process that preceded this collaborative agreement determined the configuration of the services and collections. Although each institution remains as an independent, distinct organization reporting to and under the auspices of the university and the city of San Jose respectively, one of the initial goals of the collaboration was to provide a seamless learning experience for both the university and public communities. Therefore, service points and collections were merged when possible, while others remained separate. For example, there is a single service point and print collection for the Reference section. Periodicals services and collections are also merged. Services that remain separate include a laptop program for the SJSU community and university course reserves. SJPL continues to provide services to children and young adults, and to maintain a popular collection of materials in more than fifty languages. The circulating collection of the SJSU Library is classified in the Library of Congress classification system, while SJPL's collection is classified in Dewey. These collections are housed on separate floors. The SJSU Library is designated as a depository for both federal and state government publications, while the public library focuses on collecting city and county government publications.

The SJSU Library provides services and scholarly resources that meet teaching, learning, and research needs of a community of approximately 28,000 students and 1,100 faculty members. San Jose State is a metropolitan university, with the majority of the students commuting to class rather than residing on campus or in the neighboring environs. The average student is twenty-six years of age and has work and/or family responsibilities. The university supports distance learning programs, and student enrollment in distance education classes has increased each semester since 1999. Therefore, all SJSU students welcome the ability to access electronic databases, journal articles, and government resources from off campus.

FEDERAL DEPOSITORY LIBRARY PROGRAM AT SJSU

The FDLP in the United States has had a long history of serving local communities. Initially, resolutions of the years 1857 and 1858 identified the need to send copies of congressional publications to selected libraries. The Printing Act of 1895 (28 Stat.601) expanded the distribution categories to include federal agencies' publications. This act also established the concept of free public access to government publications. Free access was later codified in the United States Code as a part of Title 44 (44 USC 1911).

Congress passed the Depository Library Act of 1962 (82 Stat. 1282), which increased the number of libraries eligible to participate in the depository program. Previously, only one library for each congressional district was authorized as a depository.[2] The SJSU Library took advantage of this opportunity and applied for membership in the FDLP. The library has served as the depository for California's 16th Congressional District since 1962.

The SJSU Library is a partial depository library, that is, a library that selects a percentage of the items published by the Federal government. The library has, until recently, selected about 53 percent of these publications. With federal agencies offering more digital resources, SJSU Library is currently (as of 2005) at a 62 percent selection rate.

The SJSU Library had limited the selection of government publications to items that corresponded to the needs of the university curriculum. The librarians could easily identify the courses that would be supported by specific federal agency publications. With the merger of the university and public libraries, the selection of government publication titles was expanded to include subjects that would serve the local community.

THE PROBLEM OF TRACKING ELECTRONIC
GOVERNMENT RESOURCES

FDLP libraries must provide free access to the federal government publications as mandated by Title 44, Chapter 19 of the U.S. Code (44 USC 1911). With this requirement in mind, many libraries have included bibliographic records for tangible government publications in their online catalogs to provide access. The SJSU Library decided to also add bibliographic records for the electronic government resources. The addition of these records provides the same ease of access as exists for the tangible resources. Circulation statistics and in-house "pickup counts" identify the usage of tangible government publications. However, tracking the usage of the electronic resources is more difficult.

Burke, Gerald, Germain, and Van Ullen questioned the validity of incorporating electronic resources into the catalog. Would bibliographic information, which might contain an inaccessible link, be a disservice to the patron? Would statistics on usage justify the inclusion of these bibliographic records (Burke et al., 2003)?

At the SJSU Library, discussion of adding government resources with PURLs to the online catalog raised the question concerning the viability of the catalog in the age of such Internet powerhouses as Google and Yahoo! Were students, faculty, and community members still using the online catalog to locate information?

The SJSU Library currently uses Innovative Interfaces' integrated library system (ILS). The online catalog provides standard access points such as name, title, and Library of Congress subject headings, as well as keyword searching and limiting capabilities. In 1995, in order to provide bibliographic records for tangible government resources, the Library began a subscription to the Marcive service that supplies these records. In 2000, the Library determined that the inclusion of records for electronic government resources would be of benefit to the users and subscribed to the Marcive service, Documents without Shelves.

The SJSU government publications coordinator believed that tracking the usage of these electronic government resources was necessary. These statistics would identify if, indeed, the catalog was used to locate government information in the electronic format. Another objective was to generate a report for the university librarians of the titles that patrons were retrieving. This report could assist librarians in collection development decisions and in library instruction design.

In 2003, the government publications coordinator attended the Fall Annual Depository Library Conference. A presentation on tracking electronic government publications was given by Christopher C. Brown from the University of Denver.[3] Brown developed a software program to track usage of electronic government resources via the online catalog. His program uses Microsoft Access and also requires a working knowledge of ColdFusion software. SJSU librarians discussed the tracking concepts and the possibility of implementing his software program. Unlike the University of Denver, the SJSU Library does not have a government publications department. SJSU Library elected to design a program that automatically generates reports. This program would provide the government publications coordinator an easy way to generate reports that documented the use of electronic government resources. Also, the program would require minimal data manipulation by the Technical Services unit.

METHODOLOGY

The initial step was to establish a design team that included two key individuals: the database analyst from the Technical Services unit and a programmer from the Library's Information Technology department. The database analyst was knowledgeable of cataloging practices, the MARC (Machine-Readable Cataloging) format, Marcive services, and programming languages, and was experienced in working with large files of bibliographic records. The programmer was skilled in writing ColdFusion code. Previously, these two individuals successfully collaborated to generate a monthly list of new titles added to the collection that was mounted on a library Web page. This new titles list is automatically updated. It was assumed that similar strategies could be applied to capturing usage statistics for electronic government resources.

In conjunction with the program design, it was necessary to identify how to search and sort the statistics into meaningful reports. The team decided to capture data from two fields: SuDocs number (MARC field 086) and title (MARC field 245 $a). Bibliographic records may have multiple 086 fields, but only the first instance is captured, that is, the current SuDocs number. The title field is primarily used as an identifier. Because the URL address (MARC 856 field) is not searchable in the local online catalog, the team needed a way to connect the URL to a specific bibliographic record. The proposed solution was to add a subfield to the URL that contained the unique local bibliographic record number (Bib ID record number). It was necessary to test this proposed solution before trying large file manipulation. After a successful test, the database analyst confirmed that she was able to add the Bib ID record number to a URL subfield for a large file of records. The programmer determined that she would need approximately four weeks to create the ColdFusion code. She also created the URL prefix that captures the usage data for each specific title. The database analyst identified all existing records for government resources containing a URL link. It was estimated that it would require about one week to add the URL prefix with the unique Bib ID record number to these records. The database analyst also created a mapping table that automatically added the prefix when Marcive records were downloaded into the local catalog. She then modified the URL by adding the unique Bib ID record number.

The team initially met in early June 2004, and created a timeline for the project with the goal of completing all the steps, including testing, by August 1, 2004. The program was mounted and debugged by August 1, 2004, and the use count officially began on August 3, 2004. The statistics were mounted on the Library's Web-based server that can only be accessed by staff.

FINDINGS

The team continued to test the program during August 2004, and identified and resolved a few minor problems. There were 193 accesses to electronic government resources via the online catalog during August 2004. The Government Publications Coordinator was concerned because the number was so low, but the fall semester did not begin until the end of that month and there was an expectation that class assignments would prompt greater use of these resources.

While the program does not identify the status of the user, whether a student or community patron, it was believed that perhaps the access pattern would reflect the university semester schedule. If this assumption was correct, there would be low access at the beginning (September) and end of the semester (December). October and November would reflect higher use, when students were researching assignments (Figure 9.1). In September, there were 386 accesses and in December,

FIGURE 9.1. Screen shot of November 2004. Titles accessed sorted in SuDocs sequence. Reprinted with permission.

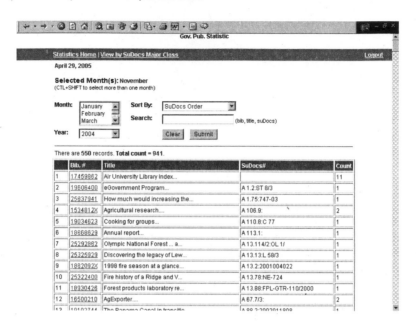

there were 399 accesses. The December 2004 statistics were interesting in that the university classes concluded on December 9, 2004, and the university closed from December 24, 2004, to January 2, 2005. The peak semester months did indeed have significant increases in use. In October 2004, there were 826 accesses, and in November 2004, there were 941 accesses.

Library instructional efforts and the subsequent research process for papers and projects may account for the increase in usage. The SJSU librarians teach many instructional classes at the beginning of each semester designed to assist students in their research. Emphasis is placed on using authoritative sources, such as the online catalog and article databases. As noted previously, usage statistics more than doubled in October and November.

January 26, 2005, was the first day of instruction for the spring semester. Once again, usage has followed the pattern established in the previous semester. January 2005 statistics show 302 accesses as compared to 193 accesses in August. As the semester progressed, February 2005 had 577 accesses and March 2005 statistics increased to 789 (Figures 9.2 and 9.3).

CONCLUSIONS

Usage statistics answered the question whether patrons were using the online catalog to locate government information. Usage during

FIGURE 9.2. Usage statistics.

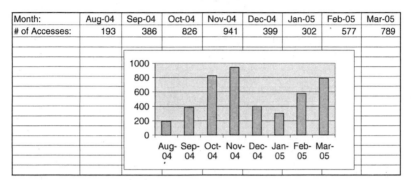

Month:	Aug-04	Sep-04	Oct-04	Nov-04	Dec-04	Jan-05	Feb-05	Mar-05
# of Accesses:	193	386	826	941	399	302	577	789

FIGURE 9.3. Screen shot of November 2004. Titles accessed sorted in alphabetic sequence. Reprinted with permission.

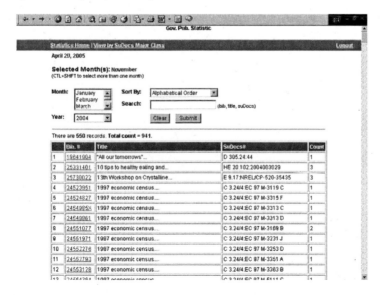

the fall and spring semesters was higher than usage during non-semester times. One could assume that the major users of these electronic resources were university students and faculty.

In addition to library instruction, each university librarian is responsible for collection development in several disciplines. One objective was to provide these librarians with a monthly report on the titles accessed. This report would assist the librarians in collection management decisions as well as library instruction design.

In April 2005, the Government Publications Coordinator assigned SuDocs numbers to each subject discipline. The health sciences librarian was asked if she would be interested in participating in a pilot project to receive a monthly list of titles in the area of health sciences. This librarian was selected for several reasons. First, there are many electronic government resources in health sciences. Second, this librarian is also responsible for working with the university's distance learning programs. She is in daily contact with off-site students and faculty and recognizes of the importance of electronic resources. The first list for health sciences was produced. It included titles, federal agencies, and numbers of accesses per title. Once a routine for harvesting this information is established, other university librarians will be contacted concerning the availability of these reports.

It is assumed that during summer, use will be predominantly by the community, as SJSU offers limited summer sessions with reduced enrollments. This assumption is derived from the usage patterns during non-semester times in August 2004, and January 2005 (see Figure 9.4). The summer of 2005 will provide a greater span of time to evaluate use of electronic government resources. If this pattern of less use during non-semester sessions continues, this would seem to indicate a need for increased outreach to the community. The next step would be to develop and implement an outreach program and then to evaluate usage patterns. This outreach would include instruction in the use of online catalog and the relevance of electronic government resources. In addition, research is needed to identify titles relevant to the community's information needs. The current title selection profile should then be evaluated and, if necessary, modified to incorporate the needs of the community with those of the university.

FIGURE 9.4. Screen shot of November 2004. Titles accessed sorted in highest number sequence. Reprinted with permission.

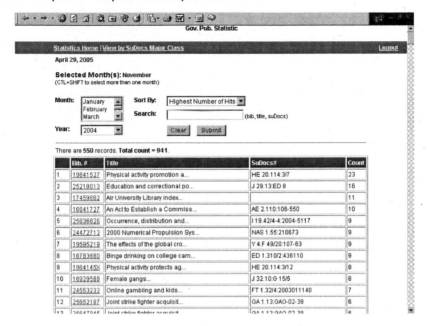

NOTES

1. Judith C. Russell, *The Federal Depository Library Program: Current and Future Challenges of the Electronic Transition.* (http://www.gpoaccess.gov/about/speeches/062003_alatoronto.pdf)

2. Joe Morehead. *Introduction to United States Government Information Sources.* 5th edition. (Englewood, Colo.: Libraries Unlimited, Inc. 1996. pp. 38-39).

3. Christopher C. Brown, *Statistics for Online Document Use.* (http://www.gpo.gov/su_docs/fdlp/pubs/proceedings/03prot.html)

REFERENCES

Bauer, Kathleen. "Who Goes There? Measuring Library Web Site Usage." *Online* 24, no. 1 (2000): 25-31.

Beam, Joan T., and Nora S. Copeland. "Electronic Resources in Union Catalogs: URLs and Accessibility Issues." *Serials Review* 27, no. 3/4 (2001): 33-47.

Bertot, John Carlo, Charles R. McClure, William E. Moen, and Jeffrey Rubin. "Web Usage Statistics: Measurement Issues and Analytical Techniques." *Government Information Quarterly* 14, no. 4 (1997): 373-396.

Blecic, Deborah D., Joan B. Giscella, and Stephen E. Wiberley, Jr. "The Measurement of Use of Web-Based Information Resources: An Early Look at Vendor-Supplied Data." *College & Research Libraries* 62, no. 5 (2001): 434-453.

Brown, Christopher. "Knowing Where They're Going: Statistics for Online Government Document Access through the OPAC." *Online Information Review* 28, no. 6 (2004): 396-409.

Brown, Christopher C. "Statistics for Online Document Use." http://www.gpo. gov/su_docs/fdlp/pubs/proceedings/03prot.html

Burke, Gerald, Carol Anne Germain, and Mary K. Van Ullen. "URLs in the OPAC: Integrating or Disintegrating Research Libraries' Catalogs." *Journal of Academic Librarianship* 29, no. 5 (2003): 290-297.

Goldberg, Tyler, Melissa Laning, and Weiling Liu. "Statistically Challenged: The Need for an Electronic Resources Measurement Standard." *Kentucky Libraries* 67, no. 1 (2003): 4-9.

Hernon, Peter. *Use of Government Publications by Social Scientists.* Norwood, NJ: Ablex, 1979.

Hoffman, Luise, and Ronald M. Schmidt. "The Cataloging of Electronic Serials in the Union Catalog of the North Rhine–Westphalian Library Network." *Serials Librarian* 35, no. 3 (1999): 123-129.

Jana, Sangharmitra, and Supratim Chatterjee. "Quantifying Web site Visits Using Web Statistics: an Extended Cybermetrics Study." *Online Information Review* 28, no. 3 (2004): 191-199.

McClure, Charles R., and Cynthia L. Lopata. *Assessing the Academic Networked Environment: Strategies and Options.* Washington, D.C.: Published by the Association of Research Libraries for the Coalition for Networked Information, 1996.

Morehead, Joe. *Introduction to United States Government Information Sources.* Englewood, CO: Libraries Unlimited, 1996.

Morgan, Eric Lease. "Adding Internet Resources to our Opacs." *Serials Review* 21, no. 4 (1995): 70-72.

Peterson, Christina A. "The Martin Luther King, Jr. Library: Joint-Use Library as an Urban Educational Corridor." *Metropolitan Universities* 15, no. 3 (2004): 30-40.

Renton, Margaret A. "Government Publications: A Comparative Use Study." *Government Publications Review* 18 (1991): 353-370.

Russell, Judith C. "The Federal Depository Library Program: Current and Future Challenges of the Electronic Transition." http://www.gpoaccess.gov/about/speeches/062003_alatoronto.pdf (accessed on January 12, 2005).

Schuyler, Michael. "Cutting-Edge Statistics." *Computers in Libraries* 21, no. 3 (2001): 51-53.

Shim, Wonsik, and Charles R. McClure. "Data Needs and Use of Electronic Resources and Services at Academic Research Libraries." *Libraries and the Academy* 2, no. 2 (2002): 217-236.

Wilson, Rita L., and Grace A. York. "Government Resources on the Web: Will It Change Public Services?" *Library Hi Tech* 61, no. 1 (1998): 60-70.

Xue, Susan. "Web Usage Statistics and Web Site Evaluation: A Case Study of a Government Publications Library Web Site." *Online Information Review* 28, no. 3 (2004): 180-190.

doi:10.1300/J123v53S09_10

Chapter 10

The Implications of Usage Statistics As an Economic Factor in Scholarly Communications

Heather Morrison

THE NEED FOR, AND DEVELOPMENT OF, USAGE STATISTICS

There are, and probably always will be, real needs for usage statistics for information in the electronic format. Authors, publishers, and funding authorities, as well as libraries themselves, need to know whether or not costly resources are being used. A lack of usage can alert a library to a resource that has not been set up properly. Low usage rates may indicate a resource that needs better promotion. High usage is an indication of the value of a resource to the library's users. The timing of usage statistics tells us the hours of the day that library users are active, which can inform other decisions such as scheduling of virtual reference hours.

Usage statistics can also provide information to assist us to better understand users and their information-seeking behavior and needs. Through usage statistics, Ohiolink discovered that about 15 to 35 percent of the titles received through the "big deals," which no Ohiolink library had previously subscribed to, were actively used (Gatten and

[Haworth co-indexing entry note]: "The Implications of Usage Statistics As an Economic Factor in Scholarly Communications." Morrison, Heather. Co-published simultaneously in *The Serials Librarian* (The Haworth Information Press, an imprint of The Haworth Press, Inc.) Vol. 53, Supplement No. 9, 2007, pp. 173-182; and: *Usage Statistics of E-Serials* (ed: David C. Fowler) The Haworth Information Press, an imprint of The Haworth Press, Inc., 2007, pp. 173-182. Single or multiple copies of this article are available for a fee from The Haworth Document Delivery Service [1-800-HAWORTH, 9:00 a.m. - 5:00 p.m. (EST). E-mail address: docdelivery@haworthpress.com].

Available online at http://ser.haworthpress.com
doi:10.1300/J123v53S09_11

Sanville 2004). Statistics have helped the open access Stanford Encyclopedia of Philosophy (SEP) to make a case for funding for ongoing open access, by providing evidence of heavy usage, and also by providing details about who is using the resource. In other words, statistics indicate that the SEP is used not only by the professional philosophy researchers for whom it was designed, but also by many departments across many campuses; thus, the case was made that the SEP was a good resource, and that libraries, as well as philosophy departments, should financially support the project (Zalta et al. 2005).

Important strides have been made toward the development and standardization of usage statistics for electronic resources. This is largely due to the efforts of the International Coalition of Library Consortia (ICOLC) and the COUNTER (Counting Online Usage of Networked Electronic Resources) project (http://www.projectcounter.org/). ICOLC developed a set of guidelines, "Guidelines for Statistical Measures of Usage of Web-Based Information Resources" (ICOLC 2001). COUNTER further developed the ICOLC guidelines, and provided a means of auditing compliance with the standards.

Thanks to these efforts, librarians are now beginning to see usage statistics based on these standards that are comparable across resources and platforms. A great amount of work needs to be done, however. There are still many vendors and publishers who still need to either adopt usage statistics reporting mechanisms or bring the quality of their statistics up to the COUNTER standard. Nevertheless, there are currently enough quality usage statistics available that this is now a factor in making financial decisions, such as the cancellation and retention of journals.

The remainder of this chapter will explore the potential impact of usage statistics as an economic factor in scholarly communications. Selection and cancellation decisions based upon usage statistics may have one set of implications when viewed from the perspective of the individual library or library consortium. The same decisions may have a totally different set of implications when viewed from the perspective of scholarly communications as a whole. The availability of quality usage statistics raises the possibility of developing pricing models based upon usage. Factoring in usage has some advantages in developing pricing models in the short term, as a transitional measure. In the long term, usage-based pricing is not optimal as an economic basis for scholarly communications, most notably because usage-based pricing provides an economic disincentive to use. For example, usage-based pricing creates a situation where a cash-strapped university could save money by canceling research-based assignments and/or information literacy programs at early undergraduate levels.

USAGE STATISTICS AND THE INDIVIDUAL LIBRARY OR LIBRARY CONSORTIUM

Usage statistics makes it possible to calculate the cost-per-use on a database or title-by-title basis. For instance, this kind of cost analysis has been very useful for Drexel University in their shift from print to electronic-only journals. Carol Montgomery, the Dean of Libraries Emeritus and research professor at the College of Information Science and Technology at Drexel, has done a comparison of the cost-per-use for e-journals (for Drexel, these averaged from one dollar to six dollars per use) to the cost-per-use of print (e-journals averaged two dollars per use; unbound print issues were six dollars per use, and bound print volumes were thirty dollars per use) (Montgomery 2004). This cost-per-use analysis facilitated the move from print to electronic-only for Drexel University.

Hahn and Faulkner (2002) have shown how usage-based metrics can be used by the individual library, not only to make informed decisions about cancellations and help faculty understand cancellation decisions, but also to develop benchmarks to help determine a rationale for future purchases. Gatten and Sanville (2004) analyzed usage statistics at individual library and consortial levels, and found that aggregated usage statistics are a reasonable method for a consortium to retreat from the "big deal" if financial, or other, factors made that necessary.

This approach to selection and cancellation makes a great deal of sense at the individual library or consortium level. If libraries cannot afford to purchase everything, it makes a great amount of sense to prioritize the titles that library patrons are actually using.

USAGE STATISTICS AND SCHOLARLY COMMUNICATIONS AS A WHOLE

What happens to scholarly communications as a whole, if library decisions based on usage become standard, and if journals continue to rely on subscription income? Consider the implications of such decisions in relation to open access, conservatism in science (that is, the tendency to favor a predominant viewpoint and filter out new evidence that does not fit), important but less popular or less-adequately funded academic areas, small research communities, and titles in different languages.

Over ninety percent of publishers allow authors to self-archive a copy of their own work (SHERPA 2005). Authors' tendencies to self-archive vary by discipline. Physics, for example, has a strong tradition of self-archiving, starting with preprints, in the arXiv e-print archive (http://www.arxiv.org). In some subdisciplines, such as high-energy physics, the rate of author self-archiving approaches 100 percent. Researchers will be likely to have read many of the articles as preprints, before their formal publication. It then makes sense that this would have an impact on usage statistics for purchased resources. In physics, this has not made any difference to the subscriptions. However, is it possible that in other disciplines a failure to take into account the usage rates of articles that are openly accessible could result in many libraries canceling journals, even though the articles are very much used?

Thomas Kuhn, in "The Structure of Scientific Revolutions" (Kuhn 1962/1970), described one form of scientific advance as a process of revolution from one paradigm, or set of beliefs, to the next. Concepts that fit within a prevailing paradigm are readily accepted, while concepts that do not fit are considered to be anomalies, and thus discounted. Picture then, the usage statistics of a journal focusing on topics that fit within a prevailing paradigm, as compared with the usage statistics of a new journal startup reflecting the concepts of what, all else being equal, could become the next paradigm at some point in the future. It seems plausible that the usage statistics would be higher for journals that fit within the accepted paradigm and lower for journals outside of that paradigm. If usage statistics are used as the basis for selection and retention decisions, could one type of result be a reinforcement of an inherent bias toward conservative concepts in science?

At any given time, some areas of scholarly endeavor are likely to be more popular and/or better funded than other endeavors, regardless of their underlying merit. A current example is the present emphasis on science, technology, and medicine, with relatively less emphasis and funding for the humanities. This does not necessarily reflect any inherent lesser significance of the humanities, but rather reflects current societal values favoring more financial support of technologically based fields.

Within any given discipline, some areas are likely to be more popular or better funded than other areas. Consider, for example, the implications of making decisions about canceling medical journals at the time when a particular health crisis is occurring. For example, did outbreaks of Severe Acute Respiratory Syndrome (SARS) have an impact on the usage of biomedical journals dealing with the basic science of virology? If the world economy took a downturn during a similar crisis, and many libraries were canceling journals as a result, would these journals be protected, perhaps at the expense of other basic biomedical journals of equal importance in the longer term? What if an economic downturn occurred at a time when the world's attention was on nonviral medical factors–could key journals in virology be canceled, perhaps hampering the progress of research, just before the next viral crisis? These are cautionary questions that library managers must keep in mind when utilizing usage statistics, without considering other factors, in their collection development decisions.

For a variety of reasons, the global research community in any given discipline may be small or large, depending on various factors. Heart disease, for example, is a major killer throughout the world. The size of the research community that is investigating the causes, prevention, and treatment of the disease is very large. Core heart journals are likely to be well used, wherever they are available. Many other illnesses are less common or occur primarily in isolated geographic areas. The research communities in these areas are likely to be much smaller, and journals devoted to such less-common problems are likely to be more vulnerable to cancellations based on usage statistics. If journals in such a geographic area are relying on subscription income, and many libraries cancel their subscriptions due to similar low usage patterns, the journals may cease to exist. Opportunities to publish in these areas could decrease, which could lead to fewer researchers pursuing research in these areas. The end result could be a decrease in diversity of research, which has a concrete impact on real people and in many fields, such as medicine.

Usage-based selection decisions have a particular significance in relation to titles in languages other than English. A conversation with the author's professors at the University of Alberta in the 1970s may be instructive. It was during the time of the Cold War and a serials cancellations process was underway. The debate at the time was about the cancellation of journal titles produced behind the Iron Curtain. From the usage point of view, this made a great deal of sense. These journals were written in languages (e.g., Russian and Ukrainian) that few people at the University of Alberta could read. Most of those who could read these languages were foreign language specialists, and not likely to be interested in or sufficiently familiar with the scholarly disciplines these journals covered, to find any particular journal title useful. Using articles in these journals required an expensive translation process that was rarely undertaken. This scenario was no doubt repeated at research libraries throughout North America. When the library is focusing on the needs of the University of Alberta and its library clients, canceling journals that receive little or no usage makes eminent sense. What happens, however, when a large number of libraries, all facing the same financial pressures and coping with the same serials crisis, make basically the same cancellation decisions? What happens to journals, publishers, and authors when many libraries choose to target their particular journals for cancellation? What happens to the desire for cross-cultural communication, keenly felt during the Cold War, when one of the most hopeful avenues, scholar-to-scholar communication, decreases or disappears?

This is not merely a historical problem. Given the difficulties libraries are facing in purchasing even the most necessary scholarly information for our clients, how are librarians, as a profession, doing today with collecting journals in other languages from other countries and cultures? In the future, with China expected to become an economic superpower, will important research journals be published in Chinese only? If so, will libraries with few Chinese readers simply not purchase these journals, anticipating little use?

There is more than one approach to this question of language and journals. Libraries could decline to collect titles in languages that the majority of its patrons do not understand. Given sufficient financial resources, libraries could provide translation services. Another option would be for our educational institutions at various levels to choose to prioritize and strengthen the teaching of different languages, perhaps as a requirement, along with other academic disciplines. This latter option not only offers the potential for enriching our understanding of the world, but it also provides us with a better foundation for competing in a future world where important research results may not necessarily be uniformly reported in one language only.

To summarize this section, if journals are relying on subscription income for financial survival, and if libraries faced with an ongoing serials crisis are making selection and cancellation decisions on the basis of usage statistics, there are very serious potential implications for scholarly research. These kinds of decisions could lead to the cancellation of journals whose articles are well used, but in their open access form. This approach could also lead to a more conservative, popularity-based scholasticism that is less diverse in topic, language, and culture. While research is needed to confirm these possibilities, there are enough obvious reasons to give a pause for thought before too many libraries begin to rely solely upon usage statistics in their selection and cancellation decisions.

If these assumptions are correct, the collective effect of these kinds of decisions, which make so much sense at the individual library level, potentially have a very unfortunate effect on scholarly communications as a whole. What, then, is the remedy? Does it make sense for libraries to include consideration of the overall impact on scholarly communications in their collection development policies?

The good news is that open access not only can, but almost certainly would, counter most of these trends. The new paradigm might make it difficult to publish in traditional journals, or to start up a new traditional-style journal with an existing publisher. With open source publishing software available, this research community can easily begin their own open access journal and leave the question of reading and accepting their ideas with the reader. The issues are more difficult for research communities whose journals may be subject to cancellation; however, converting to an open access model or starting up new journals is an option for these communities as well. Journals in languages that are less likely to attract a significant subscription base can opt for open access as the best means to enhance the impact of their authors.

THE DANGER OF USAGE-BASED PRICING

The ready availability of quality, reliable usage-based data raises the possibility of pricing based upon usage. At face value, usage-based pricing does seem fair. Those who use a resource most heavily pay the most and smaller users pay less. Indeed, there is much to say for considering usage when developing pricing models. Usage data can be useful, for example, to determine the relative value of a resource for different types or sizes of libraries, and price accordingly. One example, using a full-time equivalent (FTE)-based pricing model, would involve comparing the relative usage of resources at two-year colleges to that at four-year universities. A resource that is used somewhat less at two-year colleges could be weighted to 75 percent FTE for colleges, while a resource that is used a great deal less at two-year colleges could be weighted at 50 percent FTE for these colleges.

There is much to be said for offering usage-based pricing, or the "pay by the drink" model, on an optional basis, when some libraries are unable to afford the required subscriptions. For obvious reasons, this is much better than no access at all.

However, if a pricing model based on usage were to become prevalent, there are some real dangers, as there are disincentives to use with usage-based pricing.

As Andrew Odlyzkow, the director of the Digital Technology Center at the University of Minnesota, characterized it when referring to Internet usage pricing models: "Usage-sensitive pricing is effective. The problem is that many of its effects are undesirable. In particular, such pricing lowers demand, often by substantial factors" (Odlyzkow 2001). For example, when America Online (AOL) switched from usage-based pricing to flat pricing for its users in 1996, usage tripled. This effect has been replicated in other countries and cultures. Research has shown that even small charges discourage Internet usage, even if the charges are small enough that even heavy usage would be less than flat pricing.

While this research is based on Internet, rather than on print information resources, and on individuals rather than libraries, it makes sense that the same principles would apply to libraries and institutions as well. Picture, for example, a cash-strapped university looking for ways to cut the budget. With usage-based pricing, eliminating research papers at the first- or second-year level, eliminating the hands-on or exercise-based portion of an information literacy program, or scrapping the information literacy program altogether, would all be methods to achieve cost savings.

If the cost of use is known, there is a danger that a cash-strapped library will pass the cost along to the user, resulting in the direct disincentives to the user that Odlyzkow describes. This has been the tendency for many libraries with interlibrary loans, an area where libraries themselves have implemented usage-based fees deliberately, in order to limit demand (Budd 1989). Clinton (1999) discusses how libraries in the United Kingdom have implemented user fees for interlibrary loans to discourage what they see as indiscriminate use of the service.

With a print-based collection, users are free to browse to their heart's content. As a researcher, the author has browsed extensively, often in journals not obviously related to the research topic, looking for new approaches or research methods, or possibly knowledge from one discipline that might have implications in another. If libraries move to electronic-only collections and charge on the basis of usage, this kind of cross-disciplinary research might well be perceived as costly. Readers and researchers might be discouraged from browsing for the sake of curiosity, and be asked to limit their reading to what might be clearly justifiable economically. Learning, and certain types of research, such as interdisciplinary research, would suffer.

To conclude, pricing based upon usage does not appear to be optimal for scholarly research, due to the likelihood of this pricing model discouraging use.

CONCLUSIONS

There are real needs for quality usage statistics, and it is encouraging to see some developments in this area, thanks largely to ICOLC and Project COUNTER. There are some benefits to considering usage in the economics of scholarly communication, particularly for the individual library, and as an informational measure to determine levels for other pricing models.

However, there are some real potential pitfalls if usage becomes prevalent as the basis for selection and cancellation decisions. There is reason to suspect that the cumulative effect of such decisions, made separately by many libraries, could create a tendency toward an overall increase in scholarly conservatism; the loss of important, but less popular or less well-funded areas of research; detrimental effects on smaller research communities; and less linguistic and cultural diversity. Journals allowing open access options such as self-archiving also could be adversely affected. Happily, open access not only can, but also almost certainly will, counter many of the unfortunate effects of such decisions. The question of whether broader implications for scholarly communications, as a whole, should be incorporated into collection development policies is also being raised.

The possibility that usage statistics will form the basis of a usage-based pricing system has also been examined and found to be inadvisable, as usage-based pricing tends to discourage usage.

Economics is concerned with the allocation of scarce resources, which have potentially competing alternative uses. This is one of the most basic principles of economics. Consumption has an impact in determining what is produced, and for whom. Raising prices of products can control consumption by consumers who have either less desire for a particular product or less ability to pay (Allen 1967).

The scholarly journal article in the electronic form does not fit within the realm of economics, as there is no reason to see a scholarly journal article as a scarce resource. An openly accessible article can be downloaded by millions, and its value will not at all be depleted. There are other kinds of goods that can gain value by creating a false scarcity; for example, commercial movies in electronic form. This does not fit with the model for scholarly knowledge, however; scholarly knowledge, unlike goods and services produced primarily for profit, gains in value the more it is used.

Science works in a series of steps, or blocks, which build upon one another. If one researcher finds a next step, the more researchers there are who read the results and who build on them, the faster that the research community as a whole can advance to the next step. Consider, for example, the cancer researcher. When research is concluded and the results are published, we could be a step closer to a cure, treatment, diagnosis, or basic understanding of how cancer works. The more people there are who find out about this step and move forward to the next step, the sooner we can all reach the ultimate goal (a cure, treatment, etc.). There is no value to be gained for the researcher in withholding this information. There is nothing to be gained from a pricing model that will result in reasons for discouraging potential users from reading an article.

REFERENCES

Allen, C.L. *The Framework of Price Theory.* Belmont, California: Wadsworth Publishing Company, 1967.

Budd, John M. "It's not the principle, it's the money of the thing." *The Journal of Academic Librarianship,* September 15, (1989): 218-222.

Clinton, Pat. "Charging users for interlibrary loans in UK university libraries–A new survey." *Interlending & Document Supply* 27:1 (1999): 17.

Gatten, Jeffrey N., and Tom Sanville. "An Orderly Retreat from the Big Deal: Is it Possible for Consortia?" *D-Lib Magazine* 10:10 (October 2004). http://www.dlib.org/dlib/october04/gatten/10gatten.html

Hahn, Karla L. and Lila A. Faulkner. "Evaluative Usage-based Metrics for the Selection of E-Journals." *College & Research Libraries* 63:3 (May 2002): 215-217.

ICOLC. Guidelines for Statistical Measures of Usage of Web-Based Information Resources (Update: December 2001). http://www.library.yale.edu/consortia/2001webstats.htm

Kuhn, Thomas. *The Structure of Scientific Revolutions.* 2nd edition. Chicago: University of Chicago Press, 1962/1970.

Montgomery, Carol. Presentation. XXIV Annual Charleston Conference: All the World's a Serial. (2004).

Odlyzkow, Andrew. Internet pricing and the history of communications. Revised version (February 8, 2001). http://www.dtc.umn.edu/~odlyzko/doc/history.communications1b.pdf

SHERPA Publisher copyright policies & self-archiving. http://www.sherpa.ac.uk/romeo.php. (April 14, 2005).

Zalta, Edward N., Colin Allen, Uri Nodelman, and Daniel McKenzie. Stanford Encyclopedia of Philosophy. Open Letter to Librarians. http://www.plato.stanford.edu/fundraising/librarians.html (April 17, 2005).

doi:10.1300/J123v53S09_11

Chapter 11

E-Journal Usage Statistics in Action:
A Case Study
from Cancer Research UK

Angela Boots
Julia Chester
Emma Shaw
Chris Wilson

INTRODUCTION

This case study is based on an evaluation of e-journal titles with
COUNTER-compliant usage statistics. By comparing online usage levels with journal costs, Cancer Research UK (CRUK) has been able to
develop a simple "cost-per-download" model, which can then be compared with the average cost of obtaining a copy of a journal article from
document supply sources. It is appreciated that the number of downloads, while giving an indication of usefulness, does not accurately represent the full value of an online journal. This is the first step in the
ongoing development and refinement of a process for more accurately

[Haworth co-indexing entry note]: "E-Journal Usage Statistics in Action: A Case Study from Cancer Research UK." Boots, Angela et al. Co-published simultaneously in *The Serials Librarian* (The Haworth Information Press, an imprint of The Haworth Press, Inc.) Vol. 53, Supplement No. 9, 2007, pp. 183-198; and: *Usage
Statistics of E-Serials* (ed: David C. Fowler) The Haworth Information Press, an imprint of The Haworth Press,
Inc., 2007, pp. 183-198. Single or multiple copies of this article are available for a fee from The Haworth Document Delivery Service [1-800-HAWORTH, 9:00 a.m. - 5:00 p.m. (EST). E-mail address: docdelivery@
haworthpress.com].

Available online at http://ser.haworthpress.com
© 2007 by The Haworth Press, Inc. All rights reserved.
doi:10.1300/J123v53S09_12

assessing the value a journal delivers against its cost. It is hoped that this case study will be of interest to other information professionals engaged in the perennial struggle to balance user demand for easy access to a rich and extensive journals collection with the need to control the library budget.

CANCER RESEARCH UK

Cancer Research UK was formed in 2002 by the merger of the Imperial Cancer Research Fund (ICRF) and the Cancer Research Campaign (CRC). It is the world's largest independent organization dedicated to cancer research. It funds over 3,000 scientists, doctors, and nurses based throughout the United Kingdom through grants to scientists in universities, hospitals, and independent institutes, and by supporting work in its own research institutes and units.

The Library and Information Services (LIS) department of Cancer Research UK serves the information needs of 1,300 laboratory and clinical scientists working primarily in the field of biomedical research. Five hundred researchers are located at the London Research Institute, where LIS is also based. These researchers include graduate students studying for doctoral degrees, post-doctoral fellows, scientific officers, and laboratory heads. Other researchers are spread across the United Kingdom, typically attached to universities or teaching hospitals, and use library services remotely.

The main objective for LIS is to provide researchers with electronic access to a range of relevant and up-to-date information sources and services. Researchers' current information needs are primarily met by providing them with access to databases such as PubMed and ISI Web of Knowledge, weekly alerting services that are centrally managed by LIS, and online access to full-text articles in peer-reviewed biomedical journals. The strategy of LIS for the next eighteen months to two years is to convert from a hybrid collection, using the print plus online journal model, to a wholly electronic information model. Research interests can frequently change direction and LIS must be sufficiently flexible in order to respond quickly to new demands. Unlike many medical libraries, Cancer Research UK's collection development policy is not restricted by an ongoing commitment to maintain a large and broadly focused collection. Subscriptions can be canceled as soon as a journal ceases to be useful to researchers, or as soon as it becomes so expensive that it fails to deliver adequate value for the money it costs. This apparent ruthlessness means that funds can be diverted to acquire new titles to support changing research interests with relative ease. It also requires the development of a reliable and effective methodology for defining and assessing "usefulness."

BACKGROUND

The immediate priority for LIS is to identify appropriate methods for establishing both the level of usage and the value derived from our online journals collection. Traditionally, the collection of usage statistics for print journals has been problematic. It has largely depended on self-reporting by users, observation of reader behavior by library staff, knowledge about patterns of usage gained from reshelving, or by counting error photocopies discarded by users. All these methods for assessing usage are unreliable. It is also far from being clear that simply counting usage is a valid indicator of value. In academic libraries, other factors must also be considered. For instance, there can be variations in the levels of usage between different departments, faculties, and disciplines, and in a large and multidisciplinary institution, it may be important to protect the needs of small user groups. The last point is not a major issue for Cancer Research UK, as journals required by only one researcher or research group are not funded from the library budget, and must be purchased from the laboratory research grant.

Much of the literature currently available on electronic journals usage statistics pre-dates the COUNTER Code of Practice. The lack of more recent literature may indicate that the profession is still evaluating the implications of COUNTER. However, revisiting the concerns that were expressed about usage statistics in the pre-COUNTER age is a useful way to establish the background for this case study. A number of authors highlight the general concerns and key requirements shared by librarians and publishers, which fed the debate that resulted in the COUNTER Code of Practice. The main issue was the lack of reliable and comparable data provided in an easy-to-use, standardized format. Variations in definitions of terms, collection processes, and systems made it difficult to interpret the available data and put it into any meaningful context.

There were concerns about the potential risks of acquiring too much dependency on statistics produced by publishers, who may have a vested interest. However, while local or 'home grown' usage collection systems appeared to offer a more reliable alternative, at least in terms of data comparability, they were mainly limited to counting access rates, that is, the number of times a user clicked on a link to a journal from the library catalog or Web site. Detailed analyses of the number of searches or downloads, as well as of usage from journal home pages bookmarked by users, could not be collected locally. Much of the debate has centered on the terminology used by publishers to describe online activities and how this affected the interpretation of online statistics. Some discussion has centered on the differences between simply accessing a journal, and on actually making use of it or getting value from it. For example, do links to the home page, or to the current table of contents, searches, links to abstracts, and downloading full-text HTML or PDFs, have equal value? Kidd points out that viewing or downloading a full-text article (HTML or PDF) may not be the only indicator of actual usage or value, and that access to the abstract may, in fact, be just as useful. Commonly, usage statistics have been seen as just one part of the data required to understand the value of a journal. It is important to look at other factors as well, such as tracking usage levels over time, looking for trends, and talking to users, in order to put statistics into some sort of a context.

However, despite their reservations, a number of authors have predicted that online usage statistics would begin to play a significant role in subscription decision making. Not only would it be possible to calculate cost-per-use, but electronic journal pricing models would evolve towards reliance on usage statistics. Some authors expressed the view that while online statistics had the potential to be more useful and more accurate than print usage statistics, they should still be treated with a degree of caution and could not be used as performance indicators.

Discussion of some of the issues around journal statistics led to the development of the COUNTER Code of Practice. This started in the United Kingdom with the Joint Information Systems Committee (JISC) funded by the UK Further and Higher Education funding councils, the Association of Learned and Professional Society Publishers (ALPSP), and the Publishers Association. It has gained the agreement of many relevant professional groups and publishers. In March 2002, the COUNTER Code of Practice was launched, specifying the requirements for vendor statistics reports.

To quote from the COUNTER Code of Practice itself:

COUNTER has been developed to provide a single, international, extendable Code of Practice that allows the usage of online information products and services to be measured in a credible, consistent, and compatible way using vendor-generated data. The COUNTER Code of Practice specifies the data elements to be measured, definitions of these data elements, usage report content, format, frequency, and methods of delivery, protocols for combining usage reports from direct use, and from use via intermediaries. The Code of Practice also provides guidelines for data processing by vendors and auditing protocols. In response to librarian demand, 'Release 1' of the COUNTER Code of Practice focused on the usage of journals and databases, the products that accounted for the largest share of most libraries' materials budgets. Future releases of the Code of Practice will extend the scope of COUNTER, not only to other content types, but also to more detailed levels of reporting for each content type. (COUNTER, 2005)

Since the launch of the Code of Practice, the situation has changed substantially, and, in theory, the widespread availability of COUNTER-compliant usage statistics allows library professionals to systematically collect and compare usage data for the first time. It would seem that many of the pre-COUNTER issues have been resolved, but CRUK's experience is that there is still a difference between having better access to comparable usage statistics and actually being able to utilize them effectively.

CASE STUDY

Library and Information Services at Cancer Research UK has been experimenting with online journals usage statistics in order to develop a useful and reliable collection evaluation and management tool. CRUK has developed a very simple model of cost-per-download by dividing usage statistics into journal costs. We have proposed to use this technique as part of the annual review of journal titles for cancellation or renewal. However, CRUK still has concerns about how far download statistics accurately represent the usefulness or value of an online journal. It is important to note that this case study does not specifically address the issue of the value. The authors see this as a complex and multilayered subject, and although we have some ideas about how this organization may approach it, our initial objective has simply been to establish a practical routine for downloading e-journal usage statistics and using them to investigate and understand the actual costs. CRUK sees this as the starting point for a much longer-term exploration into the development of a range of tools for accurately assessing the value that a journal delivers against its cost. Our practical experience in collecting and using COUNTER-compliant usage statistics reveals that there are still a number of issues to be resolved.

This case study is based on a set of CRUK online journal subscriptions, all of which have COUNTER-compliant usage statistics available, either direct from the publisher or via an aggregator (Figure 11.1). Out of the total collection of 150 current online journals subscriptions, COUNTER-compliant usage statistics are available for all but twenty-two titles, and for these, we have no usage statistics at all. CRUK has been downloading and recording usage statistics for the last

FIGURE 11.1. Screenshot of ScienceDirect COUNTER statistics. Reprinted with permission of Elsevier Ltd.

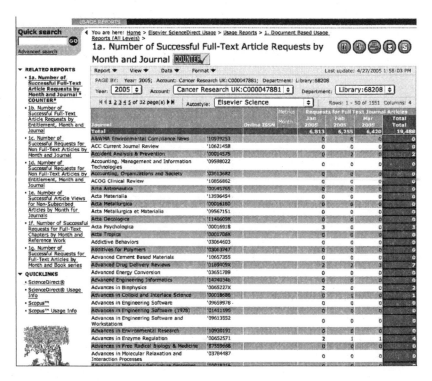

eighteen months and currently records only full-text HTML and PDF downloads. Initially we recorded a wider range of statistics (links to table of contents, abstracts, number of searches), but about twelve months prior to this writing, it was decided to focus on a more limited number of measures. This decision was made primarily on practical grounds. The range of statistics provided by publishers is not standardized, and it is often difficult to find explanations of what different publishers mean by the same term. For example, Science Direct statistics feature only the term "full-text." It is not clear if "full-text" means HTML, PDF, or both.

A number of authors have identified cost-per-use as the most meaningful measure of a journal's value (Kidd 2002; Montgomery 2002). In line with this, CRUK has been persuaded that the number of full-text downloads is the most important statistic to measure, as it enables the library to compare the cost-per-download with the cost of providing the same article through standard document-supply services. Our model is based purely on the actual subscription cost of the journal and does not include any allowance for operational or administration costs. In the longer term, CRUK may well decide that this is an element that should be included in the total cost. The literature suggests that the local cost of managing an online subscription is less than the cost of managing a print subscription, but we are very much in the early stages of managing an online collection and it is too soon to establish routine costs. The authors have accepted that there are some disadvantages in focusing on a limited number of measures, and that the full picture might not be fully seen.

Now that CRUK is developing some practical experience in collecting usage statistics, we have identified a number of problems that principally affect the ease of use. In our experience, the statistics available are not as up-to-date as would have been ideal, with an average delay of two months before the latest statistics are made available. Thus, this institution's objective is to establish a regular monthly routine, whereby we visit the publisher's site, select and download the usage statistics for the specific titles in our collection, and then upload the data into our journals management database. This, in our experience, is much easier said than done.

The sheer variety of different formats in which journals usage statistics are available makes it very difficult to select, collate, and use them effectively. CRUK feels very strongly that a greater degree of standardization in both the display and download formats for usage statistics is essential. Just to give a flavor of the practical issues that are faced, in many cases it is necessary to wade through the statistics for unsubscribed titles in order to navigate to the ones we want. Often, PDF and HTML download counts are combined. It is known that in many cases readers will first check the HTML to assess relevance before downloading the PDF, so, in effect, there is some double counting if the HTML and PDF count cannot be separated.

When exporting statistics, it is common to have to export all those available for a title, rather than the specific titles that are required. Cancer Research UK is a large organization, and in addition to the Library collection, many of the researchers have personal subscriptions. In many cases, the usage statistics for all CRUK subscriptions will be portrayed together, and it is frequently difficult to identify just those that are library subscriptions. The availability of customizable filters or export options would be a very useful modification. With a collection of only 150 titles, the task of manually editing the downloaded statistics before uploading them into the database is a difficult, but manageable task. One member of the staff spends roughly one day a month on this. In a much larger library, with many more titles, it must be a time-consuming task.

Other problems occur when a publisher launches a new Web site, or moves to a new aggregator platform. This frequently requires a complete change in the method whereby usage statistics are counted, and the format in which they are displayed. If this occurs midyear, it becomes very difficult to merge the new usage data with the old. Our conclusion is that although online usage statistics are more available, there are still a number of practical problems, largely associated with local collection, management, and storage processes, to be resolved.

Journal Selection

In July of each year, LIS reviews the collection of journals to be renewed for the following year. This assessment has previously been based on a Journals Questionnaire sent to researchers, asking them to indicate which titles they use frequently (weekly), regularly (monthly), or occasionally (less than monthly), or would be happy to see cancelled. Suggestions for new titles to add to the collection are also invited. The outcome of the questionnaire is discussed with the Library Committee, which is made up of staff representing the main groups of users, and decisions are made about cancellations and new titles for purchase. A report on document supply data for the previous twelve months is also included in the evaluation. If document supply costs are greater than the cost of a subscription then a title is automatically considered for purchase.

In the 2005 renewal round, CRUK was able to combine these sources of information with a more rigorous statistical approach. Usage statistics were downloaded and recorded in an Excel spreadsheet. This was organized with one worksheet for each publisher, with a standard format for presenting the data. The number of HTML and PDF downloads for each title per calendar month was entered where available. Total downloads by month and by year-to-date were calculated. A second Excel spreadsheet was also created to record the subscription details for each title in the collection, including the cost of the online license. This data was initially held on an Open Text BASIS database (BASIS is a proprietary database and document management software package from the Open Text Corporation), and then exported into the Excel spreadsheet for easier data manipulation and comparison with download and usage statistics.

As an initial exercise, data for 2003 usage and 2004 subscription costs were combined into a new Excel spreadsheet. This was used to calculate the cost-per-download for each journal title. There were some gaps and discrepancies in the available data. Some of the costs were in dollars, or euros, as well as pounds sterling, so an estimated exchange rate had to be applied. Some publishers charge an all-in price for a group of titles, which means the cost of individual journals cannot easily be separated from the overall total. In these cases, the total cost is divided equally across the number of titles in the deal. However, despite the difficulties, it proved possible to calculate a cost-per-download for two thirds of the Cancer Research UK collection. Immediately, it was possible to see that some of the most expensive titles, such as *Nature,* or the *Journal of Biology Chemistry,* were also the most heavily used, and–on a cost-per-use basis–there were also extremely cost-effective. It was also possible to show that some titles that were modestly priced and seemed to represent good value for the money were in fact being used so little that the cost-per-use assessment revealed them to be very expensive and much less cost-effective than we had thought. These initial findings were discussed with the Library Committee, which agreed this was an interesting and useful approach to the annual problem of evaluating the journals collection prior to making renewals and cancellations.

CRUK implemented the new approach for the first time in July 2004, as part of the renewals process for 2005 subscriptions. The following titles are examples of how this actually worked in practice. Please note that the information given is, of necessity, restricted by the need to respect commercial confidentiality about the actual deals struck.

Cell Press

The Cell Press case is a very good illustration of one of the problems with collecting statistics (Figure 11.2). Cancer Research UK subscribes to eight of the ten titles published by Cell Press. When this publisher transferred responsibility for hosting to ScienceDirect in mid-2004, this resulted in discontinuity in the usage statistics. Cell Press statistics were available for the period from January to July 2004, with HTML and PDF downloads counted separately. From August 2004 onward, ScienceDirect statistics were available, but only as a single figure for total statistics. ScienceDirect also offered some statistics for July 2004 and earlier, but these did not correspond to the Cell Press statistics, being, for example, noticeably higher for July 2004 but much lower for earlier months. It was also apparent that the monthly average for ScienceDirect downloads was higher than the monthly average for Cell Press titles, which suggested that they were being counted on a different basis. It was not clear how the library should treat these statistics; should they be combined, or would that be considered double counting? It was difficult to establish a clear picture of usage. Despite this problem, what was clear was that of the eight Cell Press titles that CRUK subscribed to, the journal *Cell* was the most popular title. Although the library was dealing with a range of possible usage rates, rather than a single definitive figure at the lower end of the range, the cost-per-download was still less than one pound sterling for all but one title. Further difficulty arose as Cell Press quoted a group or bundle rate for the eight subscribed titles, without identifying the individual costs. This meant that the library had to assume that each title cost was the same. Further discussion with the publisher will help us to identify differences in price within the bundle and improve the accuracy of our analysis.

FIGURE 11.2.

Source	Title	Type	Jan	Feb	Mar	Apr	May	Jun	Jul	Aug	Sep	Oct	Nov	Dec	Total
Cell Stats	Cancer Cell	FulltextPDF	115	130	162	100	112	127	108						854
Cell Stats	Cancer Cell	Fulltext HTML	68	81	92	84	72	41	6						444
Cell Stats	Cancer Cell	Total	183	211	254	184	184	168	114						1298
ScienceDirect Stats	Cancer Cell	Fulltext article	0	0	0	6	13	11	281	295	336	291	297	239	1769
Cell Stats	Cell	FulltextPDF	584	394	390	470	398	429	439						3094
Cell Stats	Cell	Fulltext HTML	561	473	431	385	394	296	36						2576
Cell Stats	Cell	Total	1145	867	821	855	782	725	475						5670
ScienceDirect Stats	Cell	Fulltext article	0	0	0	6	237	31	981	879	1,103	1,257	942	652	5988

Wiley InterScience

Wiley InterScience publishes thirteen *Current Protocols* laboratory manuals. Cancer Research UK subscribes to five of these (Figure 11.3). CRUK previously subscribed to these as loose-leaf, updateable print publications shelved with its book stock. These were seen to be candidates for replacement by the online version and we have already canceled the print copies. Wiley also changed the format of their statistics mid-year. From June 2004, the HTML and PDF downloads were shown as separate totals, but previously only the HTML download figures were available. The pattern of usage throughout the year appeared to be quite erratic, with a range of 28 and 218 downloads per month, for the most popular title. This may reflect that the product is a laboratory manual, rather than a peer-reviewed journal. It will be referred to occasionally as required by laboratory work, rather than browsed regularly for current awareness or cited in research. It also suggests that the statistics will be less effective in predicting the level of demand than may be the case with peer-reviewed journals. Nevertheless, the calculated cost-per-download was still less than three pounds each for articles from four of the titles, and less than seven pounds each for articles from the fifth. All titles were thus renewed.

Highwire Press

Highwire Press is a journals-hosting service offered by Stanford University. To quote their Web site, "Highwire focuses exclusively on the online hosting of full-text, peer-reviewed journals and other scholarly content" on behalf of scientific societies and not-for-profit publishers

FIGURE 11.3.

Title	Type	Jan	Feb	Mar	Apr	May	Jun	Jul	Aug	Sep	Oct	Nov	Dec	Total
Current Protocols in Cell Biology	Fulltext HTML	*					39	3	47	7	34	36	17	183
Current Protocols in Cell Biology	FulltextPDF	74	48	107	25	19	63	1	23	6	17	14	13	410
Current Protocols in Cell Biology	Total	74	48	107	25	19	102	4	70	13	51	50	30	593
Current Protocols in Human Genetics	Fulltext HTML	*					40	1	1	0	0	2	1	45
Current Protocols in Human Genetics	FulltextPDF	14	45	6	1	8	0	0	1	0	0	0	1	76
Current Protocols in Human Genetics	Total	14	45	6	1	8	40	1	2	0	0	2	2	121
Current Protocols in Immunology	Fulltext HTML	*					7	2	4	3	2	19	4	41
Current Protocols in Immunology	FulltextPDF	35	67	47	14	33	0	1	1	3	34	3	42	280
Current Protocols in Immunology	Total	35	67	47	14	33	7	3	5	6	36	22	46	321
Current Protocols in Molecular Biology	Fulltext HTML	*					201	81	16	40	53	89	15	495
Current Protocols in Molecular Biology	FulltextPDF	81	142	131	414	64	17	11	12	59	26	16	29	1002
Current Protocols in Molecular Biology	Total	81	142	131	414	64	218	92	28	99	79	105	44	1497
Current Protocols Protein Science	Fulltext HTML	*					23	8	52	10	0	31	14	138
Current Protocols Protein Science	FulltextPDF	38	26	61	12	17	1	7	39	5	10	4	1	221
Current Protocols Protein Science	Total	38	26	61	12	17	24	15	91	15	10	35	15	359

(Figure 11.4). They host the Web sites of, and provide online usage statistics for over 850 journals. They do not, however, provide subscription services for publishers, and Cancer Research UK deals with the individual publishers for renewals, albeit through a subscription agent. CRUK subscribes to forty-eight journals from eighteen different publishers using Highwire Press. In spite of the apparent potential for confusion, Highwire Press has been, in our experience, the least problematic of usage information providers, and it has been possible for us to collect a consistent set of statistics across the range of titles. Following a change in our named administrator for some titles, CRUK experienced some short-term problems, as not all our titles were recognized as belonging to us, and thus we could not access any usage statistics. However, once this problem was recognized, it proved to be relatively simple to rectify. With the help of Highwire, we were able to link the ad-

FIGURE 11.4. Screenshot of HighWire statistics. Reprinted with permission from HighWire Press, Stanford University Libraries.

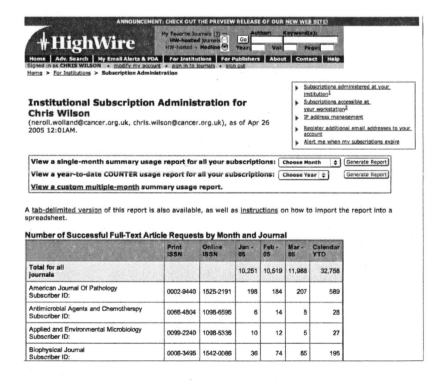

ministrators for each title, and therefore act as if there was a single administrator.

The American Society of Microbiology (ASM) is one of the publishers that hosts their journals on Highwire Press. LIS subscribes to all eleven titles they publish. Analysis of their usage statistics revealed a varied pattern of use. Some titles were markedly more popular than others, with *Molecular and Cellular Biology* having over 10,000 downloads, while *Clinical Microbiology Reviews* had less than fifty. Earlier evaluation, by means of a journals questionnaire, had revealed that only five titles were actually required by Cancer Research UK researchers, but it was more cost-effective to subscribe to a complete package than subscribe to individual titles. The statistics clearly showed that while the five core titles were consistently the most heavily used, it is still–for the time being–more cost-effective to subscribe to a package. However, we now have the reassurance of knowing that this decision is based on a better understanding of both the costs and the usage levels.

The Genetics Society of America publishes *Genetics,* also through Highwire Press. Cancer Research UK had subscribed to the print version, and this entitled us to have free online access only at our main laboratory. Because this journal was hosted by Highwire, CRUK was able to collect statistics on the level of usage. These statistics showed 1,800 downloads during 2004. When renewing *Genetics,* the library asked for a quote for multisite access across the whole of the organization. This quote was cost-effective for the level of use we were already experiencing. Given that access for extra sites would most probably increase the level of usage, it was decided to take a multisite subscription.

Nature Publishing Group

Cancer Research UK subscribes to twenty-one titles from the Nature Publishing Group. These are split into two separate deals: the *Nature* research journals, of which there are fourteen titles that we subscribe to, including *Nature Reviews,* and the academic and society journals, of which there were seven titles to which we subscribed. For the academic and society journals, the library was quoted individual prices for each journal title. It was therefore simple to calculate the cost-per-download for each of them. This demonstrated that all the journals were cost-effective. Interestingly, the two most expensive titles, *EMBO Journal* and *Oncogene,* were also the most heavily used and therefore the least expensive per download. This fact may never have been apparent without conducting this analysis.

As discussed earlier, we believe it is useful to separate out HTML and PDF downloads, as users may review the HTML version of an article before downloading the PDF full-text version. It is therefore interesting to note that the PDF downloads represent between 78 and 92 percent of the total downloads of these journals. Even if it is assumed that all HTML downloads are double-counted, and that only PDF downloads should be counted, the increase in the cost-per-download is less than thirty pence for these titles.

Our subscription to the thirteen *Nature*-branded journals (but not the journal *Nature* itself) is priced as a package, rather than by individual titles. For the purposes of statistical analysis, we assume that each journal costs one-thirteenth of the total cost, and calculate the cost-per-download accordingly. Nine journals cost less than one pound per article. Only one, *Nature Reviews Neuroscience,* stood out as having a high cost-per-download and worth considering for cancellation. On consulting the publisher, however, it was clear that the potential savings of removing this journal from the deal were less than appeared from the initial calculation, and not substantial enough to justify its cancellation.

CONCLUSIONS

The aforementioned examples show how Cancer Research UK is using statistics of online journal use to quantify some aspects of the value we receive from our electronic journal subscriptions. What has been presented is the first application of this approach. From 2006 onwards, CRUK intends to cancel our print subscriptions, except for a small core collection, and to use online-only journals wherever possible. As we do this, we will use cost and usage data to provide a clear picture of the cost-effectiveness for our users of different journals, and to be more rigorous in our decision making about what to renew or cancel.

Looking at the future of e-journal usage statistics, there are some issues the authors believe merit further examination and research. The first of these is value. We have statistics on how often the full-text of an article has been downloaded by our users from any given journal, and the costs of these downloads. These do not directly indicate the value or importance of that journal to our users. It is not yet fully understood how the behavior of our users is reflected in these statistics. It is not known if an article is downloaded because it might be useful or because it is definitely needed, if a user will download an article once and save it or download the same article several times, or what the choice of an

HTML or a PDF format signifies. We do not know who within the organization is using any given journal, and whether it is used a little by many staff members, or a lot by only a few staff. We do not know what value is attached to an article by the person who has downloaded it, and who is using it for their work. One of the authors, Shaw, is currently undertaking research for her master's dissertation to try and understand this dynamic better. It is a subject which will repay examination, as librarians try to ensure that they use their organization's assets as effectively as possible and for the greatest benefit of their users.

The next area that would merit further examination is the practicalities of downloading the statistics from publisher Web sites, and how that practice could be simplified. LIS has recently had discussions with MPS Technologies (part of Macmillan Publishers) who, together with IBM, have been considering providing a service to consolidate usage statistics for libraries. This may provide one model for relieving the administrative task of the library staff involved in cutting, pasting, and formatting data from multiple publishers' Web sites.

The final area that may need thinking through is the effect this increased amount of information has on publishers' pricing models. It may be that the increased amount of data available to libraries and publishers will alter the balance of advantage in licensing negotiations. It seems predictable that the pricing of online journals will be decreasingly similar to that of print journals, where there is unlimited use for a set price at one site. As publishers have more sophisticated information about how users behave on journal Web sites, there may be scope for more sophisticated pricing models as well. Those of us in the library profession who remember paying per download fifteen years ago may find we have indeed "come to a full-circle."

REFERENCES

Cole, Louise. "Usage Data–The Academic Library Perspective." *Serials* 13, no. 2 (2000): 97-102.

COUNTER. 2002. Counter Code of Practice. Release 1: December 2002. In, http://www.projectcounter.org/code_practice.html (accessed on April 26, 2005).

COUNTER. 2005. Counter Code of Practice. Release 2: April 2005. www.project counter.org/code_practice.html.

Davis, Susan. "Serials Spoken Here: Reports of Conferences, Institutes, and Seminars." *Serials Review* 27, no. 2 (2001): 78-81.

De Groote, Sandra L, and Josephine L Dorsch. "Measuring Use Patterns of Online Journals and Databases." *Journal of the Medical Library Association* 91, no. 2 (2003): 231-240.

Duy, Joanna, and Liwen Vaughan. "Usage Data for Electronic Resources: A Comparison between Locally Collected and Vendor-Provided Statistics." *The Journal of Academic Librarianship* 29, no. 1 (2003): 16-22.

Hulbert, Terry. "Measuring up to Expectations? Usage Data and Electronic Journals." *Serials* 15, no. 1 (2002): 7-10.

Kidd, Tony. "Electronic Journal Usage Statistics in Practice." *Serials* 15, no. 1 (2002): 11-17.

Liu, Weiling, and Fannie M Cox. "Tracking the Use of E-Journals: A Technique Collaboratively Developed by the Cataloging Department and the Office of Libraries Technology at the University of Louisville." *OCLC Systems & Services* 18, no. 1 (2002): 32-39.

Luther, Judy. 2000. White Paper on Electronic Journal Usage Statistics. In *Journal of Electronic Publishing,* http://www.press.umich.edu/jep/06-03/luther.html (accessed on January 18, 2005).

Montgomery, Carol Hansen, and Donald W King. 2002. Comparing Library and User Related Costs of Print and Electronic Journal Collections: A First Step Towards a Comprehensive Analysis. In *D-Lib Magazine,* http://www.dlib.org/dlib/october02/montgomery/10montgomery.html (accessed on February 11, 2005).

Obst, Oliver. "Patterns and Costs of Printed and Online Journal of Usage." *Health Information and Libraries Journal* 20 (2003): 22-32.

Pinfield, Stephen. 2001. Managing Electronic Library Services: Current Issues in UK Higher Education Institutions. In *Ariadne,* http://www.ariadne.ac.uk/issue29/pinfield/intro.html (accessed on January 21, 2005).

Stemper, James A, and Janice M Jaguszewski. "Usage Statistics for Electronic Journals: An Analysis of Local and Vendor Counts." *Collection Management* 28, no. 4 (2003): 3-22.

doi:10.1300/J123v53S09_12

Chapter 12

Lies, Damn Lies, and Usage Statistics: What's a Librarian to Do?

Rickey Best

INTRODUCTION

As Bernard Rous has noted, the appropriate relationship between usage, value, and price for scholarly works has never been satisfactorily defined. Certainly, within libraries, the value of scholarly materials has never been measured purely by usage, but rather by vague[1] notions of perceived value. As financial pressure on library budgets increases, we look to user data for our electronic acquisitions to support our decisions for acquiring (or for not retaining) materials.

Faced with the increasing emphasis upon electronic resources and combined with static or declining budgets, libraries are being forced to consider the value of their licensed databases and electronic journals. In 2001, it was estimated that larger academic libraries were spending 20 percent of their budgets on electronic materials.[2] The pressures faced by Association of Research Libraries (ARL) libraries as well as by smaller, regional institutions create several common concerns: Is our money being spent wisely? Are our users finding all the information they need? Are there other resources that will meet our users' needs, albeit at a lower price? How are we to decide the answers to these vital issues?

[Haworth co-indexing entry note]: "Lies, Damn Lies, and Usage Statistics: What's a Librarian to Do?" Best, Rickey. Co-published simultaneously in *The Serials Librarian* (The Haworth Information Press, an imprint of The Haworth Press, Inc.) Vol. 53, Supplement No. 9, 2007, pp. 199-214; and: *Usage Statistics of E-Serials* (ed: David C. Fowler) The Haworth Information Press, an imprint of The Haworth Press, Inc., 2007, pp. 199-214. Single or multiple copies of this article are available for a fee from The Haworth Document Delivery Service [1-800-HAWORTH, 9:00 a.m. - 5:00 p.m. (EST). E-mail address: docdelivery@haworthpress.com].

Available online at http://ser.haworthpress.com
doi:10.1300/J123v53S09_13

The explosive growth of electronic collections forces us to ask how much the materials are being used. Is the expense for these items always justified? Even though these questions may rightly be asked of books and journals in print, the transparency of the electronic resources lends itself to an increased sense of pressure. Whereas a print volume will sit quietly on a shelf (at a relatively low cost) awaiting use, the expense of making many electronic resources available is significantly greater and usually ongoing. Computer hardware and software, printing stations, Web page development, electronic reference and help services, as well as electronic resource cataloging; all require significant investments of time, money, and energy. So what justifies our efforts in the electronic arena?

Libraries, whether academic or public, are being hard pressed to demonstrate to their funding bodies (provosts, chancellors, and faculty members, or city councils, county boards of supervisors, and the public) that the funds allocated to them are being spent wisely and effectively. In addition to reporting to our funding bodies and demonstrating that we are being good stewards of public finances, the usage statistics we keep may help us to focus our efforts in bibliographic instruction and even in the development of library Web sites.[3] To measure print resources without conducting significant user surveys, we have primarily relied upon anecdotal data. Now with electronic resources, we have access to actual numbers that either are provided by vendors, or are collected directly by the library. Unfortunately, the numbers do not tell us the whole story. First, some inconsistencies remain within the vendor numbers being reported. Second, there is no universal consensus as to what constitutes acceptable or adequate amounts of usage. Without access to data for peer institutions with similar collections, it is doubtful that we will ever be able to provide proper benchmarks for usage rates. Usage data, however, is not and should not be the main driver for decisions on selection and retention.

Selection and retention decisions for electronic resources, just as for print, must be made with a proper understanding of the users being served, the users' needs, and the overall strength of the resources of the entire collection, so as to enable public services and other staff to provide adequate support for electronic resources users. Usage data greatly assists in formulating informed decisions, but as noted by Rebecca Kemp, the data is only one component. Content is equally important,[4] and for smaller institutions, it may be argued that content is even more so. This chapter will look at the efforts of one regional university to intersect its curricular needs for resource selection with usage data for the resources once acquired.

AUBURN UNIVERSITY AT MONTGOMERY

Auburn University at Montgomery (AUM) is a regional university, and a part of Auburn University, located in the state capital of Alabama. AUM has a total enrollment of approximately 5,200 students, with a full-time equivalent (FTE) enrollment of some 3,700. Nearly 85 percent of the enrollment is at the undergraduate level. The university consists of the Schools of Business, Education, Liberal Arts, Nursing, and Sciences. The AUM Library has a collection of 320,000 books, 2,140 current periodical subscriptions, and access to 40,000 electronic books through subscriptions to netLibrary consortial collections offered through the Southeastern Library Information Network (SOLINET). The library also has access to 110 electronic databases, which provide full-text articles and reports from more than 15,000 journals.

The library began investing in electronic, Web-based resources in 1997. The electronic resources were licensed following the basic guidelines of the library's collection development policy statement, which emphasized the value of content rather than format of materials. Currently, the library spends 22 percent of its regular materials budget on electronic resources, and receives an additional $75,000 from student technology fees to apply towards the licensing of electronic materials. The library also benefits from legislative funding for the Alabama Virtual Library (AVL). The AVL was formed in 1999 to begin providing access to electronic resources to benefit the students and citizens of the state of Alabama. Constituents include public colleges and universities, two-year colleges, public libraries, and school libraries.[5] Because of the legislative funding for AVL and a number of databases from EBSCO, Gale, Infotrac, and Sirsi Dynix are included in the total, the library's breadth of access is significantly increased without additional cost to the library. The library does provide direct links to database sites that are appropriate to college-level students, and also provides a link to the AVL Home page. Because there is no direct cost to the library, there is no attempt to measure usage costs for Virtual Library sites. Apart from AVL, the library participates in consortial agreements with SOLINET and the Network of Alabama Academic Libraries to access other needed licensed resources. Overall, the AUM Library collects usage data for forty-three vendors in specific databases, which provide abstracting, indexing, and full-text resources for our students.

The AUM Library has made a concerted effort to set up its electronic resources in a simplified manner, as much as possible. The library has specific electronic journal titles it has licensed, available from hot links in the online catalog. Serials Solutions is also used in order to provide our users with an additional access point, and information from which electronic databases' specific titles are available. Electronic databases are accessed through a link on the Home page labeled "databases" and these are subdivided by general subject areas to facilitate locating relevant databases for library users. Databases that are interdisciplinary are listed in all appropriate subject areas to assist in facilitating user retrieval. The following is a screen capture of the library's Home page, to illustrate how access points are constructed (Figure 12.1).

THE VALUE OF NUMBERS

Usage data can have variety of different values for libraries. Many types of reports can be generated by vendors or integrated library systems

FIGURE 12.1. AUM library Web site. Reprinted with permission from Auburn University at Montgomery.

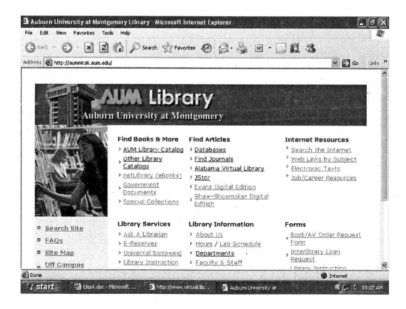

to meet a variety of operational purposes. Among the types of reports that can be generated are those reports documenting personnel and financial accountability and record keeping, support and justification for funding requests, strategic planning, and managerial decision making.[6] The reports that are prepared may include cost analysis in order to assess the effectiveness and efficiency of a product or a service; trend analysis reports which allow the examination of electronic usage over time in an effort to determine evolving trends in user information needs and related demands for resources; management reports to provide analyses of electronic resources utilized and user demands. in order to assist in the decision making process for the acquisition of new resources; and finally, faculty and administrative liaison reports which can be used to demonstrate to library funding bodies that the cost-benefit ratio for resources is sufficient to warrant additional funding or to protect current funding levels.[7]

As vendor data becomes more standardized over time in terms of reporting, these usage figures will become increasingly influential in the decision making process. A number of factors go into the decision process on whether to add or retain a journal or a database. For journals, examples of decision points may include cost, relevance to the university's research priorities (or curricula), and faculty input.[8] Citation reports such as those prepared by Institute for Scientific Information (ISI) may also be used to support decisions to cancel titles.[9] Some of the difficulties with early usage data, however, have been the inconsistency with which such data has been historically reported. Early reports did not provide sufficiently detailed usage information, such as statistics by individual journal or database titles. Reports were also inconsistent because vendors used their own in-house terminology and failed to provide adequate definitions to enable library staff to easily understand reported statistics. Reports were also not comparable because they came in different formats and contained different statistical data points. In this, libraries were unable to compare usage figures with each other.[10]

Since the mid-1990s, the International Coalition of Library Consortia (ICOLC) has been working toward a standard set of definitions for the reporting of usage statistics. In its original release of the publication, "Guidelines for Statistical Measures of Usage of Web-Based Information Resources" (November 1998), ICOLC listed the following requirements for vendors to report usage data:

1. Each specific database of the provider
2. Each institutionally defined set of Internet Protocol (IP) addresses/ locators to the subnet level

3. Report usage data for the entire consortium
4. For special data elements used by the subscriber (e.g., account or ID number)
5. Each time period[11]

The vendor systems were required to report minimal data by month, and for the month reported, each type of use was to be reported for each hour of the day. Twenty-four months of historical data were requested. Usage elements in the reports were to include:

1. Number of queries (searches) categorized as appropriate for the vendor's information
2. Number of menu selections categorized as appropriate to the vendor's system
3. Number of sessions (logins), if relevant, was to be provided as a measure of simultaneous use
4. Number of turnaways, if relevant, as a contract limit
5. Number of items examined (that is, viewed, marked, selected or downloaded, e-mailed, printed) to the extent that these can be recorded and controlled by the server rather than the browser, to include:
   (a) Citations retrieved for abstract and indexing databases, and
   (b) Full-text retrieved, categorized by title, International Standard Serial Number (ISSN) with title listed, or other identifier as appropriate.

A critical element in the ICOLC recommendations had to do with searches. The guidelines defined searching as representing "a unique intellectual inquiry. Typically, a search is recorded each time a search form is sent/submitted to the vendor's server. Subsequent activities to review or browse the number of records retrieved or the process of isolating the correct single item desired do not represent additional searchers."[12]

In 2001, the ICOLC guidelines were revised. Minimum requirements were changed from "total consortium" to "overall consortium, aggregated at the consortium level." The reporting of "full-text displayed" was altered to report the number of "full-content units examined, downloaded, or otherwise supplied to the user," and included electronic books as part of the reporting mechanism.[13]

In April 2000, the ARL began the E-Metrics project. One of the aims of the project was to engage in a collaborative effort with selected database vendors to establish an ongoing means of producing selected descriptive statistics on database use, users, and services.[14] The value of ARL's involvement with the vendors, in addition to ICOLC, was that substantial influence was being brought to bear on vendors to provide meaningful data from which libraries could begin making decisions. Through the efforts of ICOLC and ARL, all libraries, including smaller academic and public libraries, are now benefiting from improved data reporting.

USAGE DATA:
WHAT IS THE VALUE?

Regardless of library size, usage data is vitally important. In spite of the inconsistencies in vendor reporting, the data prompts librarians to begin thinking about and formulating their decisions on issues relating to cancellations or additions to electronic collections.

At AUM, in order to garner data to demonstrate how its print journal collections were being utilized, the library checked either circulation records (if the items circulated) or conducted relatively expensive usage studies in-house, measuring the journals that were removed from the shelves by patrons. The latter has generally been deemed to have underreported actual use due to users "assisting" the library by reshelving the journals they were looking at. Even if this were not a factor, for print journal use, the library had no information on which particular issues were used if the title was bound, nor did it know how many articles were examined. Electronic usage statistics provide the AUM Library with more information regarding usage–not necessarily better data, but certainly more of it. The library now knows how many times a particular journal was accessed in each of the databases. The library can determine which articles were most heavily used. The library can also see how many times the article was downloaded, printed, or e-mailed. What AUM cannot know, however, is how successful the integration of the article into the user's work ultimately was. The library assumes that the article met the need, but for a heavy undergraduate population that may rely on the title only to judge an article's relevancy (often without looking at the abstract), students may not discover the inadequacy of the article until later in their research process. This same vagueness applies even to print materials, but the illusion of "information" provided by the usage statistics we receive electronically has and is influencing our perception of the ultimate "value" of our electronic resources to our users.

At Auburn University at Montgomery, the addition of electronic resources are "valued," whether they are in aggregated databases, are
single e-journal subscriptions, or are subject-focused collections, primarily
by the potential support they bring to the curriculum. Does the material
in question fill gaps in our print holdings? Is the convenience of the access such that library users will benefit from the time saved that would
have otherwise been spent looking at multiple print resources? The next
most important factor to the library is examining the average per-use
cost (in terms of searching) for titles, and the average per-access cost for
titles. Because the library is chronically short of space, and because of
the lack of subject-area breadth in its print journals, the library has
sought broad coverage of titles through the acquisition of aggregator databases. When Kenneth Frazier warned libraries about the dangers of the
"Big Deal,"[15] the AUM Library listened. Frazier's warnings about subscriptions to aggregator databases, which bundle their journals, have
proved to be essentially correct. While some modifications in the title
mix can generally be made, that amount is fairly minimal. Aggregators
do bundle their weaker titles with their strongest titles. As a result, libraries end up paying for titles they neither want nor need. In this situation, smaller institutions may end up paying more for more titles, when
costs are averaged out. The AUM Library currently accesses approximately seventy-eight subscribed electronic databases, which provide
access to over 15,000 titles. For these electronic titles, the library pays
roughly $190,000 per year, which is less than two-thirds the cost of its
print subscriptions, but this cost also provides access to more than 700
times the number of titles that are subscribed to in print. Gatten and
Sanville have recognized the importance of increased access, stating,
"Electronic access stimulates a great deal of use both on titles previously available in print and those not previously held."[16] Gatten and
Sanville go on to state, "While sheer volume of use (that is, cost-per-use
analysis) is not the only measure of value, to fail to recognize use as the
dominant starting point is to deny reality."[17]

AUM USAGE

In analyzing usage, AUM has established a timeframe of three years
as being the optimum time required for users to become acquainted with
the existence of a new database. As reported in Luther's "White Paper
on Electronic Journal Usage Statistics," it takes users from sixteen
months to as much as three years to integrate a new resource into their

routines for accessing information.[18] The availability of more than one year of access promotes the heaviest use, along with the provision of user instruction in the library.[19] The three-year baseline used by the AUM Library allows time for the staff to get the database established and well integrated into the library instruction program and also to evaluate and determine the best means of integrating the site into the library Web page.

In addition to using the three-year baseline, the library has worked to determine the average cost-per-access (search) for the databases, utilizing the methodology established by Karla Hahn and Lila Faulkner.[20] Because the library deals with a number of aggregated databases where information on the average number of articles online is not easily available, the library has altered its method for determining the average cost-per-article. Instead of dividing the subscription price by the number of articles online, the library has resorted to utilizing the number of articles printed, e-mailed, and/or downloaded as being representative indicators of usability. The AUM Library continues to rely on Hahn and Faulkner's original approach for those electronic resources, which provide easily identifiable and accessible article data.

As an example of the library's approach, Table 12.1 contains selected library databases, which compare the average cost-per-use over a three-year period. The cost-per-use is then averaged for the three years. Usage is defined as the number of searches.

Following the principle of length of availability, all of the databases declined in cost-per-use over the three-year period. The cost-per-search in each of the three years shows a decline indicating that even with the database costs increasing, the number of searches also increased. The in-

TABLE 12.1. AUM average cost-per-database use.

Database	FY 2001-2002	FY 2002-2003	FY 2003-2004	3-year average
EBSCO World History Full-Text	$6.95	$7.28	$4.51	$6.25
JSTOR	$5.61*	$1.56	$1.11	$2.76
ACS Publications	$147.34	$134.29	$33.70	$106.21
Engineering Village	$248.40	$134.29	$58.42	$147.03
Science Direct	$14.69	$7.59	$5.15	$9.14
Database Average	$84.60	$57.66	$20.58	$54.28

*The figures reported for JSTOR in 2001-02 represent a partial year.

creased familiarity with the database is due, in part, to the library's promotion of the databases via formal instructional sessions and one-on-one
instruction with students by the reference staff.

While the yearly cost-per-search declined, the average cost-per- article unfortunately did not show the same consistency. As Table 12.2
demonstrates, the average cost-per-article during the second year increased for both the EBSCO World History Full-Text database and the
ACS Publications database. The number of articles retrieved for each database during the second year of availability declined for reasons that
the library has not been able to identify. One possibility is that the students were able to target specific articles, lessening their need for broad
subject searches.

It should be noted that the library does provide print subscriptions to
some of the journals in the aforementioned databases. Where the subscription costs for print journals are extra, the additional costs have been
added to the appropriate database cost to help determine a true average
cost. The print usage has also been added to determine average usage
cost, although not for determining the average article cost. This is because the library has no way of tracking article access for print copies.

While recognizing that there are many additional elements of usage
statistics for electronic resources that may be considered, the library
chose the two that seemed to have the greatest impact for its users and
for the library's collection. The average use cost demonstrates to the librarians that the electronic resources have the potential to be cheaper
than subscriptions to print copies. Even taking into account those data-

TABLE 12.2. AUM library average cost-per-article.

Database	FY 2001-2002	FY 2002-2003	FY 2003-2004	3-year average
Ebsco World History Full-Text	$7.66	$12.04	$8.77	$9.49
JSTOR*	$7.32	$1.89	$1.19	$3.47
ACS Publications	$68.59	$129.38	$31.69	$76.55
Engineering Village	$84.40**	$53.88**	$25.56**	$54.61**
Science Direct	$15.61	$7.73	$4.91	$9.42
Database Average	$36.73	$40.98	$14.42	$30.71

*Again, the JSTOR data represents a partial year.
**For Engineering Village, instead of articles the data indicates pages of information shown.
The pages include journal articles, conference reports, and trade publications.

bases which require the maintenance of print, or which add a surcharge on print, the convenience and expanded access for users, particularly during periods when the library is not open, is a great benefit for all. This is especially true on the AUM campus, where many students commute from home. The cost-per-article data for the most part indicate that by providing electronic access, the library is able to limit increasing costs for interlibrary loan. The cost-per-article based usage has a drawback, however, of potentially ignoring the importance of lesser-used titles, which have a significant impact on research.[21] While recognizing this as a limitation, the library also realizes that the major portion of patron usage comes from undergraduate students and is fairly interdisciplinary. As Duy has observed, undergraduates may access a journal's content most frequently by a full-text aggregator database.[22]

It is important to bear in mind the library's collection policy and scope when reviewing databases. The collection policy statements at AUM were developed in conjunction with the teaching faculty in the college disciplines. When the library reviews a database for selection, staff must ask the following questions:

1. Does the database in question fit within the scope of the library's collecting policy?
2. If the library has identified its collection focus in a particular field, for instance, Business at a level 3, how many electronic resources, mapped against its print materials, are necessary for it to maintain or improve on that level of coverage?

Libraries do not, as Jennifer Weintraub noted, make selection decisions solely upon the basis of usage statistics.[23] Assessment and evaluation will be key components to determining the adequacy of the library in areas of its collecting focus. For example, in assessing the AUM Library's holdings in Political Science and Public Administration, the library staff came across numerous books that were only available through the netLibrary collections held by the Library. These titles counted toward the percentage of library holdings, but when staff analyzed usage, electronic access was found to be greater than that for print. Out of twenty-seven titles available electronically only, there were thirteen circulations electronically. For those titles available both in print and electronically, there were seventeen electronic circulations versus four circulations for in-print titles. Assessment, however, requires not just a reading of the utility of items for subject specific collections, but also a broader level of assessment in order to determine utility for inter-disciplinary usage.

Many assessments for journals and journal access take place at the point of finding titles (or databases) to cancel. Most assessments in this regards are impacted because they are discipline-based. Researchers in other disciplines who might be using a journal in another field may be affected by another discipline's decision to cut a title. As Hill notes, "a more appropriate way of evaluating usage is to measure use across the entire community served."[24]

Usage statistics, however detailed and useful they may be, are only a part of the decision making process. Two years ago, the AUM Library decided to drop the ABI/Inform database and instead acquire EBSCO's Business Source Premiere. In examining the access for the two data-bases, the library discovered that Business Source Premiere appeared to offer greater coverage than ABI/Inform for the curriculum offered in the University's School of Business. In addition, the coverage for titles that appeared interdisciplinary also seemed greater. The library ran the title-lists for the two databases and identified the overlaps and unique titles. We then examined the average cost of access for ABI/Inform, which for the library was $4.23 per search. Further, per article access was deter-mined to be $1.19 per article. The library next calculated the per search cost for Business Source Elite, for which there was access through the Alabama Virtual Library. The average cost-per-access, had AUM been paying for it, would have been $0.77 per search. The cost-per-article would have been $0.42 per article. AUM anticipated that by migrating to Business Source Premiere, with its larger pool of titles, it would be able to further decrease the access cost and the per article cost. This in-deed turned out to be the case. By starting access to Business Source Premiere in mid-year, AUM saw an average per use cost of $0.51 and an average per article cost of $0.37. As noted by Shim, Murphy, and Brunning, values such as cost-per-search and cost-per-article are in ef-fect, ratios. Costs for databases are sunk costs, which must be paid for regardless of the level of use.[25] These ratios can, however, anticipate the value upon which our users place on electronic resources.

By determining that EBSCO's Business Source Elite offered a better value for the library's users, AUM was able to extrapolate that value and, in discussions with the teaching faculty, was able to demonstrate that by mov-ing to the Premiere version of the database, there would be: (a) an increase in the number of valuable titles available to the schools' curriculum; and (b) a familiarity with the database structure, such that retraining the students or faculty to search the resource would not be required. Integrating the Premiere version of the database into the Library's instructional program was simplified because of the familiarity with the search interface. The AUM Library was able to exchange its "sunk" cost of ABI/Inform for a product that better met its users' needs, and at a lower cost as well. This lower cost, in turn, freed up financial resources for the library to utilize to add materials in other areas, both in print and in electronic formats.

Usage data has also been helpful in directing the library's acquisition of other electronic resources. The AUM Library has subscribed to OCLC's netLibrary collections, offered as consortial purchases through SOLINET. AUM costs for these collections are paid in advance. Because consortial costs are shared with other libraries throughout the region, the AUM Library has been able to acquire access to more than 40,000 titles at the relatively minimal cost of approximately $2.75 per title. Because the library was acquiring in broad parameters, there was no initial concern about targeting specific subjects for acquisition. In analyzing usage data, it was discovered that over a three-year period, business, economics, and management was the most heavily used category of electronic books. Surprisingly, literature was the second heaviest used subject, followed by computers, social science, medicine, and history. The library subsequently began investigating the addition of more electronic titles in computer science based upon this data. As of this writing, the precise selection of those titles has not yet been identified. Because of the level of use for history, however, the library has agreed to license access to the titles in the American Council of Learned Societies' E-History Book Project. The collection, boasting more than 1,000 titles at present, will provide library users with access to core titles in the subspecialties of history, and the library anticipates significant usage of this collection.

The AUM Library has made a conscious decision to add electronic resources in the disciplines in line with the levels of collection emphasis described in its policy statements. AUM has attempted to include both journals and electronic books within its collection, but as a first priority, it has relied upon increasing journal access. The library's first attempts have aimed at providing broad, interdisciplinary coverage through products such as EBSCO's Academic Search Elite and Infotrac's Expanded Academic ASAP databases. Following this, the AUM library next began focusing upon products for specific subject needs: ACS for Chemistry, Business Source Premiere for the School of Business, MathSciNet for the Mathematics Department, CINAHL for the School of Nursing, and Engineering Village for the Department of Information and Decision Science.

CONCLUSIONS

Usage data provides the library with valuable information on the cost ratios for access, or use, of the databases, and for the cost of the articles. Certainly the cost of articles that the library can provide access to electronically is, with few exceptions, less expensive than relying on traditional interlibrary loan. The library has been able to evaluate potential additions to its database acquisitions in light of the library's collecting policies. When evaluating new resources, the cost ratios of similar databases has proven valuable for understanding what the potential usage must be to make the new addition cost effective. The library has thus been able to establish benchmarks for usage costs in the disciplines, which it can use, as outlined by Hahn and Faulkner, to calculate cost-based usage and article access for new collections.[26] Numbers tell only part of the story, however.

Databases (or journal titles) with low usage may still be important to a library's collection strength. A library's collecting focus will allow it to avoid using the figures as elements of absolute truth. At a smaller institution without access to Institute for Scientific Information's (ISI) citation reports and the impact factors of journals, it must be recognized that rarely used materials may have a value beyond their local costs. When assessments are done of collections, libraries rely on core lists of journals and measure their ability to provide access, either in print or electronically. Librarians must then evaluate with the faculty what resources they see as being core to their teaching of the discipline and try to ensure that librarians meet their needs for access.

Understanding of the limitations of usage data allows librarians the opportunity to integrate the data with collection policies, and helps to focus upon the needs of the user community. The ultimate goal for library collections is to increase the ability to meet users' needs. If librarians remember to include an understanding of the level of coverage the resources offer, users benefit significantly and collections will be much stronger because of this understanding.

NOTES

1. Bernard Rous, ed. *Online Usage Statistics: A Publisher's Guide.* (New York: Association of American Publishers, 2004): 2.

2. Judy Luther. "White Paper on Electronic Journal Usage Statistics," *The Serials Librarian* 41 no. 2 (2001): 119-148.

3. Oliver Pesch. "Usage Statistics: Taking E-Metrics to the Next Level," Report of a Program at the 2003 NASIG Conference. *The Serials Librarian* 46, nos. 1/2 (2004): 143-154.

4. Rebecca L. Kemp. "Selectors' Choices; Statistics for Evaluating E-Resources." Unpublished Master's Paper. University of North Carolina. April 2004: 37.

5. Information taken from Alabama Virtual Library Web site: http://www.virtual. lib.al.us/background/funding.html. Viewed on April 4, 2005.

6. Wosnik Shim, Kurt Murphy, and Dennis Brunning. "Usage Statistics for Electronic Services and Resources: A Library Perspective" in *Online Usage Statistics: A Publisher's Guide*, ed. by Bernard Rous. (New York: Association of American Publishers, 2004): 34-46.

7. Ibid.

8. Joanna Duy. "Usage Data: Issues and Challenges for Electronic Collection Management" in *E-Serials Collection Management: Transitions, Trends, and Technicalities,* ed. David C. Fowler. (Binghamton, NY: Haworth Information Press, 2004): 111-138.

9. Nisonger, Thomas. "Use of the Journal Citation Reports for Serials Management in Research Libraries: An Investigation of the Effects of Self-Citation on Journal rankings in Library and Information Science and Genetics," *College & Research Libraries* 61 no. 3 (May 2000): 263-275.

10. Wosnik, Shim and Charles R. McClure. "Improving Database Vendors' Usage Statistics Reporting through Collaboration between Libraries and Vendors," *College & Research Libraries* 63, no. 6 (November 2002): 499-514.

11. International Coalition of Library Consortia (ICOLC). "Guidelines for Statistical Measure of Usage of Web-Based Indexed, Abstracted, and Full Text Resources (November 1998). Available at: http://www.library.yale.edu/consortia/ webstats.html. Viewed on March 21 2005.

12. Ibid.

13. International Coalition of Library Consortia (ICOLC). "Guidelines for Statistical Measures of Usage of Web-Based Indexed, Abstracted, and Full-Text Resources (December 2001). Available at: http://www.library.yale.edu/consortia/ 2001webstats.htm. Viewed on March 21, 2005.

14. Wosnik Shim and Charles R. McClure. "Improving Database Vendors' Usage Statistics Reporting through Collaboration between Libraries and Vendors." *College & Research Libraries* 63 no. 6 (November 2002): 499-514. For further information on the E-Metrics Project, view the E-Metrics site at: http://www.arl.org/stats/newmeas/ emetrics/index.html. Viewed on March 21, 2005.

15. Kenneth Frazier. "The Librarians' Dilemma: Contemplating the Costs of the 'Big Deal,'" *D-Lib Magazine* 7 no. 4 (March 2001).

16. Jeffrey N. Gatten and Tom Sanville. "An Orderly Retreat from the Big Deal: Is it possible for Consortia?" *D-Lib Magazine* 10, no. 10 (October 2004).

17. Ibid.

18. Judy Luther. "White Paper on Electronic Journals Usage" *Serials Librarian* 41 no. 2 (2001): 119-148.

19. Charles W. Townley and Leigh Murray. "Use-Based Criteria for Selecting and Retaining Electronic Information: A Case Study." *Information Technology and Libraries* 18 no. 1 (March 1999): 32-39.

20. Karla L. Hahn and Lila A. Faulkner. "Evaluative Usage-Based Metrics for the Selection of E-Journals." *College & Research Libraries* 63 no. 3 (May 2002): 215-227.

21. Judy Luther. "White Paper on Electronic Journal Usage Statistics." *The Serials Librarian* 41, no. 2 (2001): 119-148.

22. Duy, Joanna. "Usage Data: Issues and Challenges for Electronic Resource Collection Management," in *E Serials Collection Management: Transitions, Trends, and Technicalities*, ed. by David C. Fowler. (New York: Haworth Press, 2004): 111-121.

23. Jennifer Weintraub. "Usage Statistics at Yale University Library," *Against the Grain* 15, no. 6 (9 Dec. 2003-Jan. 2004): 32, 34.

24. Terry B. Hill. "Using Traditional Methodologies and Electronic Usage Statistics as Indicators to Assess Campus-Wide Journal Needs: Contexts, Trade-offs, and Processes. Unpublished Master's Paper. University of North Carolina (April 2004): 7. Quoted with permission.

25. Wosnik Shim, Kurt Murphy, and Denis Brunning. "Usage Statistics for Electronic Services and Resources: A Library Perspective" in *Online Usage Statistics: A Publisher's Guide*/ed. by Bernard Rous. (New York: Association of American Publishers, 2004): 34-46.

26. Karla L. Hahn and Lila A. Faulkner. "Evaluative Usage-Based Metrics for the Selection of Electronic Journals." *College & Research Libraries* 63 no. 3 (May 2002): 215-227.

doi:10.1300/J123v53S09_13

Chapter 13

Statistics Drive Marketing Efforts

Eleonora Dubicki

INTRODUCTION

Possessing subscriptions to electronic resources does not automatically guarantee their usage by library patrons. As the costs for electronic resources continue to rise, libraries must validate the expenditures for these products. Usage statistics can supply librarians with substantial amounts of information regarding the usage habits by patrons of electronic resources. These statistics are one method by which to quantify the databases that are being used heavily by patrons, as well as a method to identify those being underutilized. There are a number of factors that may influence the level of database usage, including breadth of subject and journal title coverage, full-text coverage, and the extent of retrospective coverage. However, another critical factor that affects the level of usage is the library patron's awareness of the resources available in the library to aid them in conducting their research. The rapid growth in the number of electronic resources requires the library's commitment to promoting these resources and providing efficient access to these research tools.

This chapter focuses on how academic libraries can monitor and analyze usage statistics with the goal of directing promotional efforts for electronic resources. A combination of marketing techniques will be examined, which can be successfully employed to create a heightened

[Haworth co-indexing entry note]: "Statistics Drive Marketing Efforts." Dubicki, Eleonora. Co-published simultaneously in *The Serials Librarian* (The Haworth Information Press, an imprint of The Haworth Press, Inc.) Vol. 53, Supplement No. 9, 2007, pp. 215-231; and: *Usage Statistics of E-Serials* (ed: David C. Fowler) The Haworth Information Press, an imprint of The Haworth Press, Inc., 2007, pp. 215-231. Single or multiple copies of this article are available for a fee from The Haworth Document Delivery Service [1-800-HAWORTH, 9:00 a.m. - 5:00 p.m. (EST). E-mail address: docdelivery@haworthpress.com].

Available online at http://ser.haworthpress.com
doi:10.1300/J123v53S09_14

awareness of electronic resources, thereby resulting in greater utilization of the library's electronic resources.

USE OF ELECTRONIC RESOURCES

During the past several years, there has been a significant trend among academic libraries to transition from print to electronic formats for their serials holdings. According to the Association of Research Libraries (ARL), the percentage of the average library budget spent on electronic resources increased from 3.6 percent in 1992-1993 to 37 percent in 2004-2005. ARL university libraries reportedly spent almost $330 million on electronic resources in 2004-2005.[1] Drexel University has taken an even more aggressive approach to adding electronic resources. Print serial subscriptions at Drexel have dropped from 1,700 in the year 1998, to 294 in 2004, while electronic subscriptions have increased from 200 in 1998, to 15,000 in 2004.[2]

For library administrators, the drivers for this migration to electronic resources include the continued escalation of costs for print serials, the necessity of satisfying library budget cuts, addressing space shortages, the maintenance costs of paper, including those associated with shelving, and the promise of cost reductions associated with the removal of duplication of access in several formats such as print, microform, and electronic. From the library patron's perspective, the electronic format provides the benefits of full-text content, anywhere/anytime access, ease of use, currency, simultaneous and remote user connectivity, direct linking from abstracting and indexing services, ease of printing, and powerful search capabilities.[3,4]

In a response to both administrative and patron-driven needs, libraries have now placed a higher priority on subscribing to databases and e-journals. These electronic resources can be acquired in several ways: individually from publishers, as part of a publisher's package, or from aggregators who offer journals from multiple publishers. While many titles can be ordered individually as e-journals, few libraries have the staff to track thousands of individual subscriptions to e-journals.

Increasingly, small and medium-sized libraries have turned to aggregators such as EBSCO Information Services, H. W. Wilson, Ovid, and ProQuest, all of which offer various packages of serials. Benefits from these aggregated packages are reduced cost-per-title, simplified tracking of serials renewals, and licensing from a limited number of vendors. However, concerns have been raised regarding the composition of the titles in each package, as well as archival access in the future. Subscribing to an aggregator's package precludes individual selection of titles, and libraries are bound to accept a predetermined set of titles. On the other hand, aggregator databases can economically provide broader access to titles than the library was able to maintain previously in a print collection.[5]

The proliferation of electronic resources has resulted in significant changes in patron research habits in the traditional academic library. Both students and faculty take a different approach to conducting research than was customary, when most research was completed using print abstracts and indexes. Now, patrons have easier access to full-text articles electronically and, by searching databases, patrons can compile a set of relevant articles relatively quickly. Electronic access to serials also allows for more follow-up on cited articles, resulting in more comprehensive literature reviews by faculty and graduate students conducting research.[6]

In addition to altering research techniques, there has been a significant change in the physical location of these library users. Electronic resources allow for remote access to information. Research done by Peters indicates, "Many users of our libraries have become primarily or exclusively remote users. In this sense, they are invisible to the naked eye."[7] Similarly, studies conducted by Franklin and Plum indicate that the remote users outnumber the in-house users in medical disciplines, and the authors speculate that similar trends may result in other subject areas, when electronic resources become more widely available for those disciplines.[8]

Given patron acceptance of electronic resources and the significant cost of subscribing to databases, there is a constant need to justify these costs. Usage statistics are one way of measuring the level of utilization of the electronic resources.

COLLECTING USAGE STATISTICS

The amount of time expended on the collection of usage statistics can vary greatly, depending on the number of electronic resource subscriptions, the type of statistics captured for reports, and the data collection technique utilized. Difficulties with collecting reliable electronic resources usage statistics are well documented in the library literature. To meet the challenges of managing electronic resources, a growing number of libraries have created a new position for an "electronic resources librarian," who is responsible for the multitude of tasks associated with acquiring, maintaining, and measuring the usage of electronic resources.

Some of the challenges associated with collecting statistics include deciphering the varying definitions among vendors, the varying data calculation methods, and the differences in data delivery or retrieval methods. Several organizations have been instrumental in "reshaping the metrics being used by publishers, librarians, and information aggregators," including the National Information Standards Organization (NISO), the Association of Research Libraries (ARL), and the International Coalition of Library Consortia (ICOLC). Project COUNTER (Counting Online Usage of NeTworked Electronic Resources) has built upon these initiatives to develop tools for publishers and aggregators for measuring electronic resources with results that are consistent, reliable, and comparable.[9]

Lacking common standards in data received from all vendors, librarians are forced to take a number of different approaches to the collection of usage data. Two common methods for statistical data collection are an in-house analysis of usage based on Web server logs, and the collection of data from publishers and vendors. Both approaches have certain drawbacks. Furthermore, research conducted by Duy and Vaughan found that although locally gathered data and vendor-provided data may show similar patterns of use, the two of them do not provide the same exact quantitative values.[10]

Customized programs that automatically collect usage data on a monthly basis have been developed at some institutions to gather Web server logins to electronic resources. The major benefits to using this approach are the controlled and uniform collection of data, and easy compilation of comparable data. However, a drawback to this method is that the level of data available is frequently limited to number of sessions, and it is difficult to differentiate between multiple sessions at network-based computers.[11]

Vendor-generated statistics are the more prevalent source for usage data collected by libraries. The recent efforts of Project COUNTER have provided vendors with specific terms for inclusion in statistics and methods for counting usage in each category. Detailed statistics are available for a number of categories including number of sessions, number of searches, duration of searches, abstracts viewed, and the number of full-text downloads.[12] Although not all vendors provide this data, most of the major aggregators now provide monthly COUNTER reports, which have improved the ability to do usage comparisons between multiple electronic products.

A well-defined regimen for collecting and analyzing data across multiple products is critical in creating an overall picture of the library patron's electronic resource usage. Microsoft Excel or Access 97 spreadsheets of all e-journal and database subscriptions, with regular monthly updates of usage statistics, can be used to compile the data. The initial creation of a spreadsheet may require a significant effort to identify each vendor's method of disseminating usage data, such as secure statistics Web site, electronic or regular mail delivery. Accessing data from Web sites is often flexible, with customization of reports possible. However, since the exported data formats are not always consistent, it is often necessary to manually reenter data into a spreadsheet rather than import the data from vendor sites directly into local applications.

Another variable in time and complexity required to collect statistics is the richness of the data collected. An analysis of usage statistics for the number of searches/queries conducted by users provides a very basic point of comparison. Alternately, measuring the number of articles downloaded by patrons provides the data most closely related to actual use of print journals, since it reports which articles are being viewed.[13]

Analyzing Usage Statistics

The value of collecting usage statistics can be realized once the data has been analyzed and actions are taken based on the findings. Usage statistics are an invaluable source of data for librarians to better understand how users are accessing electronic resources. While the primary application for collecting usage statistics has been for making subscription and budget decisions, a growing number of libraries have been realizing the potential for utilizing statistics in order to improve marketing, promotion, and library instruction.

Although librarians may look at the statistics for individual resources when making renewal decisions, reviewing usage for all electronic resources provides a better overall picture of how a library's patrons are using its electronic resources. Usage data stored in a spreadsheet can easily be sorted by frequency of usage in order to identify the most heavily utilized databases. Resources that are used less frequently will fall to the bottom of the list, and can serve as initial targets for marketing efforts. Even low-usage databases can benefit from promotion, although the audience of patrons addressed with target marketing may be much smaller than is the audience for a multidisciplinary database that addresses the research needs of multiple academic departments.

Joanna Duy has proposed, "If usage data is low for a resource, it may mean that users are not finding the product and not that the product is not useful."[14] Townley and Murray found that "the longer a database is available, the more likely it is to be known, the more likely users will know how to use it, and the more likely it is to be considered preferable by at least part of the user group." They also found that a resource must be available for twelve to eighteen months before heavy usage can be observed.[15] A number of other factors can influence usage data, such as alternative resources, breadth of coverage, discipline, full-text access, and the implementation of link resolvers.

A one-time snapshot of database usage provides little insight into patron usage patterns and can be very misleading. Usage data should be analyzed over a period of months or, preferably, several years, in order to capture trends in resource adoption and use. In addition to comparing usage over time for single electronic resources, comparisons can also be made with similar-type products from different vendors or usage patterns at peer institutions.[16] An overlap analysis of titles included in a database can also provide additional insights on comparisons between similar-type products such as, if the resources have the same titles, or if certain titles are more heavily accessed.

MARKETING IN ACADEMIC LIBRARIES

The explosive growth in patron usage of electronic resources is an area of technology that has dramatically changed the manner in which students and faculty conduct research, and has radically redefined the role of academic libraries. In recent years, there has been a concerted effort to improve the marketing or promotion of library services in order to address the changing needs of library patrons. As libraries continue to expand their collections and services, they must ensure that patrons are aware of the new products and services, which are now available to them when and where they need them.[17] The transition to electronic access has created multiple issues for libraries, such as the need to keep users informed about the availability of new resources, providing easy access to these new resources, and training the user base as new resources are introduced.

A primary objective of libraries, as well as of other service-oriented institutions, is to ensure that electronic resources are being used successfully by all customers. A successful promotional campaign requires creating an awareness of the product, communicating the features and benefits of the products and services, and providing information on how to access the product.

The efficient use of library resources requires that patrons be able to find the information they need, and that the library gets a return on its investment in the collection. The delivery of services electronically to remote users creates another challenge for libraries. These patrons want their information available from anywhere and anytime with a desired goal of self-sufficiency. Research conducted by Linda Ashcroft and McIvor indicates that "electronic journals require more promotion and evaluation than is currently taking place in most academic libraries."[18] Innovative outreach methods are necessary to market to the largely invisible group of patrons using electronic resources. Promotional techniques that can effectively reach these remote users must be employed, in addition to the traditional in-library promotions such as brochures and flyers.

Linda Ashcroft proposes that, given the complexity of the current electronic environment, "there is a clear need for marketing strategies, which go beyond mere notification if users are to reap the full benefits of electronic journals." End users must be made aware of the information available, be provided directions in how to access the information, and be given the skills to best use that information.[19]

There are a number of promotional tactics that can be employed in a multifaceted approach to create awareness of electronic resources among library patrons:

- Announcements on the library's Home page and database gateway page that highlight individual databases or other electronic resources on a rotating weekly or monthly basis. Alternatively, creating a "top five" list of databases could direct attention to these resources.
- Library newsletters that provide descriptions of new databases and offer search tips on improving research. These should clearly discuss how the database could benefit users with the type of materials it covers.
- Discipline-specific targeted e-mails to faculty and to students by major, in order to highlight databases specific to that discipline, using examples of types of questions that can be answered.
- Posters, signs, flyers, bookmarks, and brochures for patrons visiting the library and lab locations with brief descriptions and information on accessing electronic resources. Vendor-supplied materials could be adapted for use in the library.

- Incorporation of electronic resources into the library catalog as another point of access in addition to the electronic resource gateway page. The inclusion in the catalog would allow subject searching in order to identify discipline-specific services.
- Conducting demonstrations and workshops for faculty, staff, and students on using electronic resources. Several levels of workshops, from beginner to advanced, could be offered, in order to explain the complexities of using new electronic products and to highlight search techniques for new databases, or for new search interfaces.
- Outreach programs directed at faculty to develop instructional sessions supporting class work and research assignments. Sessions could focus on improving search techniques in order to maximize information gathered by covering key databases and identifying supplementary print materials.
- Setting up automatic topic "alerts" for faculty from databases, with immediate notification of new research in their discipline.
- FAQ pages and online guides to help users improve research skills including defining topic areas, selecting databases to search, and developing search strategies. Help pages could be created for vendor databases.
- Using creative ideas for delivering promotional messages. Promotional materials could be inserted into mouse pads at each public access computer in the library. Business card sized "database information cards" could be created for discipline-specific databases, which could include directions for access that could be distributed after an instructional workshop, or after demonstration of the database.

Not only do libraries need to use marketing messages in order to keep users informed about the availability of new resources and to train the user base as new resources are introduced, but patrons also need to be reminded of resources that are already available in the library, but which are underutilized. Paula Wilson explained, "Each electronic resource that the library subscribes to has a potential audience. Find out who they are, then determine how to reach them."[20]

Communications should be clear and concise, focusing on a specific topic and acquainting users with the benefits of tapping into the electronic resource.[21] In an academic setting, communication among faculty and students is primarily via e-mail, and this offers an effective way of reaching library patrons. Tailored e-mail messages to a particular faculty or student group are much more effective than using generic messages to an entire user group, which may result in e-mail overload. By focusing on the relevance that a research tool has for a particular group and providing discipline-specific examples of searches, users are more likely to see the benefit of using suggested resources and are more likely to become repeat users. Patrons will be motivated to use a database if they can realize how searching the database will improve the convenience and ease of acquiring materials to complete their assignments, and show improvements in the quality and quantity of the information obtained. Similarly, communication regarding underutilized resources can help draw attention to resources in particular areas.

Promotional messages should not be a one-time event. Repetition reinforces the message and increases the likelihood that patrons will change their usage patterns.[22] A promotional campaign should be a series of messages with a similar look and feel (Figures 13.1 and 13.2). Following initial notifications regarding a new resource, targeted follow-up communications should be accomplished using brief alerts to highlight new features or training opportunities. Furthermore, every opportunity should be taken to promote new and old resources during any interactions with patrons–at the reference desk, helping at computers, or in general conversations–and not just during training sessions.

Publisher or vendor Web sites can offer ideas for library promotions. Specific benefits and examples of searches are usually incorporated into a vendor's promotional material for a database and those ideas can help tailor a message to users. Some vendors offer collaborative marketing programs that can extend the library's marketing efforts. E-journal publisher Elsevier offers several aids on their Web site that libraries can use in developing promotional materials, as well as in presentations on issues for library marketing.[23]

TIMING OF PROMOTIONS

A thorough analysis of monthly usage data will also provide indicators for the optimal timing of marketing efforts in order to coincide with patrons' research needs. In an academic setting with a fall and spring semester, higher electronic resources usage can be expected during the second and third months of a semester, when students are completing research projects. Institutions with three or four semesters per year will have different times for peak database usage, which can be identified through a full-year trend analysis. Intersession and summer sessions are

FIGURE 13.1. Research made easy @ your library.

Research made easy @ your library ®

Need to research a company? We have **Standard &**
Poor's NetAdvantage online. Try It!

FIGURE 13.2. Literature resources online.

To: English Faculty & English Majors
Subject: Literature Resources Online

Literature Resource Center provides access to biographies, bibliographies, and critical
analyses of authors from every age and literary discipline.Covers more than 120,000
novelists, poets, essayists, journalists, and other writers, with in-depth coverage of
2,500 authors. Examples of research questions that can be answered:

- Biography of Edgar Allan Poe
- Literary critique of Eugene O'Neill's *Beyond the Horizon*
- Timeline of literature of the Middle Ages

Literature Resource Center can be accessed from the Library's Electronic
Resources webpage: (link)

typically lower-use periods, with fewer students and faculty utilizing the library's resources.

The analysis of long-term trends in the library patron's electronic resources usage will show which months have higher-than-average usage, corresponding to peaks in research needs. Discussions with faculty, in order to review the timing of research assignments, can be a very effective method to corroborate usage trends and to identify the most opportune time for delivering targeted promotions. "Just-in-time" promotions, when patrons can immediately utilize the information on resources in order to aid in the completion of class projects, are the most effective. Otherwise, users may not immediately try the databases when they receive a marketing promotion and are thus less likely to remember the database in future months when they are completing assignments. In Table 13.1, a summary of searches performed in a selected group of databases indicates that the months with the highest usage of electronic resources are February, March, April, October, and November. This

TABLE 13.1. Database usage trends.

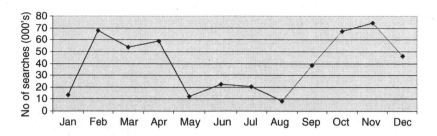

example illustrates usage at an institution with two full semesters and several shorter sessions during the summer. Promotions during these periods are likely to be the most successful in stimulating additional usage.

MARKETING UNDERUTILIZED DATABASES

Libraries can identify which electronic resources are receiving high usage and those being underutilized by analyzing usage statistics. Data collected in a spreadsheet can easily be sorted by the number of searches or other criteria. Once the resources having low usage are identified, the intended customer for that resource should be identified, and a promotional campaign targeted to that group can be developed. For example, *CQ Researcher,* a database with reports on topics of current interest, can be promoted to the English faculty and all freshmen, who will typically write a research paper for an English 101 class or freshman seminars on popular or controversial topics. By talking to faculty members, the timing of the promotion can coincide with the assignment of the project. Promotions can take several forms, including targeted e-mails, posters in the library, special notices on Web pages, and instructional sessions (Figure 13.3).

If multiple discipline-specific databases are available for patrons to search, a further analysis comparing the usage of these databases may show how they are being used. Table 13.2 illustrates usage in several business databases. By looking at additional data on the number of full-text journals available in the database, as well as the number of full-text articles reviewed, a more comprehensive perspective of the usage emerges. Masterfile Premier, while including the largest number of titles, is not the most heavily used database in terms of searches or articles

FIGURE 13.3. Help on current topics research.

To: English Faculty & Freshman Students
Subject: Help on current topics research

Looking for a current topic for your research paper?

• cosmetic surgery	• media bias
• celebrity culture	• gun control
• sports & drugs	• social security reform
• cloning	• migrant farm workers
• youth suicide	• middle east peace

CQ Researcher reports cover a wide range of political and social issues, including topics in health, international affairs, education, the environment, technology and the U.S. economy.

Access **CQ Researcher** from the Library's Electronic Resources webpage: (link)

For related journal and newspaper articles search: **Academic Search Premier, Wilson Omnifile, or Lexis/Nexis Academic.**

TABLE 13.2. Business database usage.

Database	# Searches	Full-text articles viewed	Full-text journals
ABI Inform Global	11,738	8,859	1,756
Accounting and Tax	7,873	341	267
Masterfile Premier	5,740	1,946	2,137
Business FT	3,001	553	463
Business Source Elite	2,234	1,640	1,121

viewed. A number of factors may influence this usage. However, a targeted e-mail to the business department that highlights the Masterfile Premier database could increase awareness of the database, and could probably boost usage. Later, promotions could be used to promote some of the other business databases, or their subscriptions should be reevaluated for cost-effectiveness.

Another approach in determining the need for promotion is a comparison of a library's database usage against usage at similar-sized institutions. Excellent examples for this type of analysis are usage statistics for JSTOR, a digital archive of scholarly journals. Statistics available from JSTOR include a comparison of the subscribing library's title usage with that of similar-sized libraries. An analysis of usage by discipline category may reveal that certain academic departments may not be utilizing the resources as effectively as possible. In the statistics sample illustrated in Table 13.3, it appears that journals in business and economics disciplines are being underutilized by library patrons compared to use in 539 other medium-sized libraries. On the other hand, users in education, history, and language, and literature appear to be using JSTOR in greater proportions than users at other libraries.

The low usage can be addressed by sending a very specific marketing message to the business and economics department faculty, as well as to students majoring in this area on how they would benefit by using JSTOR to meet their research needs. While some general information on the database can be included, it is imperative to tailor the benefits that this specific audience will achieve by using the database to conduct research. A sample message is illustrated (Figure 13.4), which includes very specific examples for research projects in economics.

PROMOTING NEW DATABASES

Promotions for new databases should commence immediately upon subscription. A brief announcement to draw attention to the new resource should be posted in multiple locations on the library's Web site, such as the Home page and electronic resources gateway page (Figure 13.5). The objective is to capture the users' attention several times, and from multiple potential access points to the electronic resources.

It is also important to offer training sessions or to create online tutorials for subject-specific databases, offering concrete examples of search strategies. These should focus on what is unique to the database,

TABLE 13.3. JSTOR relative usage by discipline.

Discipline	Your site (%)	Your site size (%)	All sites (%)
Business	4.0	10.3	12.0
Economics	3.4	6.9	8.7
Education	7.7	3.0	2.3
History	20.7	10.1	7.6
Language and Literature	20.6	10.1	7.6

FIGURE 13.4. Help with economics research.

To: Economics Faculty & Majors
Subject: Help with economics research

JSTOR provides a deep electronic archive of scholarly journal literature. Each journal in JSTOR can be searched or browsed back to its first issue, some dating back to the 1880's.

Examples of research questions that can be answered using this database:
   Articles discussing the gold standard and money supply
   Articles analyzing reparations after WWI and the international flow of capital
   Review of D. Patinkin's book, *Keynes' Monetary Thought: A Study of Its Development*

The **JSTOR** database can be accessed via the alphabetical list of databases on the Library's Electronic Resources webpage: (link)

FIGURE 13.5. New @ your library.

New@your library®
We now have ***Sociological Abstracts*** online. Try It!

The Library has acquired ***Communication & Mass Media***. Try It!

especially, the terminology that should be used to improve search results. Furthermore, one should point out that the discipline-specific nature of these databases allow for a very narrow searching on a specific subject with customized results, rather than the general search that would be done in a multidisciplinary database producing a large set of results, which may only be peripherally relevant to the user's topic.

EVALUATION OF PROMOTIONS

Research conducted by Linda Ashcroft found that the majority of respondents "did not specifically evaluate effects of promotional initiatives." There is a heavy reliance on usage statistics to evaluate marketing, but it is critical to create a baseline for measuring actual effectiveness of promotions. Further methods of evaluation include electronic questionnaires, customer surveys, and citation counts. Ashcroft suggests that new skills in marketing and market research need to be employed by librarians to evaluate promotions.[24]

Other means of evaluation could include qualitative methods, such as focus groups with users and faculty in order to discuss which promotional techniques received the best reaction, and also to solicit alternative ways to reach users.[25] Townley and Murray state, "It is important to develop a model that any library can use to evaluate any database in terms of its ability to meet local demographics."[26]

Working from another perspective, collaboration with faculty can be used to create an awareness of resources among faculty, and lead to instructional sessions to deliver database training for specific assignments, and a subsequent evaluation of the quality of the completed student assignments. Follow-ups can be done with faculty members to review the benefits of instructional sessions, and to identify which aspects of the instructional session were the most helpful for students in conducting their research. These findings can then be used to modify future instructional programs.

Evaluation of promotions may also indicate the necessity for more detailed data collection than simply counting the number of database sessions or searches. It may be necessary to expand data collection to capture the number of downloads of articles or usage at the journal-level, rather than by database.

CONCLUSIONS

It is essential to apply the knowledge gathered from collection and analysis of electronic resource usage statistics. By applying that knowledge to targeted promotional efforts, librarians can improve the library patrons' experience in acquiring the information they need. Creating awareness of the available electronic resources will also improve patrons' perceptions regarding the value of library products and services. We as a profession cannot defer to the "if we build it, they will come" mentality. Librarians must justify costs associated with their collection, but even more important, libraries need to entice users to fully experience the benefits of using the collection.

Furthermore, benchmarking library data against peer institutions may lead to identifying best practices in marketing being utilized by libraries that can be emulated at other institutions. Ultimately, the more the analysis that is done, the more useful the results will be in defining future promotional efforts that increase awareness of library products, improve the library's return on investments in electronic resources, and create an environment for improvements in user satisfaction with library services and the quality of research.

NOTES

1. Martha, Kyrillidou, and Mark Young, *ARL Statistics 2004-05*. (Washington, DC: Association of Research Libraries, 2006).

2. Carol Hansen, Montgomery, "E-Journals Only at Drexel: After Four Years," *The Charleston Conference*. Charleston, SC: November 6, 2004.

3. Sulekha, Kalyan, "Non-Renewal of Print Journal Subscriptions that Duplicate Titles in Selected Electronic Databases: a Case Study," *Library Collections, Acquisitions, & Technical Services* 26 no. 4 (2002): 410.

4. Martin J. Brennan, Julie M. Hurd, Deborah D. Blecic, and Ann C. Weller, "A Snapshot of Early Adopters of E-Journals: Challenges to the Library," *College & Research Libraries* 63 no. 6 (2002): 524.

5. Judy, Luther, *White Paper on Electronic Journal Usage Statistics*. October 2000. http://www.clir.org/pubs/reports/reports.html

6. Brennan, "A Snapshot of Early Adopters" 522.

7. Thomas, Peters, "What's the Use? The Value of E-Resource Usage Statistics," *New Library World* 103 no.1172/1173 (2002): 42.

8. Brinley, Franklin and Terry Plum, "Library Usage Patterns in the Electronic Information Environment." *Information Research* 9 no. 4 (2004) [available at http://www.informationR.net/ir/9-4/paper187.html]

9. Peter T. Sheperd and Denise M. Davis, "Electronic Metrics, Performance Measures, and Statistics for Publishers and Libraries: Building Common Ground Standards." *Portal: Libraries and the Academy* 2 no. 4 (2002): 659, 662.

10. Joanna, Duy and Liwen Vaughan, "Usage Data for Electronic Resources: A Comparison Between Locally Collected and Vendor-Provided Statistics." *The Journal of Academic Librarianship* 29 no. 1 (2003): 21.

11. Ibid., 17.

12. Joanna, Duy, "Usage Data: Issues and Challenges for Electronic Resource Collection Management." *E-Serials Collection Management Transitions, Trends and Technicalities*, edited by David C. Fowler (Binghamton, NY: Haworth Press, 2004), 124.

13. Ibid.

14. Duy, "Usage Data: Issues" 126.

15. Charles M. Townley, and Leigh Murray, "Use-Based Criteria for Selecting and Retaining Electronic Information: A Case Study," *Information Technology and Libraries* 18 no. 1 (1999): 38.

16. Peters, "What's the Use" 44.

17. Association of College and Research Libraries (ACRL), 3M, Inc and A.B. Reynolds. *Strategic Marketing for Academic and Research Libraries, Participant Manual*, p.19.

18. Linda, Ashcroft, and Stephanie McIvor, "Electronic Journals: Managing and Educating for a Changing Culture in Academic Libraries." *Online Information Review* 25 no. 6 (2001): 385.

19. Linda, Ashcroft, "Win-Win-Win: Can the Evaluation and Promotion of Electronic Journals Bring Benefits to Library Suppliers, Information Professionals, and Users?" *Library Management* 21 no. 9 (2000): 466.

20. A. Paula, Wilson, "Take It to the Street," *Netconnect* (Summer 2004) Supplement, 13.

21. ACRL, Strategic Marketing, 34.

22. Ibid., 41.

23. Elsevier, http://www.info.sciencedirect.com

24. Ashcroft, "Electronic Journals," 386.

25. Ibid.

26. Townley and Murray, "Use-Based Criteria," 37.

doi:10.1300/J123v53S09_14

Chapter 14

Uses of Necessity
or Uses of Convenience?
What Usage Statistics Reveal
and Conceal About Electronic Serials

Norm Medeiros

INTRODUCTION

The standardization and assessment of processes related to managing electronic resources have necessarily lagged a few years behind the inception of such processes. As an example, electronic journals (e-journals) had been available for several years before Nancy Olson's *Cataloging Internet Resources* was published in 1995.[1] Until the publication of Olson's seminal text, pioneering catalogers developed uncoordinated local practices within the construct of AACR2 and MARC to provide bibliographic description for these elusive resources. Several years before the Digital Library Federation (DLF) commissioned Tim Jewell of the University of Washington to investigate management issues associated with electronic resources, many academic libraries had been recording administrative metadata about e-resources within spreadsheets and homegrown databases. As a result of Jewell's study, the DLF sponsored the Electronic Resource Management Initiative

[Haworth co-indexing entry note]: "Uses of Necessity or Uses of Convenience? What Usage Statistics Reveal and Conceal About Electronic Serials." Medeiros, Norm. Co-published simultaneously in *The Serials Librarian* (The Haworth Information Press, an imprint of The Haworth Press, Inc.) Vol. 53, Supplement No. 9, 2007, pp. 233-243; and: *Usage Statistics of E-Serials* (ed: David C. Fowler) The Haworth Information Press, an imprint of The Haworth Press, Inc., 2007, pp. 233-243. Single or multiple copies of this article are available for a fee from The Haworth Document Delivery Service [1-800-HAWORTH, 9:00 a.m. - 5:00 p.m. (EST). E-mail address: docdelivery@haworthpress.com].

(ERMI) to investigate the needs of libraries with respect to electronic resources. The final report of the ERMI group, two years in the making, was released in August 2004.[2] It contained detailed, comprehensive specifications that identified the elements, values, and relationships that formed the foundation of e-resource administration. Functional specifications 40.1 through 40.7 are devoted to usage statistics, one of the next important challenges for libraries.

A BRIEF HISTORY
OF E-JOURNAL USAGE STATISTICS

Measuring the use of serials is not a new phenomenon. One needs only to browse the dusty bound volumes of *Library Literature* to see how ubiquitous this activity was in past decades. Goehlert,[3] Maxin,[4] and Broadus[5] have described the value of usage statistics when making collection development decisions about print journals. Impetus for these studies of the late 1970s and early 1980s was the rising cost of serials, especially scientific/technological/medical (STM) journals. Sadly, the serials cost crisis has not only persisted, but also been exacerbated by the advent of the e-journal.

In 1997, the JSTOR Users Group created a Web Statistics Task Force to investigate desirable usage statistics reporting.[6] Early in their work, the Task Force discovered that reporting inconsistencies and other problems, more plentiful than had been anticipated, might be alleviated if the vendor community adopted a common set of standards. In response to the JSTOR investigation, the International Coalition of Library Consortia (ICOLC) developed guidelines in the following year that were adopted by dozens of consortia throughout North America and Europe, citing a "responsibility to their library members to ensure the provision of usage information of licensed electronic resources."[7] These guidelines included elements such as number of queries, logins, turnaways, and item-type displays (for example, tables of contents; abstracts; full-text articles). These data were considered desirable for learning how and how often e-resources were being used. On the heels of the ICOLC guidelines, Project COUNTER (Counting Online Usage of NeTworked Electronic Resources), an international initiative developed in 2002 in large part by publishers in the United Kingdom, sought to create "services to be measured in a credible, consistent, and compatible way using vendor-generated data."[8] This code, which dictates how sessions and file types should be counted, recorded, and delivered to libraries, has been adopted by a growing number of e-resource suppliers. The gradual increase in "COUNTER-compliant" suppliers has been a significant step toward realizing a global set of standards for measuring usage of electronic resources. Although other means of usage reporting have been implemented, COUNTER has become the de facto standard for the scholarly publishing community.[9]

WHY DO WE TRACK USE?

Libraries have long been fond of measuring usage of the resources they provide. As Weintraub notes, "Librarians in the all-print library were happy with their relative understanding of how much their collection was used. They could get information by keeping records of circulation, journal browsing, and even a cursory look at how well worn their books were. In the electronic world, we do not have those cues."[10] Circulation is among the most tracked statistic in libraries, but other statistics, both for collections and services, are also monitored. Commonly tracked statistics include reference interviews, Web site accesses, and gate counts. Libraries are often asked for these and other data from statistics-collecting agencies. Consequently, reporting to these bodies is a key reason for maintaining such statistics.

Although, recently, at least one statistics-collecting agency has asked about e-journal usage for a certain set of resources, libraries that track usage do so because they feel such data can help with current or future collection development. Usage statistics often contribute to, and at times dictate, retention and cancellation decisions. Tracking usage, in a manner that incorporates financial review, can determine whether it makes sense fiscally to retain a subscription or, instead, to gain access to needed articles through a document supplier. With respect to print journals, this practice has never been exact. As Galbraith reminds us, "Usage studies of print collections assign one use per journal issue or volume, regardless of how many articles within the issue or volume were reviewed."[11] The inexplicable nature of article-level usage with print journals creates a fundamental flaw with the data collected. As a result, comparing or integrating print journal usage with e-journal usage, which is recorded at the article level, is worthless. In light of this "apples to oranges" comparison, and of the continued migration of print holdings to electronic, the need for maintaining statistics on print journal usage must be called into question. Yet, the continued rise of serials subscription costs, the splintering of journal titles, and the multi-payment of content (e.g., paying for current issues as well as back issues as well as aggregator content) are strong catalysts for maintaining e-resource usage statistics.

SPREADSHEETS GALORE

Despite the adoption of COUNTER-compliant usage statistics by a growing bloc of e-journal providers, the maintenance of usage statistics is a labor-intensive activity. COUNTER statistics by rule port to spreadsheets ably, as do many usage reports provided by non-COUNTER-compliant providers. Merely accumulating spreadsheets of e-journal usage, however, does not provide the kind of immediate and longitudinal analysis libraries need, in order to make both informed and on-demand collection management decisions. Still, the practice of storing countless spreadsheets of usage data predominates among statistics maintainers, since no agreeable alternative presently exists.

Complicating matters is the desire to analyze usage against expenditures. Since fee-based document suppliers can provide immediate online access to a large body of current journal articles, determining whether a journal subscription or a pay-per-use approach to article provision is the more fiscally sensible route has become an important decision making factor. Typical usage analysis compared to cost data might look like the following:

Journal title	Use	Cost	Cost-per-use
XYZ Journal	25	$1,000.00	$40.00

If individual articles from the notional *XYZ Journal* could be purchased for $20 through a document supplier, a library might consider surrendering its subscription to that journal, since the cost of maintaining a subscription ($1,000) is greater than the amount the library would spend to purchase the needed articles ($500). This example presupposes that the cost-per-use measurement is accurately calculated (although, it is not); that the number of uses from *XYZ Journal* would remain constant if a subscription was not maintained by the library (although, highly unlikely); and that the staff costs of mediated or even unmediated article delivery are comparable to staff costs associated with maintaining a subscription (although difficult to determine, but probably not).

COST-PER-USE:
MEANINGLESS AND ERROR-LADEN DATA

The easiest of these three presuppositions to discredit is the cost-per-use calculation. As already noted, an important reason for tracking the usage statistics of e-journals is for collection development purposes. The disaggregating of "big deals" is opportune, but it also means that libraries must understand the curriculum and the research needs of faculty and students in order to identify the specific e-journals within a publisher's stable that are most valuable to their academic community. Part of this identification process is determining whether the retention of a subscription versus reliance on document delivery is the more fiscally sensible option. Cost-per-use, as illustrated in the previous section, is the means most commonly employed to make this determination. The figure is calculated by dividing the number of full-text uses reported in a year by the subscription cost of the e-journal (cost/use = cost-per-use). This calculation ignores staff costs incurred in maintaining a subscription, as well as staff costs that would be incurred if an article-based document delivery medium was employed in favor of a subscription. Staff costs aside, the cost-per-use calculation as generated in this section is flawed.

This easily recognizable flaw is somehow overlooked or purposely ignored by most libraries maintaining such cost-per-use statistics. Holmstrom illustrates this flaw, replacing the phrase cost-per-use with "return on investment."[12] Holmstrom argues that cost-per-use calculations do not consider uses of journals from years other than the subscription period under review. Using our *XYZ Journal* as an example, if the 2004 subscription cost was $1,000, and the e-journal was accessed twenty-five times during that year, the cost-per-use of *XYZ Journal* as typically calculated would equal $40. This calculation is inherently flawed, however, since publisher-provided statistics do not reveal the percentage of these twenty-five uses that were of 2004 journal issue content only. Even COUNTER-compliant usage statistics do not yet require this level of specificity–the age of the material being accessed–probably because few libraries are prepared to utilize such detail. Nonetheless, if collection development decisions are being made based on cost-per-use calculations, libraries ought to apply a more rigorous calculus.

Holmstrom suggests an algorithm drawn from studies performed by Carol Tenopir and Donald King in the 1990s, and documented in their seminal text, *Towards Electronic Journals*.[13] Tenopir and King conclude that issues from the current year of science journals constitute 58.5 percent of all uses of these journals in a given year, whereas, the remaining 41.5 percent of uses are from issues published in previous years.[14] In the *XYZ Journal* example, the 25 uses recorded in 2004 would equal 14.6 uses from calendar-year 2004 content, using the Tenopir-King formula. Instead of a cost-per-use equaling $40, the cost-per-use would equal $68.49 ($1,000 divided by 14.6). Yet, this cost-per-use calculation is not quite accurate either, since it does not take into account the future uses of 2004 journal content. According to the Tenopir-King formula, articles from the 2004 issues of *XYZ Journal* would represent 12.3 percent of the uses recorded for the journal in 2005. If usage for *XYZ Journal* grew by 20 percent in 2005, meaning the journal was accessed 30 times, the Tenopir-King formula estimates that 3.7 of these 30 uses, or 12.3 percent, would be from 2004 journal issue content. When added to the 14.6 uses of 2004 journal content accessed during 2004, the new cost-per-use figure is $54.64 ($1,000 divided by (14.6 + 3.7)). Looking outward one additional year, during calendar year 2006, usage of 2004 journal content would represent 6.2 percent of all uses, according to the Tenopir- King model. If usage of *XYZ Journal* in 2006 grew, once again by 20 percent, bringing overall usage to 36, 2.2 of these uses would be from 2004 content. When factored into the 2004 equation, the new cost-per-use equals $48.78 ($1,000 divided by (14.6 + 3.7 + 2.2)). Given the limitation of current statistics-reporting capabilities, cost-per-use should be derived from a Tenopir-King-like formula, which factors in all uses of an e-journal over the lifetime of that e-journal. This model seems to be a more precise means of calculating cost-per-use.

Unfortunately, usage statistics measure only utility, not value. As Luther notes, "It is dangerous to assume that a popular title, which is used by many students, is worth more than a research title that is used by only a few faculty members working in a specific discipline. Other factors need to be considered."[15] Indeed, caution must be exercised when considering how to weigh publisher-provided usage statistics within the decision-making framework. In the era of print-only serials, librarians recognized that usage studies in open-stacks environments underrepresented actual use. Consequently, the role of these studies in journal renewal/cancellation decisions was comparatively inferior to the role that usage reports for e-journals are tending to play in today's libraries. The ability to count article-level uses of e-journals, a relative impossibility with print journals, contributes to the exalted role that online usage statistics play in collection development decisions. One fundamental and critically important difference between library-administered journal use studies and publisher-provided usage statistics is motive. Libraries want to know which journals are being used and not being used by patrons, in order to make informed journal renewal and cancellation decisions. Publishers' interest in what usage statistics reveal about their e-journals may not be so impartial.

TRUSTING USAGE STATISTICS

Some authors have alluded to the potential of e-serials providers manipulating usage statistics in order to inflate usage.[16,17] It is not hard to imagine some publishers padding actual use as a way of enticing renewal of certain middle-tier journals. Perhaps in response to this concern, COUNTER employed a rigorous auditing requirement to ensure the authenticity of statistics. The *COUNTER Code of Practice* details the measures used to enforce "credibility, consistency, and compatibility" of usage statistics.[18] The audit test for the most coveted statistic, "Journal Report 1: Number of Successful Full-Text Article Requests," includes the following:[19]

1. The auditor performs 100 requests for full-text articles from a selection of available journals.
2. The auditor records the requests he made from each journal accessed.
3. The auditor compiles a report that lists the requests, separating them by journal.
4. The publisher passes the audit test, when the auditor's report and the publisher's report are within a -8 percent and $+2$ percent reliability window.

A number of additional audit tests occur for COUNTER reports. These include testing "double-clicks" to ensure that clicks for an HTML file that occur within a ten-second window, and clicks for a PDF file that occur within a thirty-second window, are counted only once; verifying that the contractual number of simultaneous accesses (user seats) are available; and ensuring proper session and turnaway counts. This third party auditing should give libraries a measure of confidence about the credibility of publisher-supplied COUNTER-compliant usage statistics, particularly comforting as pricing models based on use begin to appear. At the same time, perhaps this rigorous auditing procedure is a reason why at least some e-resource providers remain outside the COUNTER initiative.

USES OF NECESSITY, USES OF CONVENIENCE

As useful as they may be, COUNTER-compliant usage statistics cannot record motive for use. As Phil Davis states, "While usage statistics can tell us so much about *how much* a journal or resource is being used, it cannot tell us *why* it was used" (emphasis in original).[20] Although empirical data on uses of necessity and uses of convenience will never become an available COUNTER report, clearly there is some number of e-journal uses that merely meet a professorial requirement (e.g., a certain number of journal articles necessary in a bibliography) versus satisfying an information need; that is, being an article that answers well the question at hand. Many a reference librarian has watched helplessly while a patron accepts a full-text article that can be accessed immediately and printed in place of the more-pertinent article for which only a citation exists online. Granted, if the student's paper is due in one hour, and the journal in which the more-pertinent article resides would need to be requested via interlibrary loan, accessing the less-relevant but full-text article is understandable. Time constraints, however–or more typically, procrastination–aren't always the culprit. Today's culture of convenience and immediate gratification, which encourages this last-minute behavior, is further evidence that e-resource usage statistics should only augment, not dictate, collection development practices. There are numerous reasons why an obscure e-journal might receive relatively high usage, none of which may have anything to do with ongoing curricular or research needs. E-journals with longitudinal data revealing strong usage should cause notice; one-year wonders should not.

ADMINISTERING USAGE STATISTICS

Despite flawed cost-per-use calculations, uses of convenience, and the possibility of artificially inflated usage statistics provided by deceitful publishers, the maintenance and analysis of usage statistics for e-journals are important activities. To date, most libraries that have chosen to expend the effort to compile usage statistics have created spreadsheets into which they input or download data. This means of maintaining statistics make data sharing difficult. A more attractive model is a statistics repository where various staff and/or institutions can store and retrieve statistics. For example, the centralization of usage statistics would be especially useful in a consortium environment where resources are purchased collectively and used on separate campuses. If COUNTER-compliant usage data could be ingested into a repository, statistics could be available to appropriate members of a library or consortium community in a more timely, less staff-time-intensive manner.

Before library information systems vendors begin expending energy building such statistics repositories, the library community must determine what it hopes to achieve by way of usage statistics. Caryn Anderson of Simmons College surveyed members of the Electronic Resources in Libraries (ERIL) LISTSERV in summer 2004 with just this question in mind.[21] Respondents indicated that a system that could integrate usage statistics with financial data, make comparisons with peer institutions, and provide subject analysis, would be a powerful tool. Anderson used the survey to help her develop the model for her Electronic Resource Usage Statistics (ERUS) database, a repository that can store COUNTER statistics and provide access to these by subject and resource type. Andrew Nagy, a library technology development specialist at Villanova University, has developed a similar statistics-ingesting/reporting/managing system named LibSGR (Library Statistics Gathering and Reporting). Nagy's application imports comma-delimited files of usage statistics, and is capable of delivering various reports generated from these data. Anderson, Nagy, and their colleague, Tim McGeary, a senior systems specialist at Lehigh University, have agreed to combine their efforts into building a decision support system. The system will utilize open standards and provide libraries with an application to help relate usage statistics with other decision criteria, such as resource price, impact factor, and faculty interest. The group plans to share the results of their collaboration in the future.

CONCLUSIONS

Few would argue that standardized and credible usage statistics for electronic resources should not be used as a complement to other journal utility and value measures. Fewer still would argue that usage statistics maintained in an automated fashion and fused with other decision criteria would be worthless to them. Clearly, usage statistics for electronic journals will become only more important as collections shift from print to electronic. Although libraries have little choice but to rely on publisher-provided statistics for electronic journals, at least those based on the *COUNTER Code of Practice* are standardized and audited. As use-based pricing takes hold as a viable, and perhaps, popular pricing model, libraries will have an added incentive to maintain timely statistics, whether in traditional spreadsheets, or within the framework of a centralized database along the Anderson/Nagy/McGeary model. Lastly, despite everything that usage statistics cannot reveal, they are still the best utility measure available to libraries. We must accept their shortcomings and utilize their potential.

NOTES

1. Nancy B. Olson, Cataloging Internet Resources: *A Manual and Practical Guide* (Dublin, OH: OCLC, 1995).

2. Timothy D. Jewell, et al. *Electronic Resource Management: The Report of the DLF Initiative*, August 2004, http://www.dlf.org/pubs/dlfermi0408 (April 18, 2005).

3. Robert Goehlert, "Journal Use per Monetary Unit: A Reanalysis of Use Data," *Library Acquisitions: Practice and Theory* 3 (1979): 91-98.

4. Jacqueline A. Maxin, "Periodical Use and Collection Development," *College & Research Libraries* 40 (1979): 248-253.

5. Robert N. Broadus, "The Measurement of Periodicals Use," *Serials Review* 11 (1985): 57-61.

6. Jim Mullins, "Statistical Measures of Usage of Web-Based Resources," *Serials Librarian* 36 (1999): 207-210.

7. International Coalititon of Library Consortia, *Guidelines for Statistical Measures of Usage of Web-Based Indexed, Abstracted, and Full-Text Resources, Serials Librarian,* November 1998, http://www.library.yale.edu/consortia/webstats. html (April 19, 2005).

8. *COUNTER Code of Practice,* December 1, 2002, http://www.projectcounter. org/code_practice.html (April 15, 2005).

9. Peter T. Shepherd, "Industry Initiatives," in *Online Usage Statistics: A Publisher's Guide,* ed. Bernard Rous (New York, Association of American Publishers, 2004): 47-56.

10. Jennifer Weintraub, "Usage Statistics at Yale University Library," *Against the Grain* 15, no. 6 (2003): 32-34.

11. Betty Galbraith, "Journal Retention Decisions Incorporating Use-Statistics as a Measure of Value," *Collection Management* 27, no. 1 (2002): 79-90.

12. Jonas Holmstrom, "The Return on Investment of Electronic Journals: It is a Matter of Time," *D-Lib Magazine* 10, no. 4 (2004). http://www.dlib.org/dlib/april04/holmstrom/04holmstrom.html (April 15, 2005).

13. Carol Tenopir and Donald W. King, *Towards Electronic Journals* (Washington, DC: Special Libraries Association, 2000).

14. Holmstrom.

15. Judy Luther, "White Paper on Electronic Journal Usage Statistics," *Serials Librarian* 41 (2001): 119-148.

16. Ibid.

17. Terry B. Hill, *Using Traditional Methodologies and Electronic Usage Statistics As Indicators to Assess Campus-Wide Journal Needs: Contexts, Trade-Offs, and Pro-*

cesses, April 13, 2004, Master's thesis, University of North Carolina at Chapel Hill, http://hdl.handle.net/1901/64 (April 15, 2005).

18. *COUNTER Code of Practice.*

19. Ibid.

20. Phil M. Davis, "Why Usage Statistics Cannot Tell Us Everything, and Why We Shouldn't Dare to Ask," *Against the Grain* 15, no. 6 (2003): 24-26.

21. Caryn Anderson, "Survey Results," February 2, 2005, http://web.simmons.edu/~andersoc/erus/results.html (April 15, 2005).

22. Andrew Nagy, "LibSGR: Library Statistics Gathering and Reporting," c2004, http://liboffice.villanova.edu/libsgr/ (April 15, 2005).

doi:10.1300/J123v53S09_15

Chapter 15

The Next Steps in Developing Usage Statistics for E-Serials

Elise Anderson

INTRODUCTION

Most statistics for e-serials can be accurately described as "usage data," with vendors providing basic information on the use of their products through such variables as sessions, searches, tables of contents viewed, and full-text articles downloaded. Statistical analyses, in which two or more products are compared for title overlap and relative use or are examined for long-term use patterns for the study of academic research styles, must be performed in the library, as time and personnel constraints permit. Within this complex situation, there are several levels in which to develop and improve the utility of usage statistics. Close integration with the educational and budgetary activities of the library is an essential factor to include in the total process.

Initially, there are a number of steps to be taken to improve the quality of basic e-serial statistics. Even the definition of "e-serial" may be debated by some. Electronic versions of print journals are classic e-serials; databases, e-book collections, and electronic encyclopedias can also be considered to be e-serials, because they are updated periodically, paid for on a recurring basis, and are electronically delivered to

[Haworth co-indexing entry note]: "The Next Steps in Developing Usage Statistics for E-Serials." Anderson, Elise. Co-published simultaneously in *The Serials Librarian* (The Haworth Information Press, an imprint of The Haworth Press, Inc.) Vol. 53, Supplement No. 9, 2007, pp. 245-260; and: *Usage Statistics of E-Serials* (ed: David C. Fowler) The Haworth Information Press, an imprint of The Haworth Press, Inc., 2007, pp. 245-260. Single or multiple copies of this article are available for a fee from The Haworth Document Delivery Service [1-800-HAWORTH, 9:00 a.m. - 5:00 p.m. (EST). E-mail address: docdelivery@haworthpress.com].

Available online at http://ser.haworthpress.com
doi:10.1300/J123v53S09_16

the end user. Regardless of how a library defines an e-serial, when better-quality e-serial statistics are available, librarians can enhance the decision process for a number of library activities, ranging from system administration, to budget allocations, to monitoring and guiding educational programs.

CORE USAGE DATA

The first step in developing usage statistics is to address the task of retrieving high quality usage data. This is an ongoing challenge where the impediments include missing data, inconsistent data, or even no data at all. E-journals provided through databases, such as *Contemporary Women's Issues,* often have no usage data directly attributable to a specific journal title. This is a correctable omission, which the vendor can address. E-journal aggregators, such as JSTOR and Project Muse, first offered their products as browsable collections of e-journals. Gradually, e-journal providers added many of the features found in standard database search engines, until their products had evolved to the point of effectively being databases (Guthrie and Lougee 1997). They had added these enhancements while still providing usage data at the individual serial level. Since e-journal providers such as JSTOR and database providers such as EBSCO have successfully combined database search features with title-level usage data, libraries need to make concerted efforts to encourage all database vendors to provide this same combination of services in their products.

Even when usage data are provided, it is frequently unclear what is being presented (Hiott 2004). The data most useful for the Z. Smith Reynolds Library at Wake Forest University includes sessions, searches, tables of content, images downloaded, full-text downloaded, and turnaways. However, for Reynolds Library, vendors provide usage data under approximately thirty different terms. The serials analyst may guess that, "full-text downloaded" is the same as "full-text retrieved" and close to "full-text requested," but it is often just supposition. ABC–CLIO's "session" may be Springer's "visit" or APMultimedia's "connection." Vendors also vary greatly in how precisely they define the terms they use, and rarely explain exactly how they capture the data they provide. Vendors must be encouraged to adopt standardized terms and to agree on what those terms mean. The model developed for COUNTER-compliant usage data from e-journal and e-book providers is one that could be expanded to all e-serials.

In a trend that libraries should strongly encourage, some vendors, such as ABC-CLIO and ISI, are providing Internet Protocol (IP) data as part of their e-serial usage statistics. In some cases, as with ISI Web of Science, the IP data is matched against session information and is detailed at the level of the unique computer. For ABC-CLIO databases, the IP data is consolidated at a higher level that still allows an analyst to link session statistics to specific categories of users.

Usage data for e-serials do not have to come only from vendors. In the absence of vendor-supplied usage data, libraries have other options for developing a usage history for their electronic titles. "Click through" data recorded by a library's proxy servers and stored in log files (Coombs 2005; Nicholas et al. 2006) identify the electronic serials that users have selected from a library's Web site. A number of commercial and free products are available for analyzing the use of a library's Web site, including its e-serials (Breeding 2002). University campus networks are increasingly sophisticated in structure, use, and management. IT staff at many universities already use IP data to identify hackers and crackers (Noguchi 2005) and to ensure compliance in enforcing copyright protections (Read 2004). It is possible for librarians and IT staff to work together to identify which departments used specific electronic resources. "Click through" data from the library's Web site can be linked to IP data from a building's network hubs to produce information that is useful for budget decisions and collection management studies.

In addition to the need for more usage data, libraries may increasingly be faced with the tasks of identifying and adjusting inflated use figures. A federated search system, such as *MetaLib* from Ex-Libris, provides patrons with quick, one-step access to multiple databases preselected by librarians (Helfer and Wakimoto 2005). However, this one-step access also may generate higher search figures for an e-serial than would occur if only patron choice were involved. A similar inflation of usage statistics may result when a vendor's search engine defaults to searching all the e-journal databases of a product. For the year ending April 2002, the Reynolds Library search statistics for ProQuest databases totaled 84,356 searches. In the following year, the same databases recorded a total of 393,319 searches. This huge increase in searches resulted from a change in the way ProQuest captured usage data. When an e-serial appears more heavily used than one that is not included in federated searching, it might gain an unfair advantage during the library's renewal process. Because of this issue, some libraries stopped considering search statistics when evaluating products for renewal (Hiott 2004). In an effort to address librarians' concerns about inflated usage data, ProQuest now tracks "unique searches," while ISI tracks "unique searches," "unique sessions," and "unique turnaways."

ACCESSING AND RETRIEVING USAGE DATA

Libraries are always interested in anything that enables their staff to do more with less. Technology plays a vital role in all aspects of e-serial usage statistics, from accessing to collection and storage to reporting and assessment. Most areas of statistics management for e-serials need more development, but until recently, one area in particular has flown below the radar for vendors and libraries alike–the actual delivery of usage data from vendor to library. Combining new technologies with a standardized delivery process may provide the best hope for timely and comprehensive access to e-serial data.

Currently, vendors provide libraries with usage data about e-serials and other electronic resources in a myriad of formats and delivery methods. A vendor may email its information on a regular schedule to one or more designated recipients in a library. This report may be one whose parameters are set by the library itself, as is the case for reports from SilverPlatter and ProQuest. Other companies, such as Gale, forward to all customers a report with a standard set of data elements. ProQuest also follows this convention with its *Digital Dissertations.* About 15 percent of the vendors that provide statistics to the Reynolds Library link to their usage statistics from a product's search interface or home page. Sometimes, as with *Oxford Journals Online,* this offers easy access to usage data. More often, the path to usage data may involve navigating several screens and clicking on multiple links. To reach the COUNTER-compliant reports for the Annual Reviews serials requires seven steps from the site's main page. Retrieving statistics from MIT's *CogNet* involves five steps for the user, including typing in a second URL.

The majority of vendors provide Web sites dedicated to usage statistics and, often, other administrative functions. This practice simplifies access to various data repositories, although the library must maintain a list of the access points for vendor statistics. The analyst can click on a statistics site URL, and then reach the reports or the reporting function within one or two steps, even if a login is required.

When retrieving a publisher's or vendor's usage data, there are three components to consider–selecting data to view, formatting data, and delivering the data to the user. At some sites, the user is immediately presented with one or more statistical reports grouped by time period. At other sites, the user must actually identify the data elements for a report, and is able to generate many different reports, as desired.

The data is usually viewable on-screen, but many of Emerald's reports are only available as e-mailed documents. Other vendors, such as MathSciNet and JSTOR, provide only on-screen viewing of the usage data. To have a permanent copy of the original data, the statistical analyst must print the report or save it as an HTML file. Automated extraction from on-screen data is not always possible. Manually reentering the data into local electronic storage formats is time-consuming, but often can be accomplished by lower-cost labor, such as student assistants. On-screen reports are usually displayed in tabular format for easier viewing. About two-thirds of the vendors supplying data to the Reynolds Library, allow one to view the data on-screen and also to download it, typically in .csv, .tsv, .txt, or .xls file format. This allows the transfer of data to Microsoft Excel, Microsoft Access, Oracle, or other data management systems.

The timeliness of usage data for e-serials is another factor that varies widely among vendors. Usage data is very commonly reported on a monthly basis, though some vendors also offer daily and weekly reports. ProQuest, SilverPlatter, and EBSCOHost are some of the vendors that provide the previous month's data within a day or two of the end of that period. In the case of BioOne and LexisNexis, one or two months may pass before the new data appears. Some vendors, such as BioOne and Science Direct, provide prominent notice of what is the most recent usage data on their sites; for the Chadwyck-Healey collections, a user must venture all the way through the report selection process to see whether any new data are available.

The end result of the laudable efforts by individual vendors to measure and deliver usage data to their library customers is a frustrating situation with ill-defined data in widely varying formats delivered across a range of time intervals. This is a situation ripe for improvement. Technologies that combine standardized data collection and reporting with automated delivery provide the best hope for timely and comprehensive access to e-serial data. Such innovations are in development and one step forward is the creation of Project COUNTER (Counting Online Usage of NeTworked Electronic Resources). This non-profit corporation, consisting of libraries, publishers, and intermediary organizations, offers a real benefit for libraries interested in usage statistics, both from the standpoint of data as well as from the model of standardization it provides. Project COUNTER not only defines standardized usage data elements and terminology, it also specifies the formats of the report and the time frame in which reports are made available to subscribers.

Unfortunately, COUNTER-compliant reports are not comparable across publisher platforms, due to differences in the search interfaces that affect the recording of some data elements, such as "full-text downloaded." For example, on some search interfaces a user must first select and view a full-text document in HTML form, before the user can switch to the PDF version. As a result, that platform will report a higher figure for total full-text downloaded (which reports both PDF and HTML downloads) than will an interface that allows a user to select a full-text format before proceeding (NISO 2006). Even as vendors and publishers move toward providing COUNTER-compliant reports, libraries need to further encourage them to design search interfaces that allow true comparisons of usage across platforms.

Access to, and delivery of, e-serial usage data could be significantly accelerated by the development of a standardized retrieval process to complement COUNTER-compliant reports. That is now happening with SUSHI (Standardized Usage Statistics Harvesting Initiative). Sponsored by NISO, the members of SUSHI are developing a protocol for automated transfer of COUNTER-compliant reports from e-serial providers to libraries (NISO 2006). When fully implemented in a library, this protocol would enable library personnel to focus on analyzing usage data rather than on retrieving reports from individual vendor statistics sites.

REPORTING USAGE STATISTICS

As more vendors provide some type of usage data for e-serials and other electronic resources, libraries face another set of challenges: how they can efficiently store and use this data? Technological solutions to these problems are developing from a number of sources–some from within individual libraries, others from the library industry, with still others emerging from traditional business management services.

In the infancy of electronic serials, and in the absence of commercial alternatives, libraries developed local systems to collect and store usage data. These systems use a variety of formats, including Excel spreadsheets, Access databases, and Oracle tables. These custom-developed systems often dovetail precisely with the unique needs of a library. However, these systems have the complementary disadvantage of requiring a sizable investment in time and specialized computer skills for design, development, and maintenance (Breeding 2002). Another important consideration is that these systems often do not link readily with the e-serial financial information stored in the library's integrated library system (ILS).

Libraries also developed local systems for reporting e-serials usage data. Excel spreadsheets work well for cost-per-use analyses and for more sophisticated reports linking budget data and usage. Access and Oracle offer additional reporting capabilities, but again with a higher cost in time and personnel to develop that functionality. With e-serials inexorably increasing, both in terms of numbers and in terms of their impacts on budgets, even libraries with small e-serial collections are looking for alternatives for collecting, storing, and reporting usage statistics (Hiott 2004).

To address these needs, libraries are taking advantage of commercial solutions that vary from modest in scope to all-inclusive. Some of these products are offered by traditional library vendors, such as Innovative Interfaces, Inc. (III), while others are information management tools from the corporate world.

TDNet, SFX, and Serials Solutions are among the first generation of products focused primarily on e-serials management. These products have significantly evolved from their beginnings as link resolvers, and as single-user-interfaces for e-serials users. For example, Serials Solutions has progressively included usage data functions, such as journal overlap analysis and click-through statistics, as well as other "back-office" features, such as MARC records (Watson 2003b).

To analyze their e-serials information, some libraries are relying on reporting tools originally intended to meet business intelligence needs. With products such as *Brio* from Hyperion, *Crystal Reports* from Business Objects, and *ReportNet* from Cognos, analysts can use data stored in multiple formats to generate sophisticated reports with "drill-down" capabilities that enable an audience to focus on specific subcomponents of a report. These tools typically offer several powerful features including a graphical user interface for designing custom reports and a large library of predefined reports. They also provide the functionality to modify standard reports to meet library requirements (Schwartz 2004). Marshall Breeding has reviewed recently the state of library management systems, including e-serial management and reporting components (Breeding 2006).

Business reporting tools may offer a tangential advantage to libraries as well. Universities are using business intelligence tools in conjunction with their people management systems, such as Banner and PeopleSoft.

By using the same reporting tools as a university's administrative units, a library may increase the chance that its data and reports will prove relevant to more than its immediate library constituency. For example, university administrators may wish to provide accreditation agencies with library reports documenting the range and use of library databases to confirm that the university has provided adequate library support for academic programs.

As with any product developed in another industry, corporate reporting tools also carry some significant disadvantages. There are concerns about expense and the amount of time and training required for staff to become proficient with this software. Furthermore, these tools are not fully integrated with a library's ILS. Instead, they sit outside those systems, and financial data must be pulled in, to develop reports for financial analyses. As a result, it may require additional programming by library systems personnel to ensure that financial data is consistently available for reports. Because these reporting products were not designed with libraries as their target customers, these standard reports may have little utility for librarians.

Libraries may find that their best opportunities for developing a strong e-serials statistics program will be provided by products that are just entering the market. Library vendors heard about the problems that libraries face in managing e-serials almost as soon as e-serials became available. After several years of development and the release of related tools, such as link-resolvers and digital content managers, library vendors are now marketing systems that promise to combine a centralized repository for all electronic resource information with powerful reporting capabilities. These electronic resource management systems (ERMS) include products such as *Verde* from Ex-Libris, *Meridian* from Endeavor, and VERIFY from VTLS (Visionary Technology in Library Solutions), as well offerings from Innovative Interfaces and SirsiDynix (Jewell et al. 2004; Duranceau 2004).

Most of these systems are in their first or second release, and have focused initially on license and subscription management. Vendors are building on their base of knowledge and experience with digital content managers to tackle these functions first. Unfortunately, features focusing on reporting and statistics are only now being implemented in most ERMS. These systems may include the means for inputting and storing e-serial data directly, rather than just pointing at data maintained elsewhere (Jewell et al. 2004). Better still, ERMS that can work with the SUSHI protocol can perform automated retrieval and imports of COUNTER-compliant reports. These features could eliminate the need for other storage systems for usage data, reduce workloads, and streamline the generation and analysis of data for many management decisions. ERMS should offer several advantages over most existing products for the analysis of e-serials. They are generally designed to be fully compatible with a library's ILS, even when the ILS is provided by another vendor (Duranceau 2004). Several of these products rely on batch loading of data between an ILS and an ERMS, but the published goal is true dynamic linking between the systems. As a result, librarians should soon enjoy easy and seamless linking to usage, subscription, license, and financial information through a single interface (Chang 2003).

ERMS providers are well aware of the institutional need for robust statistics and analysis capabilities (Jewell et al. 2004; Breeding 2006). Some vendors, such as Endeavor, incorporated third-party business tools into the ERMS, rather than trying to emulate existing functionality. Others, such as Ex-Libris and III, partnered with MPS Technologies in 2006 to automate the first imports of usage reports from the MPS service ScholarlyStats. Using the SUSHI protocol, ScholarlyStats reports, which are modeled on COUNTER-compliant reports, have been successfully imported into the Verde system at Yale University and the Innovative ERMS at the Washington State University Libraries. Because these systems have been developed by library vendors for libraries, reporting will be fine-tuned to librarians' needs.

A further step toward developing usage statistics for e-serials may be to have someone else do them. Outsourcing certain library functions is a widely accepted practice. Outsourced processes are as varied as cataloging records, link-resolution for e-serials, and the provision of reference services during off hours (Schneider 1998; Oder 2004; Ferguson and Grogg 2004). In the corporate world, outsourcing basic usage data work to specialist companies is already underway. There, businesses may send data about their site usage to organizations such as SAS IntelliVisor, NetIQ, Keynote Systems, and WebCriteria (Kemp 2001). Under secure conditions, the data is converted into business intelligence and returned to the originating company. Usage data for e-serials might be analyzed in a similar fashion for libraries, as an extension of services already provided by companies such as Serials Solutions.

Some of the advantages to outsourcing are obvious. Conversion of raw usage data to more valuable business intelligence would be done by experts dedicated to data conversion and through the use of appropriate technologies. Libraries would not have to invest money, time, or personnel to develop and enhance technologies for the collection, organization, and analysis of usage statistics. As a result, a library could focus more of its resources on its core functions.

A few disadvantages also derive from these outsourcing features. Data converters are most experienced with the characteristics of corporate data and with the processing of that data to address corporate management needs. Since libraries comprise a relatively small share of the current customer base for business intelligence, it may not be cost-effective for data conversion companies to devote their resources to developing a library-centric conversion process. In outsourced data conversion, a library's usage data will join a stream of conversion projects handled by a data converter. As a result, the usage reports may not be available on short notice for decision makers, unless a premium is paid for expedited processing. Furthermore, a standardized report may not be sufficient to meet the specialized needs that occur in every decision making process, from contract negotiation, to devising responses, to faculty requests for changes in library services. In contrast, in-house reporting of usage statistics can be quickly adjusted to the needs and timetables of library decision makers. Finally, outsourcing business intelligence without providing expert, ongoing supervision may well result in libraries losing control of a process that is central to the success of a library (Schneider 1998; Martin et al. 2000).

Identifying the more subtle patterns in e-serial usage, and determining their significance, requires the use of reporting, statistics, or modeling programs such as Cognos ReportNet, SPSS, SAS, and the advanced functions of Excel. This either might argue for a library to rely on outside expertise for analysis, or for the acquisition of ERMS specifically designed to support these tasks.

MAXIMIZING THE VALUE OF USAGE DATA

Since the 1990s, e-serials have come to dominate the serials collections of most academic libraries, both quantitatively and financially. A lucky few libraries may be able to provide to their patrons all the serials they want, without constraints. In their case, usage statistics may be irrelevant, and theoretically could be dispensed with. Most libraries have to choose which electronic resources they provide, including e-serials, and for them, usage statistics will be an important component of the decision process.

Each library will have to decide whether to manage its statistics inhouse, or to outsource that work with appropriate administration of the process. If statistics are managed in-house, a library will have to decide if its e-serials collection, and the usage data it generates, require an automated system to be managed effectively. Otherwise, a simpler, more low-tech system using spreadsheets to store and report usage statistics may be the more cost-effective choice.

Regardless of how a library manages it e-serials statistics, the process will require a significant investment in time, personnel, and money. The library's goal should be to maximize the return on its investment in a statistics program. One area where e-serials usage data can have an impact is the budget process. Once a library has usage data, the real benefit comes from applying it for a wide range of library functions. In the future, e-serials usage statistics may play a significant role in library activities as wide-ranging as instructional programs, collection management, and system administration.

Many libraries already rely on cost-per-use analyses to identify when to switch a serial subscription between print and electronic format. An e-serial, or an entire e-serial package, may potentially be canceled if there is insufficient use recorded. If an e-serial is available from more than one source, it may be possible to cancel the more expensive version and direct the savings toward other purchases (Moore-Jansen, Williams, and Dadashzadeh 2001). Tracking e-serial usage and cost over multiple years may enable collection management librarians to anticipate and prepare for new budget demands from developing academic programs. Linking IP data to other types of usage data from vendors would significantly enhance the utility of that usage data, particularly for budget questions. As electronic resources continue to increase in cost, libraries are more frequently making joint purchases of e-serials (Watson 2003a). If the cost of a resource is shared among multiple libraries, usage data linked to IP information could identify each library's proportionate use of the product, and possibly, the relative proportion of cost adjustments. Electronic resources are a boon for academic researchers, but carry a heavy cost for the libraries that provide those databases and e-journals. When library administrators can document the tremendous increase in usage of e-serials, as well as their even-more-rapidly increasing costs (Jewell et al. 2004; Watson 2004), it becomes easier for university administrators to accept the library's need for strong financial support in providing this medium to the university community.

Besides budget questions, e-serial usage statistics can help with other collection management tasks. If a particular e-serial has a consistently high number of turnaways, then users may benefit if the library can pay for an increase in the number of simultaneous users for the product.

Spikes in turnaways only at certain times of a semester may indicate classroom demonstrations of a product and that the current user license is generally adequate.

Combining statistics provides expanded opportunities for interesting analyses. When an e-serial shows a high number of searches for each downloaded unit, it may indicate that users are having problems with the serial. They may be misinformed about the purpose of the product, or they may have problems negotiating its search interface (Hiott 2004). Either way, a librarian may be able to enhance the user's success with the serial. In contrast, high download per session ratios usually indicate that users are pleased with a product.

New uses for e-serial statistics are multiplying beyond collection management. While bibliographic instruction (BI) programs have been staples of library educational offerings for many years, recently they have been joined by semester-long classes in information literacy. Both instructional programs, although they differ significantly in their focus and their subject matter, introduce students to the concept of electronic resources. They also educate students in the use of databases and e-journals.

Usage statistics aid in determining whether the repeated use of specific e-serials in academic programs results in the higher use of those same products by students. Because BI programs began well before the availability of usage statistics, their effects on the use of e-serials are harder to track. However, if a library tracked e-serials usage before the advent of information literacy classes, and the instructors can identify which e-serials they included in their teaching, then it should be possible to identify significant changes in students' use of those serials. If statistics can document such a change in e-serial use patterns of students, this would provide strong evidence to libraries and to university administrators of the effectiveness of these programs and of the need to carefully evaluate the resources used for teaching.

Evidence of a teacher's ability to influence students' choice of electronic resources might indicate a way in which to promote under-utilized electronic resources, as well as a need to avoid endorsement or inadvertent censorship. Many libraries have large collections of e-serials. The Reynolds Library offers users more than 200 databases and several thousand electronic journals. Students and library staff alike are faced with a daunting task of identifying which e-serials are best suited to which purpose. Many Wake Forest University students resort to using a standard cluster of products, such as ProQuest and EBSCOHost databases, to answer most of their research questions and consult other e-serials on the advice of peers, professors, and librarians. Librarians, faced with a student who has waited until the last minute to begin a research paper, can rarely interest the student in the complete range of e-serials that cover the topic. As a result, every library has purchased electronic resources that do not get the use that one might expect. Often, these resources end up being canceled because the cost-per-use is unaffordable (Moore-Jansen, Williams, and Dadashzadeh 2001; Hiott 2004).

Bibliographers, collection management staff, and library instructors could work together in a process aimed at increasing the student's knowledge of the entire range of e-resources for the best academic performance. For example, at regular intervals, bibliographers and library liaisons could review the usage statistics for e-serials and identify likely candidates for cancellation. Library instructors would then take the lead in demonstrating one or more of these underutilized serials in their classes. With usage data from before and after the instructors' intervention, it should be possible to detect if there was an effect on students' use of the targeted e-serials.

If there are generally positive results with this technique then libraries could regularly identify their lowest performers and give them wider publicity through instructional programs. If an e-serial's use fails to improve after this "probationary period," then collection managers may feel more confident that librarians are canceling products that are unsuitable for their users and not just those which are unknown to them.

Students are noted for wanting to use only products providing full-text (Dilevko and Gottlieb 2002; Black 2005; Nicholas et al. 2006). Yet, citation databases often provide the best resources for a particular research topic. Student preference for full-text resources have been attributed to multiple factors, including the convenience of electronic full-text and to the frequent situation where photocopying print materials costs the student directly, but printing out electronic text does not (Black 2005). In addition, it is also well documented that students are very confused and frustrated by the process of moving from identifying a reference in one source to retrieving the full-text for that reference from another source (Black 2005; Labelle and Nicholson 2005).

If BI and information literacy programs are effective in making students more comfortable with the library research process, then usage statistics for citation databases will rise from previous levels. If so, libraries could again target low-performing citation databases for a little extra attention in instructional programs and use usage data to monitor the results.

Additional technologies can exert both positive and negative effects on the use of e-serials. As bibliographic management software, such as EndNote or Reference Manager, becomes more prevalent on campuses, users may respond by focusing on e-serials that work best with those systems. With usage data, libraries could monitor for those changes and develop appropriate responses.

Even relatively mundane activities such as system administration can benefit from usage statistics. In 2004, Wake Forest University added a wireless component to its campus network with subsystems for guests, faculty and staff, and students. Guest users have no access to to the library's small collection of locally mounted CD databases. In the first months of the dual system, large numbers of students were using the guest wireless system rather than the system intended for them. As a result, they were unable to access local databases. Reynolds Library personnel were only alerted to the problem by the sudden tripling and quadrupling of the usage statistics for those databases. Databases that previously averaged ten to twelve sessions per month were abruptly showing fifty sessions per month, usually from a single IP address, which represented one user, attempting two and three login attempts within a period of sixty to ninety seconds. After librarians began advising students of the need to use the student wireless for these databases, the usage statistics dropped significantly, though not back to previous levels. The pattern of multiple attempts in a short time is still apparent, indicating that not all students have received the message.

CONCLUSIONS

Electronic serials have been a vital component of library collections for more than a decade, and for just as long, libraries have struggled with management issues for these resources. Libraries need to encourage all e-serial providers to offer COUNTER-compliant usage data and to standardize the process of generating basic usage statistics so that libraries can accurately compare electronic products from different platforms. In addition, vendors and publishers need to continue streamlining the process by which libraries can access their information. On their own behalf, libraries can track the e-serial usage data generated from their own systems.

Once libraries have collected the core e-serial usage data, their best hope for easier storage and reporting of usage statistics may come from the ERMS that are now being developed. These systems appear to offer better linking between usage statistics and a library's financial management systems than is currently possible internally or through outsourcing, which would be a great asset in addressing budget questions. Incorporating e-serial usage statistics into BI sessions and information literacy courses would allow instructors to track user-behavior, with multiple benefits for teaching and collection management.

Libraries have embraced electronic serials from their inception. With good e-serials usage statistics, libraries can improve their effectiveness in managing e-serials, make and defend tough budget decisions, and identify new directions in library activities for the future.

REFERENCES

Black, Steve. 2005. Impact of full-text on print journal use at a liberal arts college. *Library Resources & Technical Services* 49(1): 19-26, 56.

Breeding, Marshall. 2002. Library Web site analysis. *Library Technology Reports* 38(3):22-35.

_____. 2006. Reshuffling the deck. *Library Journal* 131(6): 40-54.

Chang, Sheau-Hwang. 2003. The DLF electronic resource management initiative. *OCLC Systems and Services* 19(2): 45-47.

Coombs, Karen A. 2005. Using Web server logs to track users through the electronic forest. *Computers in Libraries* 25(1): 16-20.

Dilevko, Juris and Lisa Gottlieb. 2002. Print sources in an electronic age: A vital part of the research process for undergraduate students. *Journal of Academic Librarianship* 28(6): 381-392.

Duranceau, Ellen Finnie. 2004. Electronic resource management systems from ILS vendors. *Against the Grain* 16(4): 91-94.

Ferguson, Christine L. and Jill E. Grogg. 2004. OpenURL link resolvers. *Computers in Libraries* 24(9): 17-24.

Guthrie, Kevin M. and Wendy P. Lougee. 1997. The JSTOR Solution: Accessing and preserving the past. *Library Quarterly* 122(2): 42-44.

Helfer, Doris Small and Jina Choi Wakimoto. 2005. Metasearching: The good, the bad, and the ugly of making it work in your library. *Searcher: The Magazine for Database Professionals* 13(2): 40-41.

Hiott, Judith. 2004. Collecting and using networked statistics: Current status, future goals. *Library Quarterly* 74(4): 441-454.

Jewell, Timothy D., Ivy Anderson, Adam Chandler, Sharon E. Farb, Kimberly Parker, Angela Riggio, and Nathan D. M. Robertson. Electronic resource management: Report of the DLF Initiative. Digital Library Federation 2004 [cited April 1, 2005]. Available from http://www.diglib.org/pubs/dlfermi0408/ and from http://www.purl.oclc.org/DLF/dlfermi0408

Kemp, Ted. The many flavors of Web tracking–Varying tools and techniques let companies gauge site performance and visitors' interaction. *InternetWeek,* November 26, 2001, 19.

Labelle, Patrick R. and Karen Nicholson. 2005. Student information research skills: Report on a Québec study on information literacy. *Feliciter* (1): 47-49.

Martin, Robert S., Steven L. Brown, Jane Claes, Cynthia A. Gray, Greg Hardin, Timothy C. Judkins, Kelly Patricia Kingrey, et al. 2000. The impact of outsourcing and privatization on library services and management: American Library Association.

Moore-Jansen, Cathy, John H. Williams, and Mohammad Dadashzadeh. 2001. Is a decision support system enough? Tactical versus strategic solutions to the serials pricing . . . *Serials Review* 27(3-4): 48-61.

National Information Standards Organization. Introduction to SUSHI for Librarians and Content Providers Webinar. May 17, 2006. https://niso.webex.com/niso/onstage/tool/record/viewrecording1.php?EventID=277481065

Nicholas, David, Paul Huntington, Hamid R. Jamali, and Carol Tenopir. 2006. What deep log analysis tells us about the impact of big deals: Case study OhioLINK. *Journal of Documentation* 62(4): 482-508.

Noguchi, Yuki. George Mason officials investigate hacking incident. *Washington Post*, January 13, 2005, E1.

Oder, Norman. 2004. When LSSI comes to town. *Library Journal* 129(16): 36-40.

Read, Brock. Lawmakers laud colleges for efforts to curb illegal file-sharing. *Chronicle of Higher Education,* October 15, 2004, A30.

Schneider, Karen G. 1998. The McLibrary syndrome. *American Libraries* 29(1): 66-70.

Schwartz, Jeffrey. 2004. Look who's calling–Business Objects, Cognos, and Hyperion want you. *VARbusiness* 20(14): 28-38.

Watson, Paula D. 2003. Acquisitions of e-journals. *Library Technology Reports* 39(2): 28-41.

_____. 2003a. E-journals: Access and management. *Library Technology Reports* 39(2): 44-68.

_____. 2004. Raised expectations/rising prices. *Library Technology Reports* 40(6): 40-41.

doi:10.1300/J123v53S09_16

Chapter 16

Usage Statistics in Context: Develop Effective Assessment Practices Through Collaboration

Joan E. Conger

INTRODUCTION

Usage statistics in context is best understood when the given three word choices this author consciously makes: customer, value, and library professional. The term "library patron" implies a captive audience, whose only recourse for information is the library. Library *customers,* especially in an era of desktop access to information, have before them a wide selection of information services, of which the library is but one. Information consumers will usually fit both learning about the research process and information gathering itself into the more inclusive activities of knowledge acquisition or knowledge creation. Within the constraints of completing information gathering in good time and to good effect, the quality and breadth of an information service must be balanced against the consumers' perceptions of efficiency and ease-of-use. When selecting a service, the intelligent consumer makes a choice that combines lowest cost in terms of time and effort with highest worth in terms of meeting the information need.

[Haworth co-indexing entry note]: "Usage Statistics in Context: Develop Effective Assessment Practices Through Collaboration." Conger, Joan E. Co-published simultaneously in *The Serials Librarian* (The Haworth Information Press, an imprint of The Haworth Press, Inc.) Vol. 53, Supplement No. 9, 2007, pp. 261-273; and: *Usage Statistics of E-Serials* (ed: David C. Fowler) The Haworth Information Press, an imprint of The Haworth Press, Inc., 2007, pp. 261-273. Single or multiple copies of this article are available for a fee from The Haworth Document Delivery Service [1-800-HAWORTH, 9:00 a.m. - 5:00 p.m. (EST). E-mail address: docdelivery@haworthpress.com].

Available online at http://ser.haworthpress.com
doi:10.1300/J123v53S09_17

Value, therefore, only in part represents that high quality and breadth of information for which libraries always have been known, and which competing information services have a difficult time delivering. Value also includes expedient ease-of-use, which library professionals must create to remain a competitive service in the world of information delivery. When library professionals create value, their library becomes the consumer's information service of choice.

Library professionals are all personnel, with or without a master's degree in library and information science, whose efforts in teaching and delivery combine to craft the value their potential customers consider when making an information service selection. Every workday, library professionals, including administrators, librarians, support staff, and hourly workers make decisions that affect both the cost and worth of the library's services to current and potential users. This makes every library employee a decision maker, from the library director to the hourly shelver.

As decision makers, all library professionals can either rely solely upon their own expertise, or they can infuse that expertise and practice with usage and experiential data from the consumer. When the consumer is considered to be a patron with no alternative service choices, the library professional can make decisions insulated from the vicissitudes of customer need. When library personnel see users and potential users as customers with a choice, they make customer-centered decisions that create value, based upon data about the customer. Three kinds of data exist: inferential data, usage data, and experiential data. Decision makers must view each of these data in the context of the others.

After a brief discussion of the influence these three kinds of data have on the decisions of library professionals, this chapter will compare the reduced effectiveness of decisions insulated inside one source of data alone, and the increased agility of decisions that are given context through multiple sources of data. In closing, this chapter will address the risk intrinsic to the agility of context, particularly changes in routine and the sharing of decision making, and it will explain how collaborative-learning can potentially be a powerful solution.

ASSESSMENT AND THE LIBRARY'S RELATIONSHIP WITH ITS CUSTOMERS

Library service is a pure relationship. Tangible products such as the book on the shelf, an article online, instruction in the research process, the online infrastructure leading to these resources, a quiet table at which to study, or the human interaction that instills understanding, are, in essence, a fine web of interaction between professional decision making and consumer choice. Assessment is the vital bond of communication in this web of relationships between librarians creating services and the service experience of library users.

When library professionals create customer value within an ever-present pool of assessment data, these decisions produce services that are both low cost and high worth to the user. Decision makers can treat assessment as a year-end activity designed to evaluate use of library service, and plan for the future, based on inferences about the past. Treating assessment as a state of yearlong mindfulness of the customer relationship infuses this decision making process with the user's experience. Much of assessment relies upon knowledge of usage data, and a thoughtful assessment requires that librarians have an awareness that usage data comes to them in three forms: the transactions tallied to create usage data, professional inference about that usage that forms inferential data, and the customer experience during transactions that generates experiential data.

Usage data, such as counts of door-traffic, questions answered, log analyses of traffic on a Web site, and electronic resource usage statistics, demonstrate the willingness of the information consumer to choose a library's services over other available options. From this data, interpreted and applied through professional expertise and experience, decision makers may infer proof of value. But usage data and professional inference alone lack an essential element: the customer's experience during use of the service, which in turn influences the customer's willingness to return and to offer a recommendation of this service to others.

Placing usage data in the context of professional inference is a natural step for creators of library services. Collection developers may see a comparatively high usage of an electronic resource and infer a high value of that resource for library users. However, when these two sources of data are placed in the context of customer experience, decisions to retain, drop, or improve that service achieve the context necessary to create the value that attracts the information consumer to the library. Upon learning, through service quality surveys or analysis of outcomes portfolios, that library users have a growing need to access the electronic resource remotely, collection developers can work with other library professionals to improve access and thereby expand usage exponentially. Direct experiential data, knowing something because the customer has stated it, give a clear imperative to an improvement that, if based on professional supposition, might have been lost in the clutter of library professionals' daily tasks.

Decision makers must keep the value that librarians pursue as close as possible to the value that library users seek. The perception of what is important for library personnel to spend time improving must remain as close as possible to what is of value to the customer. In a college or university setting, the experience of a single student can influence the information consumption decisions of tens, even hundreds, of other students by word-of-mouth. In a two-year period, the teaching of two courses per semester, with an attendance of 125 students per course, by a single faculty member can impact 1,000 students.

Inferential data are the information that the librarian derives from educated assumption, based upon professional expertise and long practice. In contrast, experiential data are received directly from the user. Alone, each of these sources of data–service use, professional inference, and customer experience–provide valuable, but incomplete, input. Used together, each data source strengthens the other to create a rich pool of information from which to make decisions about what work is important, how to best accomplish that work, whether that work positively impacted the library user, and whether that user perceived the output of that work to have had value, that is, a high level of quality coupled with a low cost of time and effort.

DECISIONS BASED ON DATA WITHOUT CONTEXT

Librarians may reference two equally important criteria in daily task management: efficacy within one's own workflow and its subsequent impact on the users' experiences with the library. Librarians do not want to willingly make life difficult for themselves. Convenience for the library professional includes adherence to the ease of routine and observance of the status quo, and such convenience may advise against the extra work required to seek corroborative data on customer value. Routine and stability are characteristics of efficient workflow and thus, effective service, but these advantages must be balanced by the acknowledgement that, although half the value of a library's services lie within the services provided, the other half lies in facilitating the experience of the library customer.

Usage statistics only record a decision by a user to activate the access point (whether a login, a search, a download of a full-text article, or another point of entry into the content for which a library purchased the resource).[1] Beyond the record of this interaction with the electronic resource, the librarian has no way to interpret the reality of the user's expectation before the interaction, the degree to which that expectation was met after the interaction, or the outcome, or impact, of that interaction on the user's life as a researcher.

As a tally of direct interaction between the product and the library customer, usage statistics give an unequivocal indication of customer interest at a time of need. Usage statistics can give the librarian a convenient quantitative description of impact on the library's community of users. Tallies convert easily into comparative benchmarks between products, time periods, geographic locations, or specific user characteristics. Usage tallies can also facilitate the calculation of ratios with other numerical data such as product cost or population size. All of these calculations can provide unambiguous support for decisions to innovate, improve, continue, or discontinue future services. Without further experiential data from the customer, however, library professionals must make assumptions about the interactions with these usage statistics.

A librarian could assume that a user found a particular access point attractive enough to select. From this, the librarian could further assume that, as a result, the user's expectations were met and that the outcome (i.e., impact on life and learning) was positive. This assumption seems logical, and because informed assumptions are easier to acquire than is gathering experiential data from customers, these assumptions are often the more practical choice in a day filled with too much to do already. The ease and seeming clarity of these numbers, however, can pull library professionals into decision making that has been insulated from the customer's experience. This decision making can easily miss an opportunity to increase value for the customer.

Through the use of inferential data alone, librarians insulate themselves against the discomfort of breaking with routine and can defend the professional identities contained within their assumptions and the routines they reinforce. Using assessment to ask the customer if a decision was the right one does require some courage. Decisions that rely only upon usage data or inferential data suffer from a vacuum of experiential data about customer experience and customer outcomes. Without this direct data, the politics of personal routine and personal identity step in to fill the power vacuum.

DECISIONS BASED ON ASSESSMENT

A reliance on usage data, inferential data, and experiential data provides library decision makers with a rich exchange of information between the library and the community it serves. Data gathered on customer experience, process, usage, and outcome provide a window to library users' realities, and this data provides appropriate context for decisions to start, continue, or stop a service; to undertake an effort to improve a service; and to invest in the human and technological infrastructure required for delivery of the service.

When librarians make assessment-based decisions, they more easily achieve that necessary balance between a workflow that is practical for them and the creation of an experience that customers will willingly repeat. Together with the quantitative truth of usage data and professional standards of inferential data, gathering information on customer experience through service quality assessment, usability testing, and outcomes assessment helps prioritize which of the myriad possible tasks are appropriate to spend time on. Customer experience helps to lift processes from an acceptance of the routine status quo into the realms of creative innovation. An interest in customer outcomes, rallies colleagues around the mutual desire for service to the community and renders safe the collaborative reconsideration of past decisions and an excitement for future improvement.

Balancing usage data, inferential data, and customer experience stabilizes the decision making process in the library users' realities and renders politics less necessary. Service quality assessment tells librarians what customers' service expectations are, and whether the library meets or does not meet those expectations. Process analysis uncovers customers' experiences during interactions with the library and uncovers how librarians can improve this experience. Output data quantifies the change in service (e.g., more instruction in online journal access) and the user reaction to this change (e.g., more full-text article downloads per month). Outcomes assessment demonstrates to decision makers how the library's services, and improvements to these services, impacted the lives of researchers. All these forms of assessment data combine to show both information consumers and funding authorities that the library's services and improvements to these services were worth the investment of either time or money to support them, and if it will be worth it yet again. The library's services have value: the low cost of usability and the high worth of quality.

A rich supply of assessment data allows library professionals to establish collaborative projects across departmental lines. The high use of one electronic resource and the low use of a complementary inhouse digital archive can trigger the collaborative efforts of subject specialist faculty liaisons, Web developers, information literacy instructors, and archivists to create an electronic learning environment that capitalizes on the popularity of the electronic resource to drive traffic to the digital archive. Student researchers benefit from a broader array of resources, and faculty members benefit from a research environment tailored to a field of study. The library has decreased the cost to the user and increased the worth of the services it provides to its community. By word-of-mouth, these positive experiences bring more consumers to the library's doors and virtual portals than ever before.

This chapter uses the university community as its backdrop, but any library can benefit from assessment integrated into strategic decision making, daily task management, and collaborative innovation of both new and improved services. A public library can also improve and publicize its value to the adult learners in its community. The high school media center can collaborate with the local public library on reading support, based on common assessment data that both organizations have on the library usage and upon the experiences of high school students. Corporate libraries can streamline document delivery services in collaboration with local university interlibrary loan departments. A consortium of libraries in a community (or a state) can pool its assessment cycle data to coordinate, for example, the purchase of electronic resources supporting the same hypothetical person as he or she moves between his or her role as a faculty member at a university, to that of a genealogy researcher at the public library, to a parent of a high school student who needs research assistance, to the spouse of the corporate engineer who is able to spend more time at home because his or her research needs are able to be filled quickly and effectively by a corporate information center.

Assessment renders a librarian's work more effective, and gives meaning to that work through proof of customer value. Assessment enriches decision making by realigning decisions away from the politics of protecting routine and identity, and toward the value of lowered customer cost in terms of ease-of-use, and higher customer worth in terms of service quality. Assessment-driven decision making will more naturally seek continuous improvement of customer value, and a library can introduce assessment into its daily practices through two organizational leverage points: collaboration supported by adaptive learning.

The next section will describe how any library can introduce a shift in decision making routines by fostering the existing inclinations toward inter- and intra-organizational collaboration and the adaptive learning that lends the resulting improvements and innovations a low degree of risk and a high degree of success.

RISKS OF ASSESSMENT-DRIVEN DECISION MAKING

Two organizational factors can make assessment-driven decisions difficult to envision. First, customer-centric, assessment-based decision making may introduce a new way of prioritizing work and conceptualizing library service, but the risk of altering existing work habits may seem rather high to a library professional. Second, when leaders place the ability to gather and use full assessment data into the hands of personnel throughout a library, these leaders must also redistribute the decision making that goes into using that data for service improvement.

Even when the innovation encouraged by assessment increases library value, and fortifies the argument for a larger library budget, formal library leaders may still feel uncomfortable redistributing authority. One can solve the related dilemmas of innovation, revision of routine work flows, and the ambiguity of redistributed power, through an iterative sequence of adaptive learning practices grounded twice over, first in a collaborative work ethic and second, in a clear and unwavering organization purpose.

Iteration seeks to improve the original idea through incremental learning shared across a pool of collaborative professionals. Iterative learning processes can choose to put a decision, an innovation, or a new concept through repeated sequences of experimentation, learning, reflection, and experimentation again; in the formal milieu of research methods, this process is known variously as action research, participatory research, or cooperative inquiry. Through iterative learning, experimentation adopts a tone of trial run over rollout; learning integrates a purposeful search for improvement; and reflection recognizes the personal and organizational import of what has been discovered. An iterative learning process accommodates every level of individual risk acceptance. The risk of creating a wrong decision, a failing innovation, or an unworkable concept is diminished across both an axis of experimentation repeated with the intention to learn and an axis of multiple perspectives within a group of competent professionals.

The risk of changing work habits. Most librarians can place themselves into one of the three categories of risk acceptance. To one side is the small percentage who enjoy the thrill of learning something new, who do not mind some experimentation and are, within limits, willing take some risks and find out where it takes them. In the middle is the larger group who will want to try out relatively new ideas, but only if they are not too cutting edge. On the other side is a small group that ventures into new enterprises once others have proven them reasonably safe and unlikely to cause undue distress. Membership in any of these groups is equally justifiable and learning processes must accommodate each group, because each of us finds ourselves in one of the three at one time or another.

The thrill-seeking group can take a crazy idea into the breach, knowing that the iterative learning process will absorb both successes and failures as learning, not as indications of personal competence. Larger and larger numbers of middle-of-the-roaders become part of the repeated process of experimentation-learning-reflection-experimentation, and the learning process includes (and influences) increasingly diverse perspectives until even the latter group has had a chance to experience what is now a not-so-new idea and contribute to its refinement. This process requires, however, an ethic of collaborative decision making authority.

The risk of redistributing authority. The second form of risk found within assessment-driven decisions juxtaposes collaborative authority with autonomous authority. Collaborative authority is the personal authority that any library professional wields in search of innovation, improvement, and increased customer value. Collaborative authority leverages collaborative relationships with colleagues and assessment relationships with users. Only within a collaborative group can multiple perspectives sufficiently interpret the truth of customer value found within usage and experiential assessment data. Only in a collaborative group practicing iterative experimentation, learning and reflection on the results of that learning, can truth not run aground on the subjectivity of an individual's singular and autonomous worldview.

Autonomous authority is usually the purview of those in higher levels of responsibility, and this responsibility creates hesitation in redistributing authority too readily. A leader who wishes to take advantage of assessment-driven decision making, however, will want to avoid the breakdown of trust and subsequent cynicism that results from the reversal of a collaborative solution with an autonomous decision. Autonomous authority creates a directive environment that puts individuals in the impossible position of being personally accountable for decisions with systemic influences and systemic impact. Successful collaborative innovation includes the concerns of leaders early and often, but does so within a collaborative learning process in which the group is accountable for results.

Collaborative authority complements, it does not replace, autonomous authority. The successful leader seeks a balance between collaboration and autonomy. Not only does collaboration diffuse knowledge and ownership throughout larger parts of the system, autonomous decisions benefit from the infusion of information gathered during moments of collaboration.

One sure way to include the concerns of leaders in all decisions is the existence of the clear (but not Draconian) purpose that the leaders hold for the organization. This purpose should be so clear and oft repeated, as litmus for the quality of any decision, that anyone working in the organization can express it at the elevator, for example: "We excel in research innovation," or "We graduate the best library users in the state," or "We are the easiest library to use in town."

A leader who expresses a clear purpose consistently and often gives librarians in the organization a way to ask the leader's intent without always consulting the leader for guidance. To understand a library's clear purpose, learn first what the library does well already, then ask users what they would like the library to also do particularly well, and finally, use professional expertise to create innovate services that serve patrons well.

A ready-made plan for shifting an organization to assessment-driven decision making is impossible. Every iteration of the learning process helps a library to build assessment-driven decision making that reflects the library's unique circumstances through a unique set of assessment applications. Through repetition, reflection, and second chances, the iterative learning process absorbs the uncertainty inherent in both the risk of new work processes and the risk of redistributed authority, and through this process, the library develops decision making processes that best fit with its own unique circumstances. Several key principles, however, can contribute to successful transitions.

ASSESSMENT-DRIVEN DECISION MAKING: THE EASY WAY

Wise principles to follow when developing an assessment-driven decision making framework are to start small, start with the organization's strengths, recognize the personal and organizational risks involved, and collaboratively integrate the necessary changes within both the spirit and the practice of librarianship. Assessment is complex and includes the skilled application of dozens of techniques to assess service quality, usability, usage, and outcomes (See Further Reading for suggested guide-books).

To do this, a librarian can ask the following questions: "What types of assessment, innovation, and marketing of successes do we already do well? In what areas would we like to become more expert? What new techniques would we like to learn? To control our workload and to head in the right direction, what do our users think is important about our services?"

Design a learning plan instead of an assessment plan. Replace the outlining of detailed action-steps in an organization-wide project with the organization-wide sharing of knowledge that comes from more distributed small-group efforts at assessment-driven decision making. Plan forums and activities that reincorporate the new knowledge back into the planning of subsequent experiments and data gathering.

Every organization has a small group of high-risk mavericks. Send them out to experiment first. Ask who would like to occupy the lower-risk positions of advisers to these risk-takers. Then, have all these students of assessment-based decision making share their learning with everyone else. These people can act as coaches for an ever-growing number of library professionals, and share this learning and create learning communities, open forums, and virtual knowledge pools (such as wikis, or online forums) in order to transmit new learning easily and allow for safe, nonjudgmental reflection on which has been learned.

A general plan for implementing assessment throughout the library provides the necessary framework and milestones to keep the shift in assessment-driven decision making habits moving forward. Clarify, in very simple terms, the library's purpose within the overall mission of the parent organization. Successful corporations sum their purpose up in one to three words (for instance, to "innovate"). Many librarians participating in workshops on assessment condense the purpose of the library profession into the term "access," often leavened with other concepts, (i.e., "educate for and provide the service of access,"). A focused purpose reinforces all decisions with a consistent point of reference known and used throughout the library.

Outline expectations for what success will look like. Design ways to measure whether success has been achieved. Set projected milestones for increasing the levels of participation and the amount of assessment used by individuals, groups, and the library as a whole. Build in time and budget allocations for training in both assessment and collaboration. Without the parameters of expectation and the support of training, a shift toward assessment-driven decision making will not take place.

Recognize the risk inherent in learning new ways of working and in opening authority to collaborative effort. Celebrate successes more often than noting setbacks. Include leaders in the process often, whether high-level leaders inside or outside the library, or informal leaders with specific professional expertise. These leaders do not have to be members of the work group in order to come to a meeting and help the group reflect on its findings for a short time. Nurture the collaborative spirit by attending workshops, reading books, and practicing new concepts. Within customer-centered decision making, collaborative group management skills are an essential accompaniment to assessment skills.

Above all, know that library personnel at all levels can accomplish change in their own spheres of influence, regardless of their level of responsibility. Most people have a superior to whom they could look to start the process of change, but waiting for someone else to begin the change could take a long time, too long when the library's perceived value is at stake. Instead, library personnel at all levels can review their immediate responsibilities and ask, "What kinds of assessment could I do to begin to forge that vital relationship with the customer in my daily decision making? Who else around me could act as my advisor? What bridges can I build to other librarians or users with whom I rarely interact, but who may be able to make a helpful contribution to how my learning can advance the value of library services? How can I both involve and support my leaders in a way that reduces their risk and increases the library's service value, for which they are held accountable? Ultimately, how can assessment change my life for the better? How can I begin to incorporate more assessment into my own decision making in such a way that it gives my work day more meaning, improves the work conditions of my colleagues, proves the value of my work, confirms the resources I need to produce valuable work, and, above all, improves and proves the value of my library for the community we serve?"

CONCLUSIONS

Usage statistics are an important indicator of consumer interest in the library's services and, when complemented with data describing customer experience, including service quality assessment, usability, and outcomes assessment, it can contribute to improvement and innovation that increase the library's value to its community. Compared to decisions made with only usage data, or only through professional inference, decisions made with usage, inferential, and experiential data can more accurately absorb customer experience into innovations and improvements and, most profitably, reflects customer value in the services delivered. The easiest path toward assessment-driven decision making includes the lower-risk iterative learning process based on a collaborative ethic and an unwavering library purpose, both of which strengthen professional relationships and ultimately the library's service relationship with its customer.

NOTE

1. An article is embargoed if it contractually cannot appear in an aggregator's database until after a specified time, usually six, twelve, or eighteen months after publication by the originating journal.

FURTHER READING

Beckwith, Harry. *Selling the Invisible.* New York: Warner Books, 1997.

Campbell, Nicole. *Usability Assessment of Library-Related Web Sites: Methods and Case Studies.* Chicago: LITA, 2001.

Conger, Joan. *Collaborative Electronic Resource Management: From Acquisitions to Assessment.* Westport, CT: Libraries Unlimited, 2004.

Hernon, Peter and Ellen Altman. *Assessing Service Quality: Satisfying the Expectations of Library Customers.* Chicago: American Library Association, 1998.

Hernon, Peter and Robert E. Dugan. *An Action Plan for Outcomes Assessment in Your Library.* Chicago: American Library Association, 2002.

Olson, Christi A. and Paula M. Singer. *Winning with Library Leadership.* Chicago: American Library Association, 2004.

Reason, Peter and Hilary Bradbury. *Handbook of Action Research: Participatory Inquiry and Practice.* London: Sage, 2001.

Wadsworth, Yoland. *Everyday Evaluation on the Run.* St. Leondards, Australia: Allen & Unwin, 1997.

doi:10.1300/J123v53S09_17

Chapter 17

Electronic Resource Usage Data:
Standards and Possibilities

Janet K. Chisman

INTRODUCTION

What to buy and how to justify a purchase is an ongoing challenge for collection development librarians. Serials offer the additional dimension of commitment of money over a period of time. The sums involved are often substantial, ranging from a few hundred dollars per subscription to over a million dollars for some consortial or package deals. Per-title usage information is an essential component that assists in these purchase decisions. The electronic resource environment provides the perfect venue to supply such usage statistics to help librarians build collections that are cost-effective and focused on user needs. For example, as print indexes and abstracts moved to online access, librarians were given large amounts of usage data, either in paper or in electronic form. However, the definitions of the data elements being provided appeared to be unique to each vendor, and the available data elements also varied. For instance, was a "search" at Database A comparable to a "search" on Database B? What exactly was a "search?" With varying data elements and varying definitions, there was no way to compare the use between and among database providers to decide which were pro-

[Haworth co-indexing entry note]: "Electronic Resource Usage Data: Standards and Possibilities." Chisman, Janet K. Co-published simultaneously in *The Serials Librarian* (The Haworth Information Press, an imprint of The Haworth Press, Inc.) Vol. 53, Supplement No. 9, 2007, pp. 275-285; and: *Usage Statistics of E-Serials* (ed: David C. Fowler) The Haworth Information Press, an imprint of The Haworth Press, Inc., 2007, pp. 275-285. Single or multiple copies of this article are available for a fee from The Haworth Document Delivery Service [1-800-HAWORTH, 9:00 a.m. - 5:00 p.m. (EST). E-mail address: docdelivery@haworthpress.com].

Available online at http://ser.haworthpress.com
doi:10.1300/J123v53S09_18

viding the access that patrons needed and that which budgets could afford. The explosion of full-text electronic journals with even more vendors and more variations on the theme of "use," "search," "retrieval," "turnaway," etc., further complicated the ability to use the data to make informed decisions.

COUNTER

COUNTER (Counting Online Usage of Networked Electronic Resources) was initiated in early 2002 to make the recording and reporting of electronic usage statistics comply to standard definitions and reporting formats.[1] COUNTER emphasizes the provision of basic usage data rather than the development of increasingly detailed usage reports. The standardization of this information benefits both librarians and vendors. Librarians analyze the data to study patron use patterns, while vendors benefit from adding value to their products by supplying a standard set of data to subscribers.

The first published COUNTER code, available in January 2003, covered journal and database reports. In March 2006, the COUNTER Code of Practice for Books and Reference Works was released. Reports that are now available include:

- JR1 = Journal Report 1: Number of Successful Full-Text Article Requests by Month and Journal
- JR1a = Number of Successful Full-Text Article Requests from an Archive by Month and Journal
- JR2 = Journal Report 2: Turnaways by Month and Journal
- DB1 = Database Report 1: Total Searches and Sessions by Month and Database
- DB2 = Database Report 2: Turnaways by Month and Database
- DB3 = Database Report 3: Total Searches and Sessions by Month and Service
- JR3 = Number of Successful Item Requests and Turnaways by Month, Journal, and Page Type
- JR4 = Total Searches Run by Month and Service
- BR1 = Book Report 1: Number of Successful Title Requests by Month and Title
- BR2 = Book Report 2: Number of Successful Section Requests by Month and Title

- BR3 = Turnaways by Month and Title
- BR4 = Turnaways by Month and Service
- BR5 = Total Searches and Sessions by Month and Title
- BR6 = Total Searches and Sessions by Month and Service

Not all vendors supply all the reports, but JR1 reports are almost universal among compliant vendors.

One indication of the success of COUNTER is the large number of compliant vendors listed on the COUNTER Web site (http://www.projectcounter.org) along with the types of reports that each supplies. The standard terminology allows usage comparison across vendor reports and provides librarians with usable data to assist in collection development decisions such as deciding to use alternative information delivery mechanisms–online document delivery, for example– for low-use titles.[2,3]

While COUNTER eased the problem of supplying consistent data across vendor platforms, a tremendous amount of staff time was needed to contact each vendor individually and retrieve the data. In addition, there were also the issues of data storage and manipulation. Many libraries developed in-house spreadsheets and databases specifically to house usage data and often to add more information about a title such as Impact Factor, interlibrary loans, cost, and so forth. These staffing and storage issues highlighted the need for emerging commercial electronic resource management (ERM) systems to automatically import and store the data. The key words here are "automatically" and "store." Automatic import would save large amounts of staff time and storing would obviate the need for a separate system for this function.

SUSHI

The drive for the automated import of usage data into ERM systems revealed the need for additional standardization not covered by the COUNTER initiative. While data in COUNTER are presented as clearly defined elements in a series of standard reports, the format of the data varies from vendor to vendor. This variation prohibits automated import since automation requires standardization. Another missing element is the functionality, which allows one computer to request data from another computer and for the second computer to respond to the request and supply the data (a Web Service, query, and response component).

As individuals worked with the COUNTER data and attempted to import them into existing ERM systems, the limitations of COUNTER became increasingly evident. An informal group of librarians, content providers, and integrated library system (ILS) vendors was formed to find a solution. The group began discussions in the summer of 2005, was recognized by National Standards Information Organization (NISO) in November, and by late 2005, had successfully tested the concept of automated import of usage data. The group named the new protocol Standardized Usage Statistics Harvesting Initiative, or SUSHI.[4] The SUSHI protocol is in a trial period until May 20, 2007.

SUSHI is a fairly simple protocol using existing Web-based products (Web Services; SOAP, or Simple Object Access Protocol; and XML schema) to request, format, and import usage data. The following brief overview of the SUSHI import process is based on NISO Webinars that contain background information for librarians and vendors as well as detailed examples of the XML request and response.[5,6]

The import process begins with a library having an ERM system plus associated SUSHI client software paired with a content provider with SUSHI server software and access to the COUNTER usage data. The ERM system sends a request to the SUSHI client–often housed on the same computer–for a COUNTER report. The SUSHI client prepares an XML request and sends it via the Internet to the content provider's SUSHI server, which reads the request, processes the requested COUNTER report into XML format, and prepares a response message formatted according to the SUSHI XML schema. The COUNTER report in XML format is added to the response and both are sent via the Internet to the SUSHI client at the requesting library. The SUSHI client processes the response and extracts the data. The data are then passed to the ERM system and processed for use/display.

At this writing, vendors participating in SUSHI include content providers with SUSHI servers that supply data: EBSCO Information Services, Project Euclid, Swets Information Services, and Thomson Scientific; and ILS vendors with SUSHI clients that receive data: Ex Libris and Innovative Interfaces, Inc (III). III has announced successful SUSHI loads into their ERM system. Other vendors actively working in this area include Ex Libris, Otto Harrassowitz, OCLC, Serials Solutions, and SirsiDynix.[7]

For any new standard to be successful, it must be accepted and used by the parties involved. Therefore, the next step in the successful implementation of SUSHI is a wider adoption by content providers and ILS vendors. Librarians here have a prime role in raising awareness of

SUSHI, emphasizing the need for this initiative, and encouraging the adoption of the protocol by noting the competitive edge that companies will gain by early implementation. This librarian advocacy will help move SUSHI into the same position now held by COUNTER–something fairly standard that content providers and ILS vendors implement because it is good for business. Information on what is required and how to implement SUSHI can be found at the SUSHI Web site (http://www. niso.org/committees/SUSHI/SUSHI_ comm.html).

SCHOLARLYSTATS

As librarians promote wider implementation of SUSHI, a new company, ScholarlyStats from MPS Technologies, has stepped in to fill the need for SUSHI-formatted data as well as to supply other value-added services.[8] ScholarlyStats is working with content providers to set up agreements that allow them to gather usage statistics from the content providers for ScholarlyStats' subscribers. ScholarlyStats collects the usage data reports, standardizes them, and puts data through additional cleanup processes to enhance the quality of the information. Scholarly Stats works with ILS integration partners to develop automated import of the data into their electronic resource management systems. To date, III's ERM system has successfully imported data from ScholarlyStats. The company is currently in beta-test with Harrassowitz' ERM system, while Ex Libris is in development work with its ERM system, Verde, to support the data transfer. Another integration partner is Thomson Scientific. ScholarlyStats and Thomson Scientific have successfully integrated Thomson's journal use data with the usage data from Scholarly Stats. In June 2006, ScholarlyStats and Thomson Scientific announced a successful import of usage data for the University of Melbourne from twenty-one vendors into Thomson Scientific's Journal Use Reports (JUR) system using the XML SUSHI protocol.[9] Several libraries are now using this functionality. This extends the information available for collection analysis by coupling usage data with Impact Factor and publication information from Thomson Scientific's JUR.

ScholarlyStats provides additional services beyond monthly collection and automated dissemination of journal and usage statistics. They administer all usage statistics platform access details in one place, perform additional data cleanup, provide consolidated reports across platforms, offer a suite of custom reports that summarize usage, and allow access to usage statistics by library staff.

PUTTING IT ALL TOGETHER–
ONE LIBRARY'S EXPERIENCE

Washington State University (WSU) is a midsized land grant university located in the agricultural region of eastern Washington. The WSU Libraries followed a fairly common path in dealing with data associated with electronic resources.[10] Librarians were frustrated in the mid-1990s trying to interpret usage data supplied by vendors where the definitions varied widely and there was no ability to compare statistics. Library staff developed a database to assist in making serials selection/deselection decisions. The maintenance of this system was very labor-intensive, and frequent upgrades in software and hardware caused many access problems.

Budgets were tight and more informed decisions were needed. WSU hungered for a more organized way to manage the data and were fortunate in 2002 in joining the Innovative Interface ERM module development team. When the product became available, we purchased it and began our implementation in earnest with reorganization in October 2004 and the formation of a Serials and Electronic Resources unit within Collections and Technical Services (CTS). While the library appreciated the ability to store basic data about our electronic resources and licenses, we were looking forward to being able to generate a cost-per-use within our integrated system. So we welcomed the opportunity to beta test the automated import of SUSHI usage data from Project Euclid in April 2006. Beta testing revealed that the Customer IDs assigned by Project Euclid were too long for the III ERM configuration area. This problem was quickly solved by III changing its system to accommodate a longer Customer ID. In beta testing, III began by running the harvests manually first and when this worked, they moved to testing an automated load. It only took three days to get the automated load to also run. This automated load showed us the potential, but we still needed SUSHI-formatted data from most of our vendors.

Thus, when WSU heard of a new company–ScholarlyStats, supplying data in SUSHI format–we realized it was the right company at the right time. Since we had just participated in the beta test of the automated import of SUSHI-formatted data into our ERM, the timing of the announcement was fortuitous. A quick e-mail to III resulted in a three-way partnership. III and ScholarlyStats would test importing to the III ERM module using the WSU system. III is also developing the capability to tie the usage data imported into ERM with the payment information so we can generate a cost-per-use from within our integrated catalog. Work with III and ScholarlyStats began in August 2006. The first test downloads were completed in October 2006. More details needed to be resolved to allow the download of data from more than one vendor on the same day. This was accomplished in January 2007. In February, data from thirty-four different vendors (representing over 150 publishers and 35,000 titles) for the previous twelve months were scheduled for download into our ERM.

A considerable amount of system work was required to accomplish this import of statistics from ScholarlyStats into the III ERM system. The exchange of information for testing was slowed by the location of the ScholarlyStats programmer in India, thus limiting the exchange of e-mails to one per day as the programmers moved through the trouble-shooting process. ScholarlyStats had to develop a method to include our account number and the platform name in the customer ID field. This allowed us to create a separate entry for each platform in our configuration field and for the imported data to locate the correct access provider for the harvested data. The first test revealed that the ScholarlyStats SUSHI server expected a Requestor ID (distinct from the Customer ID) to allow the SUSHI server to determine if the request was being made "on behalf of" the Customer ID. However, WSU was making the request directly and not using a third party or ASP service, and III was using SUSHI 0.1, with the Customer ID and the Requestor ID values the same. When III implements SUSHI 1.0, they intend to make the Requestor ID/Customer ID configuration more flexible. Both companies had to make changes to their systems, and it took about seven weeks before we had our first successful harvest of usage data for Elsevier ScienceDirect titles.

WSU then tested each platform on a different day and worked through any additional problems that arose. Failures of several loads were caused by the time difference between the settings for downloads on the ScholarlyStats server and those on the WSU client. Another problem that was identified during beta testing was the inability of ScholarlyStats to handle more than one request from WSU per day due to the need to make manual changes in the system to change the Requestor ID each time a request was made from the WSU III ERM. The solution for this was found, and WSU Libraries moved into the ScholarlyStats production environment in late December. In January 2007, we were able to import statistics for all of 2006. In February 2007, we encountered another download problem, which was quickly resolved.

The work in setting up the needed configuration table in III ERM and entering information into the ScholarlyStats system took several days, but was minimal compared to the repeated manual downloading of this information from thirty-four different vendors and subsequent integration into a spreadsheet. For ScholarlyStats, we provide our Customer ID and password for each subscribed platform along with the URL to the usage statistics Web site. Special instructions can also be included as needed. We estimate that a 0.5 FTE position is now available for other duties because of this change in procedures.

On the ERM system side, information needed to make the request at a specified time is entered into a configuration table. This information includes a code for the content provider, which is used to link the incoming data with the correct resource record(s) in the system, a Customer ID, day of the month to make the request, number of months of data to request, and a Web Services Description Language (WSDL) URL–that lets the SUSHI server at ScholarlyStats know what services we are requesting.

Currently, the end product of all this beta testing and setup is the ability to retrieve a resource record for a specific data supplier, such as Elsevier ScienceDirect. Opening the Usage Statistics option in the record delivers a screen showing the months of data available. An Export link opens an Excel spreadsheet with a summary of the payments for the year, total uses, and cost-per-use for the year to date at the top. Then, each title is listed with its own calculated cost-per-use, uses for each month covered, and total uses for the entire time period covered. This automated retrieval and calculation of cost-per-use is invaluable in the efficient management of usage data.

However, cost-per-use is just one factor considered in the selection/deselection process. The latest iteration of our serials database is an Excel spreadsheet with the following elements being tracked: Title, ISSN, III Record Number, Fund Code, Cost, JCR Total Cites, JCR Impact Factor, JCR Immediacy Index, JCR Articles, JCR cited Half Life, and Data Usage Statistics for each vendor. A cost-per-use is generated as needed for each title based on the subscription fees for the year and the usage statistics imported from each vendor. The title, ISSN, fund codes, and subscription costs (by limiting to a paid date range) are pulled from the order records via a create list functionality from the Acquisitions system. This information is imported into the Excel spreadsheet using a series of macros, which format the information as needed. The usage statistics are imported annually or semi-annually from each vendor supplying COUNTER-compliant statistics. The data is further refined to produce a usable spreadsheet.

A new serials decision database is currently being developed by our new Head, collections and acquisitions, with a greater WSU focus and should be operational in April 2007. We are dropping the generic JCR data from the database and are instead including the number of WSU-authored articles published in a journal, the number of times the articles in a journal title are cited in a WSU-authored article, and the number of interlibrary loan photocopy requests are placed by WSU faculty, staff, and students for articles from a journal title. Access to the dropped JCR information is available by linking to the Ulrich's Serials Analysis System. Maintenance is still labor-intensive but the increased focus on data authored and requested by WSU faculty, staff, and students will improve our ability to identify and subscribe to publications more relevant to faculty and student research, and teaching needs.

The ideal situation would be to have the ability to store the type of information in the new serials decision database in the existing ERM module or a new collection management module of the integrated catalog. We are moving in that direction with the ability to import usage statistics and associate them with costs with the paid date(s) for the same year. Unfortunately, we usually pay a subscription in the year before the subscription actually begins, so our cost data is currently a year off. This means that a subscription beginning in 2007 is paid for in 2006, so the payment costs are associated with the usage data for 2006, and not for 2007. III will be enhancing the ERM with a new field in the order record to document the subscription period. This will then associate the correct payment with the imported statistics. If we could then enhance the ERM system further to provide storage of additional custom data (for us, it would be the WSU-authored and cited articles, and the number of ILL photocopy requests by WSU-affiliated patrons) as defined by each individual library, we would have the beginnings of a very usable collection management system within the integrated catalog. We could then eliminate the standalone serials decision database and use our integrated catalog as the central store of data associated with e-resource collection management.

CONCLUSIONS

Technology is moving rapidly to provide librarians with the data needed to make informed decisions regarding the collection management of electronic resources. The development of ERM systems is providing the ability to store the needed basic information about e-resource suppliers and the associated licenses. The COUNTER protocol provides for standard usage data for journals, databases, reference works, and books. The SUSHI protocol then provides a way to format the data for automated import into ERM systems. Currently, there are a limited number of vendors supplying SUSHI-formatted data directly. However, librarian action will ensure the widespread adoption of the SUSHI protocol by content providers and ILS vendors. In the interim, those with large collections or a pressing need for usage data in SUSHI format may consider use of an intermediary, such as ScholarlyStats, that can supply SUSHI-formatted data from an increasing number of platforms via an automated import system.

Vendors who have produced ERM systems are developing the means to integrate these imported data with subscription cost information already available in the acquisitions modules of the ILS. This will make available one more vital piece of information–the cost-per-use for electronic resources. Integration of this information with journal citation data provided by other third parties will even further expand the ability to make informed decisions regarding collection development.

The author's intent, in writing this chapter, has not been to promote a specific product, but to emphasize how the development of these products, in association with the COUNTER and SUSHI protocols, is bringing the library world closer to the goal of successfully using usage data reports to improve and focus our collections. The author also looks forward to a standard license template, with a set of standard portable descriptive data elements that librarians can automatically load into ERM systems. I propose we name it Absolutely Terrific License Attributes Simply Transferred (AT LAST).

NOTES

1. "About COUNTER," COUNTER, http://www.projectcounter.org/about.html.

2. Oliver Pesch, "Ensuring Consistent Usage Statistics, Part 1: Project COUNTER," *Serials Librarian,* 50, no. 1/2 (2006):147-161. doi:10.1300/J123v50n01_14.

3. Alfred Kraemer. "Ensuring Consistent Usage Statistics, Part 2: Working with Use Data for Electronic Journals," *Serials Librarian* 50, no. 1/2 (2006):163-172. doi:10.1300/J123v50n01_15.

4. NISO National Standards Information Organization, "NISO Standardized Usage Statistics Harvesting Initiative (SUSHI)," NISO, http://www.niso.org/ committees/ SUSHI/SUSHI_comm.html

5. Adam Chandler, Phil Davis, and Tim Jewell, "Introduction to SUSHI for Librarians and Content Providers," *NISO Webinar,* (May 17, 2006), http://www.niso. org/committees/SUSHI/SUSHIWebinarslides051506.pdf.

6. Ted Fons and Oliver Pesch, "SUSHI: The Technology Unveiled," *NISO Webinar,* (May 17, 2006), http://www.niso.org/committees/SUSHI/SUSHIWebinar 052406.pdf

7. Adam Chandler and Tim Jewell, "The Standardized Usage Statistics Harvesting Initiative (SUSHI)," *Serials,* 19 (March 2006):68-70.

8. "Simplifying Statistics," ScholarlyStats from MPS Technologies, http://www.scholarlystats.com

9. "ScholarlyStats and Thomson Scientific Announce Successful SUSHI Test for University of Melbourne," NISO, http://www.niso.org/committees/SUSHI/Scholarly Stats_ThomsonScientifi.pdf

10. Janet Chisman and John Webb, "Electronic Resource Management Using a Vendor Product," *Journal of Electronic Resource Description & Access,* 8, (forthcoming).

doi:10.1300/J123v53S09_18

Index

Page numbers in *italics* designate figures; page numbers followed by "t" designate tables; *See also* designates related topics or more detailed subtopic lists.